Charles John Vaughan

The illustrated Laconian.

History and industries of Laconia, N.H. Descriptive of the city and its manufacturing

and business interests

Charles John Vaughan

The illustrated Laconian.
History and industries of Laconia, N.H. Descriptive of the city and its manufacturing and business interests

ISBN/EAN: 9783337713126

Printed in Europe, USA, Canada, Australia, Japan

Cover: Foto ©ninafisch / pixelio.de

More available books at **www.hansebooks.com**

THE
ILLUSTRATED LACONIAN

HISTORY AND INDUSTRIES

OF LACONIA, N. H.

DESCRIPTIVE OF THE CITY AND ITS MANUFACTURING
AND BUSINESS INTERESTS

COMPILED BY CHARLES W. VAUGHAN

CONTAINING

CONCISE HISTORY, OLD LANDMARKS, PRESENT AND FORMER RESIDENTS, PORTRAITS AND BIOGRAPHICAL SKETCHES OF ACTIVE MEN, MEN NOTED IN PUBLIC, BUSINESS, AND PROFESSIONAL LIFE, BUILDINGS, PICTURESQUE SCENES, COMFORTABLE HOMES, SUMMER RESIDENTS AND THEIR RESIDENCES, ITS MANUFACTURING, GROWTH, PROSPERITY, AND FUTURE POSSIBILITIES.

PUBLISHED BY
LOUIS B. MARTIN
1899

INTRODUCTION.

In the publication of this book the aim has been to give a truthful and correct glimpse of Laconia as it has been in by-gone years and as it is to-day, feeling confident that a perusal of its pages will give all Laconians a feeling of pride over the growth and development of the town in the past, and impart renewed confidence in the future growth and prosperity of the city.

LOUIS B. MARTIN, *Publisher*.

1652—LACONIA—1899

The city of Laconia was chartered by the New Hampshire legislature of 1893, is located near the geographical centre of Belknap county, of which county it is the shire town, and is also near the geographical centre of the state of New Hampshire, twenty-eight miles from Concord, and just one hundred miles from Boston, Mass. Laconia is upon both sides of the Winnipesaukee river, while Lake Winnesquam on the south and west, Lake Opechee near the centre of the city, and Lakes Winnipesaukee and Paugus on the north and east boundaries, well entitle Laconia to be known as the "City on the Lakes," which title is inscribed upon the city seal.

Laconia was first incorporated as a township in 1855, the portion north of the Winnipesaukee river, including The Weirs, being set off at that time from the old town of Meredith. Previous to this date Laconia was known as Meredith Bridge, and the portion of the village on the south and east sides of the river was a part of the town of Gilford; and previous to 1813 this portion of the city was included in the limits of the original township of Gilmanton. The portion of Laconia south of the river was cut off from Gilford and annexed to the town of Laconia in 1874, and when the city charter was granted in 1893, Lakeport was also taken from Gilford to form a part of the city of Laconia.

The early history of Laconia, therefore, is identical with that of Gilmanton, Meredith, and Gilford, and the

Endicott Rock.

future historian of the city will be sadly hampered by the fact that there are no town records of Laconia until 1855. A brief sketch of the settlement of this territory has been compiled from Lancaster's History of Gilmanton, published in 1845, and from authentic historical sketches of Meredith and Gilford.

The first authentic record of the appearance of the white man in Laconia is found upon Endicott rock, at The Weirs, near the outlet of Lake Winnipesaukee. Strange as it may now seem, the territory of Laconia was once claimed as a portion of the territory granted to the Massachusetts Bay Colony. In 1638 the Massachusetts colonists sent a party up the Merrimack river to locate the northern bound of their grant, which was understood to be three miles from the headwaters of the Merrimack river, but was afterwards decided to be three miles from the mouth of the river. The first party of surveyors sent out from Massachusetts to locate this bound, ascended the river and marked a tree near the junction of the Pemigewasset and Winnipesaukee rivers (at Franklin). In 1652 the Bay state colonists sent out a second party from Ipswich, with instructions to find and mark the headwaters of the Merrimack river. This party consisted of Captain Simon Willard and Edward Johnson, commissioners, accompanied by Jonathan Ince, John Sherman, and two or three Indians. This surveying party reached The Weirs about August 1, 1652, and the white men in the party were probably the first white men who ever set foot upon Laconia, or gazed at the beautiful Lake Winnipesaukee.

Captain Willard and his party marked a boulder on the shore of the lake, near the outlet into Lake Paugus, and returned to the lower settlements after an absence of nineteen days. The marks cut upon the rock were the initials of Simon Willard, Edward Johnson, John Sherman, Jonathan Ince, and the name of John Endicott, governor. In 1740 the bounds of Massachusetts and New Hampshire were established, and the boulder on the shore of the lake was forgotten until about 1833, when the marks were discovered by workmen who were enlarging the channel at The Weirs. In 1885 the legislature made an appropriation for raising the rock and surrounding it with the substantial granite memorial which will undoubtedly preserve the record of the white man's visit to Laconia for centuries to come.

The portion of Laconia south of the river Winnipesaukee was granted to one hundred and seventy-seven persons in 1727, as compensation for services in defence of their country, and was incorporated as a part of Gilmanton. The charter was signed by His Majesty's colonial governor, John

The Old Red House, formerly on Pleasant Street.

Wentworth. The upper side of the river was chartered by the governor and council in 1768 as a portion of the township of Meredith. Both Gilmanton and Meredith were granted to Exeter and Portsmouth people, and the meetings of the proprietors of the grants were held in Exeter for some time.

The French and Indian wars delayed the settlement of the two towns, and although it appears that several parties came here about 1750, they came as prospectors and hunters, and it was not until 1761 that any permanent settlements were effected. In 1736 a party of men cleared a path to The Weirs and constructed a blockhouse, fourteen feet square, as a shelter and defence from Indians. About this time a new obstacle to settlement arose by order of the general court, the Province road, so called, was laid out from Portsmouth to Canada, through Gilmanton and Meredith, and consequently through the present city of Laconia. "Meredith Bridge" was first constructed at this time, but "Folsom's Bridge" at Lakeport was not built until 1782, and the bridge at The Weirs was erected in 1803. "Mosquito Bridge," leading over the narrow portion of Lake Winnesquam, was built about 1805, and "Davis Bridge," leading from the mainland to Davis' island, now Governor's island, in Lake Winnipesaukee, was erected previous to 1820.

The Old Tremont Building after the First Fire.

the claims of John Tufton Mason of Hampshire county, England, who claimed all of the territory embraced in Gilmanton and Meredith, as conveyed to him by the English government. Mason sold his claims to Portsmouth people, and in 1752 the Masonian proprietors made a trade with those who received their grant from the governor of New Hampshire, and took certain shares of the territory for their claims.

Previous to 1761 the route to Gilmanton and Meredith from Epsom and Exeter was merely a path, marked by spotted trees, but in October of this year a cart-path was made, and in 1770,

With the exception of lands which were cultivated by the Indians at The Weirs and a few other places, the territory embraced within our city limits was an unbroken wilderness until about 1766. At this time Ebenezer Smith and Jacob Eaton built their log houses and commenced clearing away the forest. From the time the Endicott rock was marked no civilized man again appears until just before the construction of the block house, which was called White Hall, for some reason unknown, and which was erected in 1736. The exact location of Smith's first house is not known, but Eaton's house was built where George Hilliard now lives near The Weirs. Not long after Smith's arrival we find he had his house near where Lowell Cawley recently lived. The first road to The Weirs was from near Smith's house by Jacob Eaton's house, about where the

An Old View of Water Street.

road now runs. On the lot where Eaton built there were several apple trees which had been planted by the Indians, which were so far as known the only apple trees ever found upon any Indian lands. At this ancient home of Eaton's the first white child of Laconia was born, and the little girl was named Thamor Eaton. Where she died and the place of burial is unknown. Soon after the birth of the Eaton child, a male child was born to Ebenezer Smith. Mr. Eaton understood that the first child born in town should be entitled to a certain amount of land from the proprietors, but Smith claimed that the "right of land" was to the first male child. A friendly compromise was arranged, and Eaton took forty or fifty acres and Smith received the lion's share, about two hundred acres. Colonel Smith was above all others the principal man of the town for many years. He was born in Exeter, N. H., in 1734. He died in 1807. He was proprietors' clerk and town clerk, justice of the peace, selectman, represented his town in both branches of the legislature, and was at one time president of the senate.

Mills for sawing and grinding were commenced at Meredith Bridge soon after the Province road was built. The mills were first built on the Meredith side of the river, and in 1775 were owned by Stephen Gale but were swept away by a freshet in the year 1779. The mill privilege was purchased in 1780 by Col. Samuel Ladd, who rebuilt on the Gilford side of the river. Colonel Ladd lost his milldam three years successively, and in 1788 his mill was burned, but it was immediately rebuilt.

About this time Abraham Folsom built mills both for sawing lumber and grinding grain at Lakeport, which was then called Folsom's mills. These mills were also destroyed by fire but again constructed the following season. There were also mills at The Weirs in 1803, called Prescott's mills, but these establishments went into disuse, while the mills at Meredith Bridge and Lakeport did an extensive business, and the community around them rapidly increased in numbers and importance.

One of the first houses on the Gilmanton side of the river was the mill house, erected by Col. Samuel Ladd in

The Old Perley Corner on Main Street.

1780, near the present location of the Huse machine shops. Colonel Ladd purchased the land of Samuel Jewett, who settled half a mile above, the previous year. It is stated that Colonel Ladd paid but seven Spanish dollars for this lot of two and a half acres of land on the east side of the river, and previously owned the territory now known as Ladd's Hill, just across the city line in Belmont. The land on the north side of the river was first owned by Schoolmaster James of Exeter. Stephen Gale next purchased this territory and sold it to Colonel Ladd. This land commenced near the present Church street bridge and the bound ran in a straight line to Lake Winnesquam, near the mouth of the Winnipesaukee river, thus including all of the most valuable property to-day in the city of Laconia. Most of the land on the south side of the river was first owned by James Conner and John Lowe, but was soon afterwards purchased by Samuel Jewett. Daniel Avery and Dr. Bowman purchased some of this property about 1790.

In 1811 the inhabitants on the south side of the Winnipesaukee river, residing in what was then called Gunstock Parish, petitioned to be set off into a separate town. The voters of Gilmanton at their March meeting in 1812 declined to favor the petition, but voted not to oppose it in the legislature. The application was therefore successful, and on the 16th of June, 1812, that part of Gilmanton called Gunstock was disannexed, and by an act of the New Hampshire legislature, incorporated as a separate town, called Gilford. This town included not only the portion of the present Laconia south of the river, but also the present town of Gilford and that portion of Lakeport and The Weirs east of the river and lake.

About the year 1790, Daniel Avery came to Meredith Bridge from Stratham, and opened a store in a small building near the bridge. He erected a factory for a cotton mill, where the Belknap mills stand to-day, and did much to enlarge and build up the village. Aaron Martin early established a paper manufactory at Meredith Bridge, which was destroyed by fire some years afterwards. In 1820, an academy was incorporated, and about the same time a term of the supreme court began to be held here. There were then about thirty dwelling-houses in the village proper. Other traders were: Woodbury Melcher, George P. Avery, and Henry J. French. A post-office was established in 1824, and Horatio G. Prescott was the first postmaster.

In 1813, when the late Timothy D. Somes came to Meredith Bridge, there was but one church in the village, located just south of the present Willard Hotel property. This church was de-

Main Street before the Unitarian Church was built.

stroyed by fire, in February, 1836. The Avery mill, owned by Daniel Avery, Daniel Tucker, Stephen Tucker, and other leading citizens, was in operation at that time, but burned down some six or eight years afterwards. There was a clothing mill near the Mill street bridge, on the site occupied by the J. W. Busiel & Co. dye house at the present time. This mill was owned and operated by Samuel and Nathan Bean. Stephen Perley had an oil mill for preparing oil for painters, near the Bean mill. Daniel Tucker owned a blacksmith shop, on the site of the present Esty mill, and manufactured axes, scythes, and other tools. The well-som kept a hotel on Pleasant street, and was one of the first tavern keepers in the village. There were but thirty-four houses on both sides of the river in 1813, and some of these were mere shanties. The best house in the town was the John A. Harper residence, where Mrs. Dr. Prescott and L. A. Ladd now reside. Mr. Harper was the only lawyer at that time, was a very able and brilliant man, and at one time a member of congress. The mails were brought from Concord on horseback, and no wagons were in use here at that time.

Dr. Zodack Bowman was the only physician in town, and lived where Mrs. Mary A. Tilton's residence now stands,

The Old Mitchell and Mallard Blocks.

known Holbrooks, who afterwards removed to Massachusetts, had a bell foundry near the Tucker mill. They cast the first bell ever rung in Meredith Bridge.

The bridge across the river on Main street at this time was a small and narrow affair, with no railing. A man named French fell off the bridge and was drowned in the river about this time, and then the bridge was supplied with a railing. On the Gilford side of the river, near the end of the Mill street bridge, was a sawmill, owned by Dudley Ladd, while Jonathan Ladd operated a grist-mill near the site of the present Pitman mills. Jonathan Fol- at the corner of Main and Court streets. There was no Main street, then, above Mill street, and a little brook ran through Bank square, where the present Perley canal is located. This brook was crossed by small bridges of one or two planks.

In 1842 Meredith Bridge was a village of considerable importance. The *Belknap Gazette* was published by the late Col. Charles Lane, and the village boasted three cotton mills, a woolen mill, grist-mills, sawmills, a large tannery, sash and door machinery, a large printing-office, with bookbindery and bookstore connected. There were ten stores, three taverns, three churches, five lawyers, three clergymen, and an academy in a flourishing condition. The regular stage went through from Holderness to Boston in one day, leaving Meredith Bridge at six o'clock in the morning, making the trip via Concord

Paying an Election Bet Thirty-five Years Ago.

and Manchester on three days in the week, and via Pittsfield and Exeter on the other three days.

The opening of the old Boston, Concord & Montreal Railroad between Concord and Meredith Bridge marked an important point in the growth of Laconia. August 8, 1848, was the date of the opening of the railroad to Meredith Bridge, and a year afterwards the road was extended to Lake Village. The opening of the road was the occasion of the biggest celebration Meredith Bridge had ever witnessed up to that date. A mammoth cannon was located near Horse Point, on the shore of Lake Winnesquam, and when the special train came along, a salute was fired, which was the signal for ringing the mill bells, and the church bell of the old North church. There was an immense throng of people waiting at the depot to welcome the iron horse, the farmers driving in from miles around.

The locomotive was named "Old Man of the Mountains," and the train was in charge of Major Jake Libbey, as conductor. The chief feature of the celebration was the collation, served by the ladies of the village in the freight depot which stood on the site of Laconia's beautiful passenger station of to-day. The car track stopped near this point. The tickets for the free ride on the special train to Meredith Bridge are still preserved as souvenirs, and read as follows:

B. C. & MONTREAL RAILROAD.

OPENING TO MEREDITH.

The directors respectfully invite your attendance upon the opening of this road on Tuesday, August 8, 1848.

ARRANGEMENT.

A special train will leave the Lowell Depot, Boston, at 6 o'clock, a. m.; Lowell at 6¾; Nashua at 7¼, Manchester 8¼, and Concord at 9, on the arrival of the special from Boston.

This will pass you free over the Boston & Lowell, the Concord, the Northern and the B. C. & M. railroad on this occasion, and admit you to the collation at Meredith.

Stockholders and invited guests below Concord will be particular to take the special train.

Previous to 1855, the citizens of Meredith Bridge went to Meredith Parade to vote. At the March meeting (March 13, 1855) occurred the great catastrophe known as the falling of the town house. Soon after the opening of

Weirs before the "Booth" Arrived.

the meeting, while preparing to take a vote by ballot, there was a rush of voters, of whom there were from six to eight hundred present, and their weight broke down the floor timbers of the yet

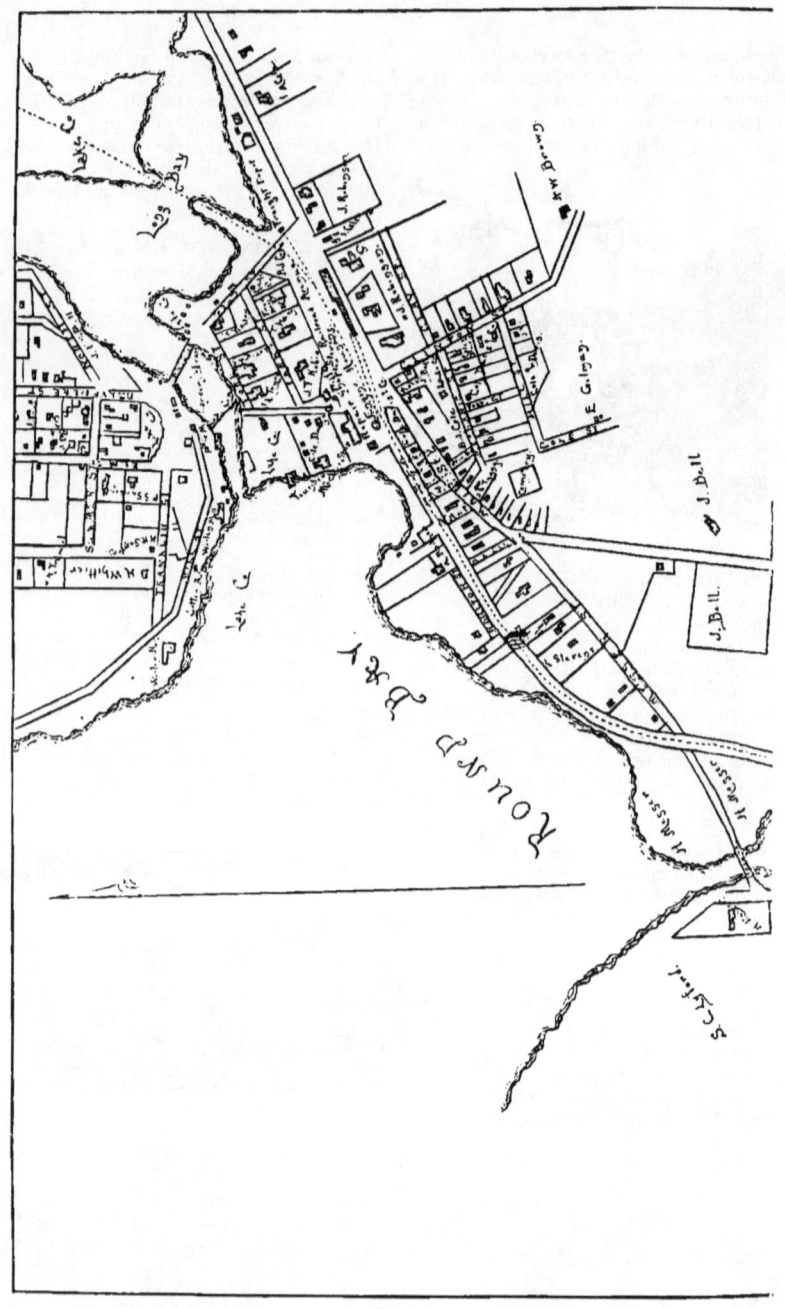

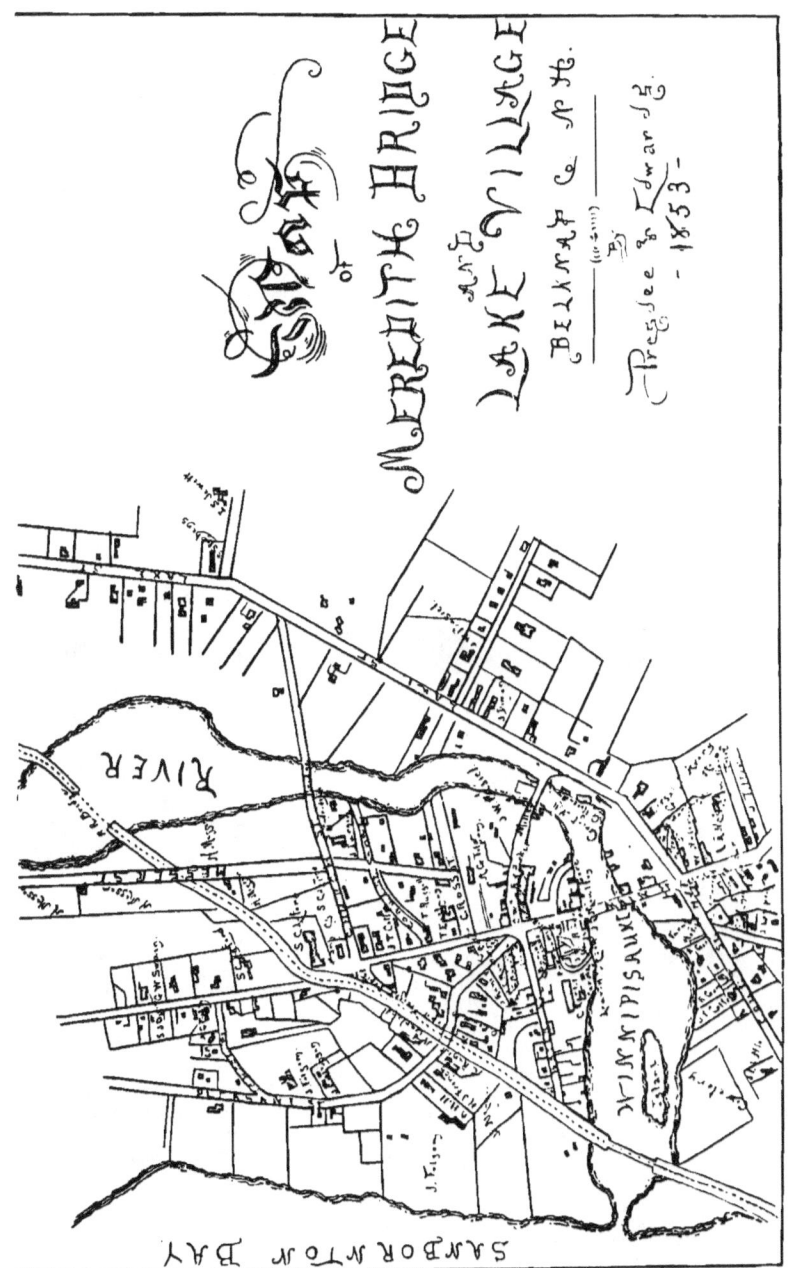

unfinished town house at Meredith village. The floor gave way, and about one hundred and fifty men were precipitated into the basement of the building. Out of this mass of struggling humanity, over sixty men were carried out seriously injured with broken bones, dislocated joints and internal injuries. Four of the injured men, James W. Durgin, Washington Smith, Benjamin D. Robinson, and Nathaniel Nichols, died in a short time, and others received injuries from which they never recovered, many being crippled for life. This was one of the immediate causes which led to the setting off of Meredith Bridge from the mother-town, and in July of the same year, by act of the legislature, Meredith was divided, and the town of Laconia incorporated.

The act to incorporate the town of Laconia was approved July 14, 1855, and signed by Gov. Ralph Metcalf. The bounds of Laconia, as created by this act of the legislature, were as follows:

"That all that part of the town of Meredith lying southerly of the following line, to wit: Beginning at a point on the easterly shore of Sanbornton bay, on the line between the lots numbered three and four in the seventh range and first division of lots in said Meredith, thence easterly on said line to the rangeway, thence northerly on said rangeway to the corner between lots numbered eight and nine in the sixth range, thence easterly on the line between said lots the length of two lots to the rangeway between the fourth and fifth range, thence northerly on said rangeway to the corner between lots numbered three and four in the fourth range, thence easterly on the line between said lots the length of two lots to the rangeway between the second and third range, thence southerly on said rangeway to the corner between lots numbered three and four in the second range, thence easterly on the line between said lots the length of two lots to the Winnipesaukee lake, thence southerly on the waters of said lake and the line between the towns of Meredith and Gilford and on said Sanbornton bay to the bounds begun at, be and the same is hereby severed from the town of Meredith and made a body politic and corporate by the name of Laconia."

The warrant for the first town meeting of the new town of Laconia was signed by H. N. Burnham, Stephen Gale, John C. Moulton, and Samuel W. Sanders, who were authorized by the legislature to call this meeting. The first meeting was held in the Boston, Concord & Montreal Railroad freight station, "near the residence of Stephen Gale," on August 2, 1855. The town officers elected at this meeting were as follows: Moderator, Horatio N. Burn-

Laconia from Vue de l'Eau Hotel.

ham; town clerk, Benjamin P. Gale; selectmen, Samuel W. Sanders, John Davis, 2d, Ebenezer S. Cate; town treasurer, Elijah Beaman; superintending school committee, John K. Young; auditors, Joseph W. Robinson, Hugh Blaisdell, John C. Moulton; surveyors of wood, Harrison Sibley, Thomas Wilder, Moses B. Gordon, and Benjamin P. Gale; surveyors of lumber, Nathan B. Wadleigh, John Davis, 2d, Joseph Ranlet, and Moses B. Gordon; town agent, Noah Robinson; weigher of hay, Horatio N. Burnham; sealer of weights and measures, James S. Hoit; poundkeeper, David Blaisdell;

legislature, and dated July 2, 1874, and the bounds of the addition are given as follows:

"That all that part of the town of Gilford bounded as follows, to wit: Beginning at a stake and stone on the easterly side of Round bay on a line with the northerly line of Thomas Durrell's land, and running easterly to and along said Durrell's land to the line between school districts No. 4 and No. 12, thence southerly on the line of school district No. 4 to the line between Gilford and Belmont, thence westerly on the line between Gilford and Belmont to Sanbornton bay, and to the line between Gilford and Laconia, thence northerly on said bay, Winnipiseogee river and Round bay, being on the line between Gilford and Laconia, to the bound begun at, be and the same hereby is severed from the town of Gilford and annexed to the town of Laconia."

Main Street, before Smith's Brick Block was Erected.

fence viewers, Ebenezer S. Cate, Chas. Smith, and Joseph W. Robinson; hogreeves, Chas. Gould, Chas. S. Gale, Moses Sargent, and Westley Maloon; constables, James S. Hoit, Hugh Blaisdell, Augustus Doe, Horatio N. Burnham, and John C. Davis; surveyors of highways, Edward Bacon, Lewis W. Boynton, Lucian A. Ladd, Reuben P. Smith, James R. Gray, John C. Folsom, Nathaniel Sanborn, John M. L. Swain, Jacob Smith, John M. Robinson, James Gordon, and Ebenezer S. Cate.

The next change in the territory of Laconia was the annexation of the portion of Gilford lying on the south side of the Winnipesaukee river. This move was heartily opposed by the old town of Gilford, but the act was passed by the

This act of the legislature united the two portions of the village on both sides of the river, under one town government, as up to this date the inhabitants on the south side had been obliged to go to Gilford village to vote, and to transact all their town business. But at Lake Village a similar state of affairs still existed, the easterly side of the river being in the town of Gilford, and the westerly side being a part of the town of Laconia. This was remedied by the act of the general court, dated July 13, 1876, as follows:

"That all that part of the town of Laconia bounded as follows, to wit: Beginning at a stake and stones on the westerly shore of Long bay, so called, at the northeasterly corner of the farm of Enoch B. Prescott, thence westerly on the northerly line of said Prescott's farm to the highway leading from Lake Village to Meredith, thence northerly on said highway to the centre of Tilton brook, so called, thence westerly down the centre of said brook to Round bay, to the line dividing the town of Gilford from the town of Laconia—be and the same hereby is severed from the town of Laconia and annexed to the town of Gilford."

The next change in the territory of Laconia was the annexation of the village of Lakeport, on both sides of the river, and the consolidation of the two towns under a city government. Lakeport had outgrown the mother town of Gilford, which was and still is strictly a farming community, and there was little or no opposition to the union of the two villages, which had grown so closely together that it was hard to tell where one left off and the other commenced.

The city charter was granted by the legislature of 1893, and dated March 24, 1893. The bounds of the portion cut off from Gilford and made a part of the city (ward six) are as follows:

"The inhabitants of the town of Laconia, in the county of Belknap, and the inhabitants of all that part of the town of Gilford lying westerly of a line described as follows, viz.: Commencing at the southeast corner of School District No. 13 in said Gilford, thence northerly on the division line or rangeway, between ranges one and two, as shown by the Gilford town plan, to the south line of lot originally owned by Joseph Libby; thence easterly on said Libby lot line to the division line or rangeway between ranges two and three; thence northerly on said division line or rangeway to Lake Winnipiseogee—shall be a body corporate and politic under the name of the City of Laconia."

The first city election held under the charter was May 2, 1893, and the first city government was inaugurated May 3, 1893, as follows: Mayor, Charles A. Busiel. Councilmen, ward one, George W. Weeks, William J. Morrison; ward two, Albert C. Moore, Francis H. Davis; ward three, Charles E. Frye, Joseph M. Folsom; ward four, Edmund Tetley, Charles W. Vaughan; ward five, Horace W. Gorrell, John W. Ashman; ward six, Benjamin F. Drake, Charles L. Pulsifer, Julius E. Wilson, Romanzo B. Priest.

Meredith Bridge suffered seriously several times in its early history from disastrous fires. Feb. 13, 1823, the large brick factory, factory store, and engine house on Mill street were burned. The fire started in the picking-room, and spread so rapidly that the girls in the upper loft were obliged to jump from the windows, and some of them were seriously injured. Clarissa Bean, one of the operatives, had her limbs broken. They were amputated, but she did not recover. In December, 1833,

Avery Dam, looking down the River.

the paper mill, sawmill, and grist-mill were destroyed by fire, and in February, 1836, the only meeting-house, located near the site of the Judge Lovell place, together with the dwelling-house and outbuildings of Lyman B. Walker, were burned. The "big fire" of Nov. 21, 1860, was the most serious conflagration in Laconia's history. It started in the stable of the Cerro Gordo hotel, which was located just below the present Moulton opera house block, swept down the street and across the street, destroying practically all the business places in the village at that time. In later years, the car shops have twice been nearly wiped out by conflagrations, but in both cases immediately rebuilt on a larger scale.

Probably nothing has contributed so much to the growth and prosperity of Laconia as the manufacturing industries. The Bean carding mill and Martin's paper mill were the first enterprises of this kind, both established about 1800. About a dozen years later, the Meredith Cotton and Woolen Company was organized, one of the first mills erected in the country for the manufacture of woolen goods. The mill was a wooden building, and much of the machinery was built here. The stock was held by citizens of the village, and the leading spirits in the enterprise were Daniel Avery, Stephen Perley, John A. Harper, and others.

Later enterprises in the same line was the establishment of the Granite hosiery mills, in 1847, by the late John W. Busiel, the White Mountains hosiery mills, established by the late Lewis F. Busiel a few years later, and the Gilford Hosiery Co., incorporated by the late John C. Moulton in 1864. The Belknap mills, the Pitman Manufacturing Co., the late J. S. Tilton hosiery industry, and the Abel machine shops should also be mentioned among the industries which have furnished employment for large numbers of workmen and helped build up the town.

The Laconia car shops are now and have been for many years, perhaps, the most important individual manufactur-

The Cerro Gordo House, burned 1860.

ing concern in Laconia. These shops were started by the late Charles Ranlet and Joseph Ranlet about 1850, under the name of the Ranlet Car Co. Perley Putnam and the late John C. Moulton afterwards came into the concern, and it was known as the Laconia Car Co. until the organization of the Laconia Car Co. Works in 1898, of which Hon. Frank Jones of Portsmouth is president and the principal owner.

Other local enterprises which have assisted in building up the town are the old Baldwin peg mill, the numerous machine shops, which sprang up from the hosiery industry, including the Abel

lage had a population of but 500. In 1890 the census showed about 3,000. After the census of 1890, and previous to the adoption of the city charter in 1893, both Laconia and Lakeport increased rapidly in population, so that it is safe to state that the population of the city of Laconia at the inauguration of the city charter was at least 10,000.

The construction and opening of the Lake Shore railroad between Laconia and Alton Bay was an important event in local history. As far back as 1847, a charter was granted to build this eighteen miles of road to connect the Cocheco road, on the eastern side of

Looking up the River, from Main Street Bridge.

shops, the Huse shops, the Cole Manufacturing Co., the J. S. Crane shops, the Wardwell needle shops, and scores of others in this and similar lines.

The lumber mills of G. Cook & Son, the Laconia lumber works, and Laconia's retail stores, especially the dry goods establishments, have also done much to advance the prosperity of the town, and make it a trade centre.

In 1855, when Laconia was set off from Meredith and incorporated as a separate town, its population was reckoned at 1,200. In 1860, the census gave the town a population of 1,806, which had increased to 2,309 by the next census in 1870, and to 3,790 in 1880. The census of 1890 showed 6,143 inhabitants. In 1830 Lake Vil-

New Hampshire, with the old Boston, Concord & Montreal railroad at Meredith. But lack of financial means prevented the construction of the Lake Shore link for over forty years, and the original charter expired. Attempts were made to renew the charter in 1868, 1869, and 1870, but it was opposed by the Boston, Concord & Montreal road. For several years the demand for this charter was made a political issue in Belknap county, and in 1883 the charter was granted by consent of both the great railroad corporations of New Hampshire, with the mutual understanding, however, that neither of them would assist in building the road. The charter was in the hands of Charles A. Busiel and his associates, and in the big railroad fight of 1887 a condition of affairs was reached where both the Concord railroad and the Boston & Maine road offered to construct the Lake Shore link. By a wise use of the opportunities growing out of this railroad fight in the legislature, the Lake Shore was constructed by the Concord Railroad corporation, and formally opened with a grand celebration in Laconia on June 17, 1890. Four special trains with invited guests made the trip to Alton Bay and return, accompanied by two bands of music, the railroad officials, the governor, and other state officers, etc. The bells were rung in the mill and in the church towers, whistles were blown, and salutes fired from cannon. The leading citizens of Dover, and other towns in that section of New Hampshire, were guests of Laconia upon this occasion, and speech-making was indulged in at Lakeport and in Moulton opera house at Laconia. The entire four train-loads of guests, and all the prominent citizens of Laconia and Lakeport, were banqueted by a down-country caterer in a large tent erected for the purpose in the rear of the City Hotel. Hon. C. A. Busiel was presented with a gold-headed cane, as a mark of appreciation from the citizens for his long struggle for the construction of the road. The crowd which thronged the streets of Laconia on that day was one of the largest gatherings of people ever seen here.

The dedication of Laconia's magnificent railroad passenger station on August 22, 1892, was another event of historical importance. Up to this time Laconia's passenger depot had been a mere wooden shell, which had done service ever since the opening of the railroad. The con

The Old Messer Bridge.

An Old View of Main Street.

Jewett Homestead, One of the Oldest Houses in Town.

tract for the erection of the present station was signed in April, 1891, and S. S. Ordway & Co., of Woburn, Massachusetts, were the contractors. The Ordway contract and the heating apparatus involved an expense of $30,000. Before ground was broken for the new depot, the railroad folks invested about $22,000 in the purchase of the Vaughan, Lane, Kelley, and O'Shea properties, removing the dwelling houses thereon, so as to clear off the entire square. The town of Laconia joined with the railroad in enlarging the railroad square, by purchasing the Tibbetts and Wilcox properties and taking a slice from the Gale property opposite the passenger station. The dedication of the depot was under the auspices of the Laconia Board of Trade, and Gov. Hiram A. Tuttle and numerous other railroad and state officials were guests of the occasion. A brass band escorted Ticket Agent E. S. Cook from the old depot to the new structure, and the first ticket, good for a ride from Laconia to Concord, was sold at public auction, and bid off by Col. F. O. Wallace for the sum of thirty dollars. The Board of Trade and their guests enjoyed a banquet at the Eagle hotel, and the depot was formally dedicated with appropriate speeches by the governor, the railroad officials, and prominent citizens. The Laconia depot at the time of its construction was pronounced by competent judges to be "without doubt, all things considered, the best structure of the kind to be found in America." Credit for the substantial and beautiful depot largely belongs to Hon. Charles A. Busiel, who was at that time one of the managing directors of the Concord railroad, and it was through his efforts and local pride that Laconia was granted such an expensive and magnificent passenger station. History will accord to Hon. C. A. Busiel the honor of constructing the Lake Shore railroad and the erection of the Laconia passenger station, and these two things will stand as monuments to the man for years to come.

To give a proper history of the record of Laconia's citizen-soldiers in the War of the Revolution, the War of

Depot Square before the Construction of the New Depot.

1812, and the War of the Rebellion, will require more space than can be afforded in the pages of this publication. The sturdy, patriotic settlers of Gilmanton and Meredith were prompt to leave their homes in 1776, and took an active part in the battles of Bunker Hill, Bennington, and other Revolutionary struggles. Major Stephen Gale, Samuel Jewett, Jacob Jewett, and Captain William Gordon were among the Revolutionary soldiers from the territory which is now the city of Laconia, and whose graves are decorated each Memorial Day by the members of John L. Perley, Jr., Post, No. 37, Grand Army of the Republic.

In the War of 1812 were James S. Hoit, Asa J. Bean, Philbrook R.

Lovett, Dudley Gilman, J. B. Pulsifer, Enoch Osgood, Josiah Randlett, James Filgate, Levi Pickering, Asa Crosby, Josiah Moulton, Capt. Wm. Heywood, Samuel Gilman, Capt. Hugh Blaisdell, J. D. Prescott, and many others who should be credited to Laconia. The late Col. Thomas J. Whipple took an active part in the Mexican War and also in the War of the Rebellion, and his military and legal fame gave him a national reputation.

When President Lincoln called for volunteers in 1861, at the breaking out of the War of the Rebellion, hundreds of the best youths and men of Laconia laid down the implements of peaceful toil and took up arms for the preservation of the Union. Laconia's record in the Civil War would require a larger volume than the "Illustrated Laconian," and some future historian must do justice to our brave citizen-soldiers, many of whom are still with us, although their ranks are growing thinner and their locks are growing grayer, as they form in line on each annual Memorial Day. The two Grand Army posts of the city now decorate over one hundred and fifty graves of deceased comrades of the war of 1861-'65.

In 1863 Laconia voted to pay a bounty of $300 to those who might be drafted, or their substitutes, and the selectmen were authorized to advance all bounties, town, state, and national, to volunteers, to the amount of $500 each. In 1864 it was voted to pay soldiers a bounty of $100 for one year, $200 for two years, and $300 for three years, to all enlisted men, and $200 to men who might be drafted. In December of the same year, it was voted to pay a bounty of $600 to enrolled men who enlisted for three years.

When the first call for three months' men came from Washington, a full company of ninety men promptly volunteered and were enlisted at the old Torrent engine house on Water street. These men served the three months, and forty-two of them re-enlisted for three years, at Portsmouth, and were attached to the Second regiment. Another company of ninety men enlisted in the Fourth regiment, with William Badger as captain, David O. Burleigh, first lieutenant, and Timothy W. Chellis, second lieutenant. The next men to enlist were a detachment of twenty men who joined the Fifth regiment, and were headed by R. R. Somes. Captain Flan-

Laconia's Passenger Station, Opened August 22, 1892.

ders next raised a company of ninety men for the Eighth regiment, and when the famous Twelfth regiment was raised in Belknap county in ten days' time, Laconia sent another company of one hundred volunteers, commanded by Capt. John Whipple, with the late Joseph S. Tilton as first lieutenant. Another company, one hundred strong, with John Aldrich as captain, went out in the Fifteenth regiment, and when the New Hampshire Heavy Artillery was organized, Laconia sent a company of one hundred and fifty men. This list does not include all the men who enlisted from Laconia in the War of the Rebellion, for detachments were formed for other regiments, and quite a number of Laconians joined the regular United States army. But for a town with a population of only 1,800, it will be seen that Laconia was not lacking in patriotism during the great civil war.

In the spring of 1898, when President McKinley issued his first call for volunteers to enlist for two years, or until the end of the Spanish-American War, practically every member of the Tetley Rifles, Co. K, of the New Hampshire National Guard, of Laconia, promptly signified his readiness to enlist. On the second day of May, Co. K marched from their armory and took the train for Concord, where they were mustered into the United States service for two years. One hundred and six men was the strength of the company which left Laconia, and this city had numerous other representatives in companies from other sections of New Hampshire. Co. K was a part of the First New Hampshire Volunteers, and the regiment was at Camp Thomas, Chickamauga Park, Tennessee, during the summer, and came back to Concord in September to be mustered out, arriving in Laconia on Tuesday, Sept.

Company K, First New Hampshire Volunteers, 1898.

13th, for a thirty days' furlough, preparatory to being discharged from the United States service. There were four deaths in the company while in camp at Chickamauga Park: Capt. William A. Sanborn, Lieut. Joseph L. Morrill, Corporal Alfred Morrill, and Corporal Earle Gilman. All died from typhoid fever, which prevailed to quite an extent in the regiment. Lieutenant Morrill and Corporal Morrill were brothers, and Corporals Morrill and Gilman were officers in the Laconia High School Cadets, and members of the graduating class of 1898, but laid aside their books and gave up the honors of graduation to respond to the call of their country.

LACONIA TO-DAY

Laconia to-day is a city of 10,000 or 12,000 population, beautifully located among the famous lakes of central New Hampshire, at the gateway of the celebrated White Mountain region. It is in the centre of one of the most fertile farming sections of the Granite state, and has been for the past hundred years the trading centre of the surrounding farms, villages, and towns within a circle of twenty miles. Boston can be reached in three hours, either over the White Mountains division of the Boston & Maine railroad system, or by way of the Lake Shore branch of the Northern division of the same system.

Laconia is bounded on the north by Meredith and Lake Winnipesaukee, on the east by Winnipesaukee and Gilford on the south by Belmont and Lake Winnesquam, and on the west by Lake Winnesquam and Meredith. The Winnipesaukee river, having its source in the great reservoir of the same name, runs directly through the heart of the city, affording valuable water privileges, which have helped very materially in the development and growth of the city.

Laconia is the recognized commercial centre of Belknap county, being the shire town and the seat of the county government. The voting strength is about 2,300, and the latest assessors'

High School Building.

figures give the city a total valuation of $4,500,000. The inventory of city property, including school buildings, fire department, street department, etc., foots up over $245,000.

The city government is vested in a mayor and fourteen councilmen, the mayor elected annually, and the councilmen elected for two years, one from each ward being elected each year, with the exception of ward six (Lakeport), which elects two councilmen each year and has a representation of four members in each city council.

The present city government is as follows: Mayor, Colonel Edmund Tetley; councilmen, Ward 1, William A. Smith, Frank M. Sanborn: Ward 2, Charles F. Richards, Rufus P. Dow: Ward 3, John T. Dodge, Joseph R. Chase; Ward 4, John P. Clay, Charles L. Kimball; Ward 5, Frank A. Edwards, Alfred C. Wyatt: Ward 6, Julius E. Wilson, Edwin D. Ward, John R. Leavitt, George E. Hull; City clerk, Simeon C. Frye; City treasurer, Arthur W. Dinsmoor; City solicitor, Stephen S. Jewett; Board of assessors, Edwin F. Burleigh, Lewis S. Perley, Charles L. Pulsifer; Collector of taxes, Fred A. Young; City engineer, superintendent of sewers, and street commissioner, William Nelson; Overseers of the poor, Arthur Tucker, Arthur C. S.

Bird's-eye View of Latakia, from Vue de l'Eau Hotel.

Bird's-eye View of Jdeidet, from Reservoir Hill.

Randlett ; City physician, Dr. J. G. Quimby; Board of health, D. L. Davis, Dr. W. H. True, Fred A. Floyd.

The police department of the city is under the direction of a board of police commissioners, appointed by the governor and council of New Hampshire. The present commissioners are Frank E. Busiel, Fred C. Sanborn, Charles W. Vaughan. The police force consists of a city marshal, Henry K. W. Scott; assistant marshal, Frank A. Bailey; and four patrolmen, Bert M. Hutchins, Charles A. Harvell, Charles E. Small,

nine companies of firemen, divided as follows : one steamer company, two hook and ladder companies, and six hose companies. In connection with the fire department is the latest fire alarm telegraph service, with steam whistle and gong attachments. The city has one hundred and six hydrants, including seventeen private hydrants, supplied with water from the Laconia water-works, and having a powerful head of water, ready for immediate use at all times. In addition to the modern hydrant service, the city owns thirteen large reservoirs, distrib-

Masonic Temple

James B. Fernald, who patrol the streets of the city both day and night. The police court of Laconia also derives its authority from the state of New Hampshire. George H. Everett is presiding justice, True W. Thompson is associate justice, and Martin B. Plummer is clerk.

The Laconia fire department is, and has been for many years, one of the most efficient volunteer fire departments in New Hampshire. The total manual force at the present time consists of a chief engineer, Albert W. Wilcox, with three assistant engineers, John M. Sanborn, Albert Griffin, William Harris, and

uted about the city, which can be used in emergencies. The steam fire engine, ladder trucks, hose carriages, etc., are kept in good condition, with plenty of good hose, and horses are available at all times to haul the apparatus to fires.

Laconia's public schools are under the management of a board of education, elected by the voters. The present board consists of Charles L. Pulsifer, William A. Plummer, Albert C. Moore, Dennis O'Shea, Mrs. Lydia E. Warner, Mrs. Mary Gale Hibbard, Dr. Clifton S. Abbott, John G. Quimby, and William H. Flanders. The city owns eleven school

buildings and hires two more, employing a corps of thirty-six teachers. Joseph H. Blaisdell is superintendent of schools, and Hoyt H. Tucker is principal of the high school. The annual appropriation of the city for this department is from $20,000 to $25,000.

Odd Fellows' Opera House.

Laconia has two public libraries, one at Lakeport with about 2,000 books, and one at Laconia with 7,000 books. These libraries are maintained by an annual appropriation from the city, and are under the management of a board of library trustees, consisting at the present time of Messrs. W. J. Morrison, Chas. C. Davis, John T. Busiel, William F. Knight, Chas. K. Sanborn, Chas. F. Locke, and A. Stanton Owen.

At the present time the libraries are in rented rooms, but by the generosity of the late Major Napoleon B. Gale, the city will soon have a magnificent public library building. Major Gale bequeathed the bulk of his large estate to the city for the purpose of purchasing a suitable lot for a park and the erection of a library or memorial building. It has been thought best to combine the legacies for the two purposes, and with this end in view, the large property of the late John C. Moulton, located on the corner of Main and Church streets, has been purchased as a site for the park and library building. The executors of the Gale will have nearly settled the estate, and announce that in a short time they shall have a fund of about $150,000 in readiness to lay out the park, beautify the grounds, erect a memorial library building, and maintain the same, which probably will not be excelled by any structure of the kind in New Hampshire.

Another institution in which Laconia takes pride is the Laconia Cottage Hospital. The late Mrs. Rhoda C. Ladd, in January, 1893, left to Laconia the residue of her estate, amounting to nearly $10,000, for the establishment of a hospital whenever the city raised an equal amount. This fund has been increased from time to time, and, pending the establishment of a permanent hospital at some future date, public-spirited citizens in 1898 fitted up and opened a cottage hospital in the former residence of the late Rhoda Ladd, on Court street. This hospital is most excellently equipped, and is main-

Mechanic Street School Building, Lakeport.

tained by charity and an annual appropriation from the city council.

Laconia is well supplied with churches and religious organizations. There is one Congregational church, two Baptist, two Methodist, two Free Baptist, two

Roman Catholic, one Christian, one Advent, one Unitarian, and one Episcopal, besides Young Men's Christian Association rooms and a branch of the Salvation Army. Nearly all of the churches own commodious, and in some cases magnificent, church buildings, and there are numerous missionary societies, Christian Endeavor societies, and kindred organizations connected with nearly all of the churches.

Two G. A. R. posts, one military company, a large Masonic fraternity with elegant rooms in a recently-erected by a private corporation. No city in New England can boast a purer or better supply of drinking-water, and the head is sufficient for fire purposes and light manufacturing. Laconia has a good sewerage system, installed a few years ago at an expense of nearly $120,000. But few cities in New England of Laconia's size can boast of more concrete sidewalks. Large amounts of money have been invested in good walks, and there are but few streets in Laconia which have no concrete sidewalk, while nearly all of the more im-

Moulton Opera House Block.

Masonic temple, the most pretentious structure in the city. Odd Fellows, Daughters of Rebekah, Knights of Pythias, Good Templars, Red Men, United Workmen, Pilgrim Fathers, Knights of Honor, two Building and Loan associations, a Board of Trade, Ancient Order of Hibernians, Foresters, New England Order of Protection, and perhaps a dozen more organizations in these lines leave but little or nothing to be desired in this direction.

Laconia has a splendid water supply, pumped from Lake Winnipesaukee and distributed throughout the entire city portant streets have substantial concrete walks upon both sides of the highway.

Among other advantages which Laconia possesses as a desirable city for residential or business purposes, might be mentioned two telephone exchanges, the New England Co. and the Citizens', the latter a local corporation, both having a large list of patrons. An electric street railroad connects the two ends of the city, Laconia and Lakeport, and during the present summer of 1899 its tracks were extended to The Weirs, affording an opportunity to ride six or seven miles entirely within the city limits, and along the lake shore among some of the most beautiful scenery of New England. Laconia's streets are lighted by electricity, and private residences are illuminated by both gas and electricity, while gas is now being largely introduced as a fuel for cooking and heating as well as illumination.

In dry goods, clothing, carpetings, furniture, and perhaps some other lines, Laconia boasts the largest stores and the largest stocks to be found in New Hampshire, and these establishments have a well-earned reputation for selling goods at retail at lower prices than can be obtained even in the city of Boston, in many cases.

Financially, Laconia is the headquarters for a large territory of surrounding towns and villages. There are three national banks in the city, with a combined capital of $250,000, besides three savings banks with aggregate deposits of over one million and a half.

Laconia has three opera houses, one of them generally conceded to be one of the handsomest in New Hampshire. All of the best theatrical companies visit this city, and there are always plenty of attractions in this line. In the summer season the entire surrounding country, at The Weirs, Lake Shore Park, and other points easily reached by the shores of the lakes, is a veritable picnic-ground, most of the shores around the lakes being open to all comers, while hundreds of summer cottages dot the islands and shores of Winnipesaukee and Winnesquam, and afford a quiet retreat for their owners in the city.

The foregoing pages give but a hint at Laconia's many advantages and attractions. Laconia is a city, with all the conveniences and facilities of city life, for business, manufacturing, and home life, and at the same time offers the enjoyment of country life in its charming location, beautiful shaded streets, magnificent views, and unsurpassed scenery of both lakes and mountains.

A Census of Laconia in 1836.

John Farmer, who was secretary of the New Hampshire Historical Society in 1836, compiled a census of Laconia, then Meredith Bridge, which is still preserved, and probably very nearly correct, reading as follows:

"Population of Meredith Bridge Village, June 1, 1836, embracing the territory one mile on the Main road leading through Meredith to Gilmanton, the village lying in Meredith and Gilford."

The heads of families, the names thereof, and the number in each family appear as follows:

"Smith Jewett, 10; Stephen Boynton, 4; Nathaniel Batchelder, 7; Mrs. Robbinson, 5; Isaac M. Parker, 10; the Rev. J. K. Young, 4; Salmon Steavens, 5; Daniel J. Dinsmore, 3; Benning Mugridge, 6; Nicholas Gilman, 2; Charles Parker, 6; Nathan Bagley, 7; Osgood Bagley, 2; Mrs. Cheney, 7; Mr. Danforth, 2; F. W. Boynton, 9; Alpha Stevens, 5; Samuel Mugridge, 2; Josiah Crosby, 7; S. C. Lyford, 1; John T. Coffin, 7; George Hopkinson, 6; Moses E. Piper, 6; Francis Russell, 12; Thomas Eastman, 13; John M. Fitch, 4; P. W. Downing, 5; M. J. Boynton, 3; Alfred Bean, 5; Mrs. Dow, 4; John Wardwell, 5; T. D. Somes, 4; I. W. Mudgett, 6; I. B. Taylor, 4; S. Perley, 9; J. L. Perley, 1; Daniel Tucker, 3; Winthrop Young, 6; Hiram Bean, 9; Samuel H. Bean, 4; Mr. Dimond, 5; A. Brigham, 5; Widow Allen, 31; A. T. Parker, 2; Hugh Wilson, 6; Widow Quimby, 6; Widow Swasey, 32; Elijah Quimby, 15; Jonathan Hill, 8; H. H. Robinson, 10; S. Lawrence, 2; J. F. Clough, 9; George L. Sibley 7; J. Sanborn, 8; J. Cookson, 11; Thomas Piper, 3; M. F. Buzzell, 6; Isaiah Merrill, 8."

The above includes a total of 58 families and a population of 384. It will be noticed that the Widow Allen is accredited with 31 members in her household and the Widow Swasey with 32. Both of these kept boarding-houses.

The Laconia Car Company Works.

The Laconia car shops, under the management of the Laconia Car Company Works, of which Hon. Frank Jones of Portsmouth is president and principal owner, with Hon. Edward H. Gilman of Exeter as general manager and treasurer, is the largest single industry in the city of Laconia, and also one of the largest, most important and most widely-known in New Hampshire.

The original Laconia car shops were started by the late Charles Ranlet in 1848, and was first known as the C. Ranlet Car Manufacturing Co. In 1849 Mr. Joseph Ranlet was taken into partnership and the firm name was the Ranlet Car Company. This partnership continued until the death of Mr. Charles Ranlet in October, 1861. In December of the following year, the surviving partner, Joseph Ranlet, formed a partnership with the late Hon. John C. Moulton, continuing the business under the name of the Moulton & Ranlet Car Company. In January, 1865, another company was formed under the name of the Ranlet Manufacturing Co., the members of the concern being John C. Moulton, Joseph Ranlet and Perley Putnam, who continued in business until April 20, 1878, at which time Mr. Ranlet retired.

In 1882 the company was re-organized under the corporate name of Laconia Car Company, Messrs. Moulton and Putnam still being the principal owners. In 1889, the late Mr. Moulton sold out his interest in the corporation to his partner, Mr. Perley Putnam, who carried on the car building industry, practically alone in its ownership and management until 1897, when the entire property passed into the hands of Hon. Frank Jones and his associates.

The new corporation, chartered under the name of The Laconia Car Company Works, was organized on Feb. 25th, 1897, and the board of officers of the corporation at the present time are as follows:

President, Hon. Frank Jones.
Treasurer, E. H. Gilman.
Directors, Hon. Frank Jones, E. H. Gilman, B. A. Kimball, C. F. Stone, Dennis O'Shea.

The original plant was comparatively a small concern, with cheap wooden buildings and old-fashioned machinery. But the wooden buildings have gradually given way to most substantial structures of brick, equipped with the latest machines in every department. The plant now covers seven acres of land in the very heart of the city of Laconia, and a large proportion of this property is covered with the foundries, wood-working shops, setting-up shops, painting shops, storehouses, etc., including the immense four-story brick structure de-

Hon. Frank Jones.

voted to the malleable iron foundry industry, which is operated in connection with the car construction business.

When the car plant was started, nothing but freight cars were manufactured, but afterwards facilities were added for turning out all kinds of passenger cars, and the Laconia car shops soon won a national reputation for building first-class cars of every description. During the past few years the introduction of electric railroads in all parts of the United States has developed a new branch of this car-building industry, and to-day one of the most important departments of the Laconia car

ment is pushed to its full capacity, and there are prospects of plenty of work in this line for months to come.

The car shops now employ about five hundred men, and as these are, of course, in many cases the heads of families, the importance of the car business to Laconia can be easily seen. Vast quantities of lumber are consumed every year (estimated at 4,000,000 feet), making a ready market for much of the better timber within a radius of fifty miles of Laconia, while, of course large quantities of Southern, Western and foreign woods are brought from a distance.

The malleable iron foundry depart

Car built for the Woonsocket (R. I.) Street Railway Company.

shops is the construction of electric street cars.

In the manufacture of all styles of electric cars, this concern has achieved a reputation second to no car company in the United States and the handsome and substantial products of the Laconia shops can be seen upon the trolley lines of Boston, New York, and, in fact, nearly all the large cities of the United States. The demand for electric cars appears to be constantly increasing and there is evidently a great future for this branch of the business. At the present time the electric car construction depart-

ment was established a few years ago, and this foundry is one of the largest of the kind in New England.

The motive power for operating the machinery in the plant includes steam, water power, and electricity. During the past two years, thousands of dollars have been invested in rearranging and improving the plant, adding modern machinery and in every way making the facilities up to date for turning out the best possible work at the least possible expense.

The Boston office at No. 50 State street is the general headquarters of the corporation, and the office of the treasurer and manager, Hon. E. H. Gilman. Mr. Peter Walling, formerly connected with the Boston & Maine railroad, as master bridge constructor, is the superintendent of the plant at Laconia. Nearly all the foremen in the various departments, and in fact a large proportion of the employés, are men who have grown up in the car-building business and have found employment in these shops nearly all their lives.

The above sketch, of course, gives but a faint idea of the completeness of the Laconia car plant, or of its importance to Laconia. From a small concern, employing less than one hundred men, it has grown to require almost a regiment of employés in its shops, and its capacity has been increased from a few rough freight cars per week, to a palatial modern passenger car per day. Under its present management the business is conducted on a substantial basis; excellence and improvement in methods and production are the aims in every department of the business and the prospects for future success and a large increase in business are most excellent.

Colonel Edmund Tetley.

Colonel Edmund Tetley, mayor of the city of Laconia, and colonel of the First regiment, New Hampshire National Guard, was born in Bradford, Yorkshire county, England, October 26,

Interior of Car built for the Woonsocket (R. I.) Street Railway Company.

1842, son of William and Mary Ann (Brayshaw) Tetley. He attended the schools in England until he was twelve years of age, when with his family he came to America. At the age of nineteen he enlisted in the United States Marine Corps at Portsmouth, and saw some active service. He was at the attack on Forts Jackson and Philip, and at the capture of New Orleans by Admiral Farragut, being on board of the

United States sloop of war *Portsmouth*, which was subsequently stationed at New Orleans for nearly four years. At the close of the war he returned to Amesbury, Mass., subsequently going to Appleton, Wis., and then to Utica, N. Y. From Utica he went to Olneyville, R. I., and thence to Lowell, Mass., where he obtained employment in a paper-box factory. Somewhat later he obtained employment in a paper-box factory in Methuen, from which he next went to Haverhill, Mass. In 1873 he came to Laconia, where he entered the employ of Mr. Frank P. Holt, a manufacturer of paper boxes. Five years later Mr. Tetley succeeded Mr. Holt and has since carried on a large and successful business on his own account.

Mr. Tetley's interest in military affairs did not end with his war service. Soon after coming to Laconia he joined Company K, Third regiment of the state National Guard. He was made lieutenant in 1873, and a year later was promoted captain, serving in this rank until his resignation in the year 1883. Some years later the old Company K was disbanded, whereupon Mr. Tetley organized another company which took the place in the same regiment, of which he was chosen captain. He was promoted to the rank of major, May 8, 1894. He held this position at the time of President McKinley's first call for volunteers, and the Third New Hampshire regiment was selected for duty at the front. Major Tetley went to Chickamauga Park with his regiment and came back to New Hampshire in September as the lieutenant-colonel of the command. After the regiment was mustered out of the United States service and the old organization of the New Hampshire National Guard was resumed, Colonel Tetley was again promoted to colonel of the regiment, a position which he now holds.

Colonel Tetley has held numerous political positions, among them selectman of Laconia, high sheriff of Belknap county, a member of the first city council, member of the state legislature in 1894, etc. March, 1899, he was elected mayor of the city of Laconia, and was inaugurated on March 21. In politics Colonel Tetley is a Republican. He is very popular in fraternal circles, and is a member of a dozen or more organizations.

Colonel Tetley was married December 9, 1868, to Ella F. Merrill of Lowell, Mass. Of their seven children, five are living: Edmund B., now a student in theology; Guy M., superintendent of the Tetley box factory; Gertrude, a resident of Lowell, Mass.; Blanche, and Charles, now at school in Laconia.

Col. Edmund Tetley, Mayor of Laconia.

Laconia Building & Loan Association.

When men of small means found out that a business enterprise, which no one of them could conduct alone, was possible for them by uniting their labor and their capital they discovered the secret of coöperation. When they found out that by uniting their surplus earnings they could provide themselves with homes of their own instead of remaining subject to the demands of landlords, they put coöperation to one of its most beneficent uses.

The concentration of capital is daily going on, for capitalists have learned that by this means (coöperation) they can conduct great enterprises with more certainty of success than by any other.

Now what is good for the man of large means is equally good for the man of small means; but the latter class seem to have been much longer in finding it out, and have always plodded along because they believed themselves too poor to accomplish anything. Single-handed a man is, but when he is afforded an opportunity to pool his savings, though small they may be, he should not hesitate to do so, for by such methods he receives valuable assistance and is enabled to raise himself much more easily from the financial "slough of despond" in which he with the ninety and nine are wallowing. With the object of coöperation in view, and to give to Laconia an institution that would be a benefit to its people, in the year 1887, the formation of this organization was begun by Walter S. Baldwin and Charles W. Tyler, who worked assiduously for its completion.

On the 14th day of January, 1888, the association was incorporated under the laws of the state, and began business January 31, 1888, by issuing its first series of shares, five hundred in number, which were promptly taken.

The Laconia Building and Loan Association is now an established fact. It has a large membership, and offers both depositors and borrowers advantages unequaled by any other system of banking known to the world. It combines the principles of a savings bank and a stock company. It is authorized to issue shares to the amount of $1,000,000, which are nominally worth $200 each, but are paid for in installments of $1.00 per month, or better, these monthly payments, together with the dividends which they have earned, will at some future date (usually about eleven years), equal $200.

If the shares have been used in securing a home, it is then the borrower's, free from all incumbrances. On the other hand, if they have been held for investment only, they will then be paid in cash. During the little more than eleven years of its existence the association has met with deserved success, and the many homes that have been built through the assistance given to its members is proof positive of its true worth and merit.

Twenty-three series of shares have been issued during the time, and its membership has numbered as high as 425, holding an issue of 2,400 shares of stock.

The following named, many of whom have been connected with the association since its formation, comprise its management: Edmund Tetley, president; Alburtis S. Gordon, vice-president; Albert C. Moore, secretary; Charles W. Tyler, treasurer; Stephen S. Jewett, attorney. Directors, Walter S. Baldwin, William F. Knight, Charles W. Vaughan, Charles F. Richards, Charles J. Austin, William A. Plummer, Frank P. Webster, Louis J. Truland, Stephen S. Jewett, Alburtis S. Gordon, Charles W. Tyler, and Albert C. Moore.

The assets of the association amount to nearly $160,000, nearly all of which are investments within the city limits.

The office of the association is located in the Masonic Temple, where it occupies a handsome apartment.

James McGloughlin.

James McGloughlin, proprietor of the Belknap Brass and Iron Foundry, is a native of England, born March 21, 1853, in Manchester, England. He came to this country during the Civil War, in 1863, with his parents, and has lived most of the time since then in Laconia. Mr. McGloughlin received his education in the little old red schoolhouse which formerly stood near the residence of Ex-Mayor S. B. Smith on Harvard street, and which was for many years the only school building on the north side of the river. This little one-story schoolhouse, with two rooms, sheltered many hundreds of Laconia's school children, forty years ago, and was finally sawed into two parts and remodeled into two tenement houses which still stand on Middle street. Mr. McGloughlin commenced to learn the moulder's trade at the foundry of the late Benjamin J. Cole in Lakeport, and finished with George Rollins in Laconia. In 1877 he removed to Concord, N. H., where he was employed at his trade by W. P. Ford. In 1889 he came back to Laconia and bought out Arthur Smith, in what was known as the Belknap Iron and Brass Foundry. This foundry business had previously been conducted by three different parties, but the concern was a failure financially up to the time of Mr. McGloughlin's advent. Under his careful management, however, the concern has prospered, and by strict attention to business and enterprising methods, he has built up a large and prosperous industry.

Mr. McGloughlin was married to Mrs. Anna Greene, March 24, 1879, and they have one daughter, Miss Florence S. McGloughlin.

Mr. McGloughlin is an Episcopalian, and a member of the Knights of Pythias, which he joined in Concord in 1879, also of the Ancient Order of United Workmen, which he joined in the same city in 1887.

He has held several public offices, being elected a selectman of Ward 4 in 1895, and a councilman from the same ward in 1896. In 1897 he represented his ward in the legislature.

As a business man and manufacturer, Mr. McGloughlin has been very successful. His iron foundry business is one of the largest in this section of New Hampshire and he supplies not only the city of Laconia, but the city of Franklin, and numerous small towns and villages with the iron castings required in the numerous machine shops, mills, and factories. Mr. McGloughlin is popular with his employés and always provides a Thanksgiving turkey for every family man in his establishment. Mr. McGloughlin is a Republican in politics and as a member of the legislature and in the city council chamber always took a prominent part in all legislation. He is a public-spirited citizen, is interested in the Laconia board of trade, of which he is an active member, and is always ready to assist in every way in his power in any movement which promises to advance the interests of Laconia.

Recently Mr. McGloughlin became interested in the development of the McGloughlin Positive Friction Clutch, of which he is the proprietor and manufacturer, handling this industry in connection with his regular foundry busi-

James McGloughlin.

ness. For the uninitiated, it may be well to explain that a "clutch" is a device attached to a line of shafting in factories and shops, whereby a portion of the shafting can be cut off and stopped, or thrown into motion again, without resorting to the manipulation of beltings, etc. By the use of the McGloughlin Positive Friction Clutch, for instance, it is now possible by the simple movement of a lever to instantly start up a heavy piece of machinery like an electric dynamo, or two-faced electric machines. The McGloughlin clutch is conceded to be the best in the market, for electricians have always found it difficult to keep a two-faced dynamo in step, but with this clutch when once in step it can never slip or strain upon the shafting, as would naturally be expected from suddenly connecting a dormant machine to a rapidly-revolving shaft. The McGloughlin clutch starts the machinery by friction alone, but as soon as the machine or shafting is moving in unison with the shafting from which the motive power is derived, the friction clutch locks automatically and becomes a positive clutch, which cannot be shaken loose or slip. In the same easy manner the machinery can be stopped and the motive power removed, without disturbing the main line of shafting or interfering in any way with other machines which may be in operation on the same line.

Inventors have for a long time sought for a device of this kind, and Mr. McGloughlin appears to have hit upon a clutch which not only answers every requirement, but apparently cannot be improved. Manufacturers and mill men everywhere who have used the McGloughlin clutch are loud in its praise, and as the field for its usefulness is almost world-wide, a large industry will undoubtedly be built up from this invention. Although the clutch is comparatively a new thing upon the market it is called for by manufacturers in all parts of the United States, and is everywhere pronounced the best device of the kind which has yet been brought to public notice. Of course the clutch is protected by patents and competent judges state that the invention is worth a fortune if properly introduced.

Carroll & Crapo.

One of the metropolitan establishments of the City on the Lakes is the tonsorial establishment of Michael J. Carroll and Joseph Crapo, located at No. 487 Main street. This shop is the handsomest and best equipped of any in the line here; the chairs are comfortable, everything is neat as wax-work, and the razors are always sharp. In addition to Messrs. Carroll and Crapo here can be found Mr. Ai O. Cox, who has a reputation second to no one in Laconia, as an artist with the razor and shears. This establishment has the steady patronage of many of our most fastidious citizens, and it surely merits the success which it receives. Messrs. Carroll and Crapo are both young men, but they pay strict attention to business and are "sure winners."

Residence of James McGloughlin.

The Laconia Hardware Company.

Until within a comparatively few years, the hardware trade of Laconia was handled by dealers in general merchandise. In 1886 Messrs. George W. Riley and Farrar & Cilley built the so-called Belmont block, on the south side of the river, on the site formerly occupied by the old Tremont Hotel. Mr. Riley put a small stock of general hardware into one of the stores in the block, and this was the first attempt in Laconia to conduct a hardware and paint store. In 1887 Messrs. Levensaler & Smart bought out Mr. Riley, in Belmont block was too small to handle the increased trade of the store, the business having thus early outgrown its quarters. Consequently, when the Masonic Temple was erected, the corner store and basement were leased, and the Laconia Hardware Co. removed to its present location in October, 1896.

This concern can boast of the largest store and the largest stock of general hardware, paints, iron and steel, mill supplies, bicycles, fishing tackle, and sporting goods, to be found in northern New Hampshire.

The motto of the firm has always

The Laconia Hardware Store.

and continued for one year. Mr. Levensaler then retired from the business, and Mr. Albert T. Quinby came into the concern. This was in 1888, and the Laconia Hardware company was born at that time. Quinby & Smart continued for about one year, and then Mr. Quinby assumed full control, employing his son, Edwin N. Quinby, as head salesman and Charles Dearborn as assistant, with his daughter, Miss Nellie P. Quinby, as bookkeeper.

The business increased rapidly, and in 1895 E. N. Quinby was admitted to the firm. It was found that the store been: First quality goods, small profits and square dealing. This motto is lived up to every hour of the day and every day in the year, and it has built up a large and prosperous business.

There are now employed in the store, besides the members of the firm, two men and a lady book-keeper, making five persons in all. Mr. Edwin N. Quinby is the buyer for the concern and also the traveling salesman. He covers the entire northern section of New Hampshire and by constant hustle and square dealing has built up an immense trade in hardware among the retail dealers of the north country.

Mr. Albert T. Quinby is the financial man of the business, having charge of the whole concern, but more especially paying attention to the settlement of accounts, collection of bills, and other financial matters.

Albert T. Quinby.

Probably but few of the general public are aware of the immense stock of merchandise which is carried by the Laconia Hardware Co. They have a large storehouse in the rear of the Masonic Temple which is filled almost entirely with iron and steel for blacksmith supply. The basement under their store is packed full of paints, oils, rope, glass, and nails galore, of every size and style. Everything in the line of builders' and carpenters' hardware is carried in stock. Cutlery is another department which receives much attention. Bicycles, horse blankets, lawn mowers, garden tools, carpenters' tools, brushes, in fact, it would take a bigger publication that the Illustrated Laconian to catalogue the stock carried by this enterprising concern.

In the line of sporting goods, Messrs. Quinby & Son are the headquarters for this section of New Hampshire. They always have a choice line of shotguns, rifles, etc., and every kind of ammunition and hunting supplies. The fishing tackle department is a treat for anglers, as their stock in this line includes both cheap and costly rods, lines, reels, hooks, baskets, landing nets and, in short, everything used for brook, river and lake fishing at any season of the year.

The Laconia Hardware establishment is a credit to Laconia and the proprietors deserve success for their enterprise, courteous treatment of patrons, and square dealing.

Albert T. Quinby, the senior member of the firm, was born in Portland, Maine, in 1845. At the age of 17 years he entered the employ of the hardware concern in Searsport, Me., and after six years took an interest in the concern. This business was continued with various change until 1888, when Mr. Quinby, who was then the head of the concern, sold out his interest in the business and removed to Laconia. Mr. Quinby has always been prominent in society and in the Masonic fraternities, being four times elected W. M. of his home lodge. Since coming to Laconia he has joined Pythagorean Council and Pilgrim Commandery, Knights Templar,

Edwin N. Quinby.

in which he has taken great interest and held offices.

Edwin N. Quinby was born in Searsport, Maine, in 1867. He received his education in the public schools and at the age of 17 years entered the employ of a wholesale hardware concern in Portland, Maine, where he remained until 1888, when he came to Laconia to enter the employ of the Laconia Hardware Co.

The Late Daniel S. Dinsmoor.

On the morning of March 24, 1883, the people of Laconia were shocked by the announcement of the very sudden death of Hon. Daniel Stark Dinsmoor. He was stricken instantly, without warning, when apparently in good health, and died immediately without returning to consciousness. The death of Mr. Dinsmoor was regarded as a public calamity. He was a scholarly and accomplished man, of fine personal appearance, and universally loved and respected. He had just reached his full and promising manhood when the summons came and his earthly career closed forever.

He was born in the village of Laconia, Sept. 23, 1837, the son of Daniel J. and Caroline (Stark) Dinsmoor, a descendant of John Dinsmoor, a man much loved and respected by the early settlers and even by the Indians as well, for his honesty and uprightness; he was also a descendant of Gen. John Stark of Revolutionary fame, "the hero of Bennington," whose family name he bore.

He received his early education in the village schools and Gilford academy, where he exhibited among other qualifications a marked ability in declamation. After the course at the academy in his native village he went to New London Literary and Scientific Institution, at that time one of the leading institutions of the state, where he graduated with high honors in 1860, his address before the society receiving especial commendation. For some time after graduating he read law in the offices of Hon. Wm. Blair, Geo. W. Stevens, Esq., and Hon. O. A. J. Vaughan, and was admitted to the bar in 1864.

In 1865 he was united in marriage to Amelia M. Whittemore, the fruit of the union being two sons, Arthur W. and A. Jameson Dinsmoor. Upon the organization of the Laconia National bank, in 1865, he was chosen cashier, which position he held until his death. He was frequently selected for political honor, holding many important offices, such as county treasurer, register of probate, representative to the legislature of 1875, besides other minor offices, and was a member of Governor Cheney's staff. In November, 1882, he was elected senator from the Laconia district, the issue being the Lake Shore railroad, although the district was conceded to be Democratic while he was always a Republican of unquestioned integrity. He was prominent in Masonic circles, having been master of Mt. Lebanon lodge; he was also a member of Union Chapter. On the year previous to his demise he was

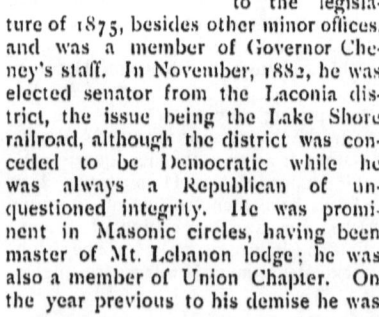

The Late Daniel S. Dinsmoor.

invited by the local post of the Grand Army of the Republic to deliver the Memorial Day poem which he complied with, and we know of no more fitting manner of expressing the esteem in which he was held by his associates, than to quote a few lines of the poem delivered on the successive year.

Standing to-night, where twelve months since
He who has served you, as a prince
Does subjects' service till his sire
Calls him to state and duty higher;
I should but partly voice your thought,
Not naming him who held, unsought,"
Your hearty and your honored call
To stand in senatorial hall.
And thus remind you of the claim,
That memory has on Dinsmoor's name.
I will but name him, any words of praise
Are needless here to you who knew him well;
The memories that his welcome name will raise
Are more than tongue or pen of mine can tell.
For with you here as youth and man he dwelt,
Gave you his service and his cordial cheer;
And you as kindred and as neighbors felt
When he was from you borne upon his bier,
The stroke that struck him down in manhood strong
Reached to your hearts, reëchoes in my song.

Rev. J. Franklin Babb.

Rev. J. Franklin Babb, although now located at Ashland, New Hampshire, is a Laconia boy, as he spent his boyhood days in Lakeport and was educated in our public schools. He was born in Lowell, Mass., May 20, 1874, his parents being John W. and Josie H. (Damon) Babb. His mother was the daughter of Rev. Joseph B. Damon, at one time pastor of the First Baptist church of Lakeport. Rev. Mr. Babb is a lateral descendant of Gov. John Hancock of Massachusetts, and a direct descendant of the famous John Tufton Mason, who was granted the region now known as Maine and New Hampshire, in the old colonial times. He was educated in the public schools of Lakeport, academic course, and then making a three years' special study for the ministry. He was ordained in Ashland, Feb. 23, 1898, as pastor of the Free Baptist church, his present charge.

Rev. Mr. Babb's father died when he was six years old, and the young man worked in factories, etc., to continue his studies and prepare himself for his chosen work in the ministry. He is a self-made man, and is popular not only as a pastor but as a citizen, and highly esteemed by hundreds of friends in this

Rev. J. Franklin Babb.

section of New Hampshire. Rev. Mr. Babb has written quite a good deal for the press, especially in the line of poetry, and articles from his pen' are frequently seen in some of our leading New England publications.

The Wardwell Needle Company.

Among the many industries that have contributed so much to the development of Laconia as a manufacturing city is the plant of the Wardwell Needle Company. This company was established in the early sixties by the late C. P. S. Wardwell and was under various managements with moderate success until the year 1885 when it passed into the hands of its present owners who immediately commenced the erection of new buildings and the installation of modern labor saving machinery, much of which is protected by patents and used exclusively by this company, bringing the whole plant to a state of perfection that has enabled the company to take a leading position in the manufacture of the celebrated Excelsior needles for all kinds of hosiery machinery. These needles are used exclusively by many of the largest knitting mills in the country and have a good reputation where known.

The constant endeavor of this company to give its customers the best that can be produced has brought them a large trade from all sections of the country and the fact that the owners of these works manufacture and sell more latch needles each year than any manufacturer in the world is a sufficient endorsement of the popularity of their goods. The stock room is filled with finished needles for all the different knitting machines in use and orders are usually filled upon same day they are received. A large number of employés are given constant work and the weekly disbursement of wages for a long series of years has been an important factor in the growth and improvement of that portion of the city. A liberal policy toward its help has always been characteristic of this concern, which has added largely to its prosperity, strikes or other labor troubles never occurring. The mechanical departments are under the personal supervision of Mr. S. A. Whitten, an expert needle maker, and the whole business is managed by Mr. Julius E. Wilson, the treasurer. He came to Laconia with the parties now owning the company and has devoted himself to the building up of a large permanent industry and that success has crowned his efforts goes without saying. In this connection a brief biographical sketch of Mr. Wilson and his connection with our city and its institutions is pertinent.

The Wardwell Needle Company.

Julius E. Wilson, manager and treasurer of the Wardwell Needle Co., was born in Swanzey, New Hampshire, July 16, 1849. His early life was spent upon a farm, and he acquired his education in the public schools and academies of that section. In 1867, after completing a course in the Bryant & Stratton Business College in Manchester, he entered the employ of the Massachusetts Mutual Life Insurance Co., at Manchester, and was engaged in the insurance business for many years. Later he became manager of a large clothing house, where he remained until he came to this city in 1885, to take charge of the Wardwell needle business.

Mr. Wilson married Morgia M. Porter of Manchester. They have no children. In religious matters he is a Unitarian.

In secret and fraternal orders, Mr. Wilson is connected with the Masonic and Odd Fellows fraternities, and he is also a member of the Home Market Club. He is an enthusiast in all matters pertaining to hunting and fishing, and was one of the organizers of the Belknap County Fish and Game League, which was formed about two years ago, and already has, perhaps, the largest and strongest membership of any similar organization in New Hampshire. Mr. Wilson has been the president of this league from the start. He is also president of the Mutual Building and Loan Association, Lakeport, and is also a trustee of the City Savings-bank at the Laconia end of the city.

In politics, Mr. Wilson is a staunch Republican. He was elected a member of the first city council of Laconia, in 1893, and has been reëlected at every subsequent election, being at the present time the oldest member of the city government in point of service. In the city council Mr. Wilson has served upon the finance committee, the roads and bridges committee, and other of the more important committees, devoting much of his time during the past six years to city affairs. His long service in the city council gives him perfect familiarity with all municipal affairs, and he has always been one of the strongest members of this body.

Julius E. Wilson.

Residence of Julius E. Wilson.

John W. Ashman.

John W. Ashman was born in Barnston, Que., Oct. 14, 1849, his parents being Edward and Sarah (Folly) Ashman. His father died Sept. 1, 1852, and John went to Walden, Caledonia county, Vermont, to live. In the public schools of this town he received his education supplemented by a term at Phillips academy in Danville, Vt.

Mr. Ashman came to Laconia Mar. 22, 1871, and entered the employ of the late Horace Whicher. He remained until November, 1875, when he entered the law office of E. P. Jewell, Esq. He was admitted to the bar in March, 1880, and continued in the prac-

tice of his chosen profession until January, 1885, when he was elected treasurer of the Belknap Savings bank, which position he now occupies.

Mr. Ashman is a Democrat in politics and has received numerous honors in the political line. He first entered the public service in March, 1880, as town clerk, and held that office five years. He was chosen librarian of the public library July, 1879, which position he held five years, and was also a trustee of the library for ten years. Mr. Ashman was one of the members of the board of education in 1881, 1882, and 1883, and was also clerk of the school district. He was a moderator at the annual town meeting, in March, 1890. He served as register of probate for Belknap county for three terms. When the city government was inaugurated Mr. Ashman was chosen a member of the first city council from Ward 5, and served as a member of the finance committee. In 1898 Mr. Ashman was elected as a Democrat to the New Hampshire legislature from Ward 5, which is one of the strongest Republican wards in the city.

Mr. Ashman is treasurer of the Laconia Hospital association, and First Unitarian society, also of the Laconia Land and Improvement Co. He was a charter member of Winnesquam Colony, No. 14, United Order of Pilgrim Fathers, and has held various offices in this order.

Mr. Ashman was a member and treasurer of Company K, New Hampshire National Guard, when this company was first formed by Captain Elbert Wheeler (now General Wheeler), and went with this company to the centennial celebration at Yorktown in 1881.

In religious affairs Mr. Ashman affiliates with the Unitarians. He is still unmarried.

John W. Ashman.

O'Shea Brothers' Establishment.

O'Shea Brothers' is perhaps the best known mercantile establishment in central and northern New Hampshire. The firm handles clothing, dry goods, and furniture, and has grown from a small beginning in the year 1875 to one of the largest stores and largest distributors of goods in their line in this section of New England.

On April 25, 1875, Dennis O'Shea and his oldest brother, the late John O'Shea, commenced the dry goods business in a little store in a building which then stood on the site of their present furniture department building. The Laconia *Democrat* office occupied the second floor of the building, and Miss Kate Feeley conducted a millinery store in one side of the ground floor of the building, leaving about 1,100 square feet for O'Shea Bros.' dry goods business. Both members of the firm had served a few years as clerks in similar establishments in Laconia, and consequently had a fair knowledge of the business. Their first year's trade was an immense success, actually turning the entire stock over seven times. Encouraged by the favor which their venture received from the public, they decided to put in a stock of ready-made

O'Shea Bros.' Store in 1875.

clothing, and in December of the same year they leased the portion of the building formerly occupied by Miss Feeley, and in this addition to their establishment put in a stock of clothing, engaging their brother, Eugene O'Shea, to take charge of this department.

This venture, also, proved a success,

O'Shea Bros.' Store in 1878.

but in a short time the firm again found itself pressed for room to accommodate their rapidly-increasing trade. In the spring of 1877, the late John C. Moulton built an addition to the rear of the building, which increased the floor space to 3,550 square feet. The stock of goods up to this time consisted only of dry goods and clothing, but next came a demand for carpetings, there being at that time only one small stock in town. To meet this demand, O'Shea Bros. leased more land in the rear of the Moulton building, and erected another addition, 35 by 18 feet, for a carpet room.

But the patronage of the establishment and the consequent demand for a larger and more varied stock had in the meantime increased faster than the

O'Shea Bros.' Store in 1882.

accommodations, and O'Shea Bros. soon found themselves again cramped for room to conduct their growing business. In the spring of 1878 they leased the land on the north side of their store, and erected a block of about thirty feet front and seventy feet depth. The old and new stores were connected and the new building accommodated the clothing department on the first floor, while the carpet and custom-made clothing departments were upstairs.

The new building gave about 4,000 square feet more floor space, making the largest store in Laconia and probably the largest in New Hampshire at that time. The establishment certainly appeared large for a town the size of Laconia, and many of our people predicted a downfall and failure. Pluck and perseverance, however, won again, and in the autumn of 1882, when the Laconia *Democrat* vacated the rooms store in New Hampshire, containing seventeen different departments.

No further changes were made until the spring of 1886, when Mr. Moulton decided to erect the present Moulton opera house block. At this time O'Shea Bros. purchased the Mrs. J. H. Story property on Pleasant street and removed their own building there (now

Present Store of O'Shea Bros.

over the dry goods store and moved to Mill street. Messrs. O'Shea Bros. leased the vacated premises and put in a stock of furniture. They also induced Mr. Moulton to add a third story to the building, while they put a third story on their own building adjoining. At this time the original store of 1,100 square feet had grown to an establishment of 13,000 square feet, the largest the Kirtland House property) to make room for the opera house block. The firm up to this time had consisted only of the two brothers, Dennis and John, who opened the original store in 1875, but in 1887 Eugene O'Shea, who had taken charge of the clothing department, was admitted to membership.

When the Moulton opera house block was completed in August, 1887, Messrs.

O'Shea Bros. leased the entire first floor and basement, in connection with the wooden furniture building, all three floors of which are devoted to the furniture and carpeting business. The floor space now occupied by this concern, including their storehouse for furniture, near the passenger depot, amounts to nearly 30,000 square feet, or about two thirds of an acre.

John O'Shea died Oct. 26, 1890, and the business has since been carried on by Dennis, Eugene, and Thomas O'Shea, the latter having the furniture and carpeting departments.

O'Shea Bros.' store is an establishment of which all true Laconians are proud. Their success is due to natural shrewdness and business tact, combined with hard work, untiring attention to the wants of the public, fair dealing, and liberal advertising.

From young men in limited financial circumstances, the O'Shea Bros. built up a business of $250,000 per annum, and made themselves among the foremost and best-known merchants of the Granite state. They have always found time to interest themselves in every movement of a public nature which promised to assist in the growth and prosperity of Laconia, and they have been important factors in nearly all our local enterprises.

Dennis O'Shea, the senior member of the firm, is a director of the Laconia National bank, a trustee of the City Savings bank, president of the Laconia Electric Light Co., president of the Laconia Board of Trade, one of the promoters, organizers, and president of the Casino Building Co., a member of the board of education, and has always found time to devote himself enthusiastically to the success of every enterprise and public position with which he has been connected.

Mutual Building & Loan Association.

The Mutual Building and Loan Association was organized June 3, 1890, with the following board of officers and directors: President, Henry B. Quinby; vice-president, Henry J. Odell; secretary, Leroy M. Gould; treasurer, Edwin D. Ward. Directors: Benjamin F. Drake, Henry Tucker, Charles E. Buzzell, Stephen B. Cole, Edwin L. Cram, Libbeus E. Hayward, Elijah H. Blaisdell, Samuel R. Jones, Charles J. Pike; solicitor, Joseph L. Odell. The association commenced business June 10, 1890, with a membership of 113, fifteen of whom were females. Its mission has been to assist mechanics and others in getting homes of their own. In this it has done its work well. It now has $30,000 assets which consist of loans to its members who are monthly drawing nearer the time when they will have homes of their own free from incumbrance, and others who are laying by something for a rainy day. Its affairs have been successfully conducted at all times, and as yet the association has not lost a dollar by injudicious investment, while on the other hand its members have been receiving a good rate of interest on their investments. From the start the officers and directors have been very careful in making all loans and herein lies one of the principal secrets of its successful career.

The business of the association is conducted in such a way that any person desiring to build or purchase a home, lift a mortgage, or engage in business may become a member at any time by paying a nominal admission fee and taking one or more shares of stock. The Building and Loan Association offers inducements to mechanics, artisans, and laboring men generally that are not found in banking and other financial institutions.

The present officers and board of directors are: President, Julius E. Wilson; vice-president, John N. Meader; secretary, Leroy M. Gould; treasurer, Edwin D. Ward. Directors: Libbeus E. Hayward, Charles L. Pulsifer, John Aldrich, Edwin L. Cram, William G. Cram, George B. Munsey, Albert M. Read, Charles E. Sleeper, Charles L. Simpson. The headquarters of the association are at Lakeport.

Cole Manufacturing Company.

In 1827 the foundation of the Cole Manufacturing company was laid by the father of Benjamin J. Cole who moved from Franklin with his family in that year to Batchelder's Mills, now Lakeport, and built a small foundry, doing his melting in a large kettle with charcoal which he burned in the neighborhood; prior to leaving Franklin he had built the second foundry erected in the state and numbered among his customers General John Stark of Hooksett. This foundry was bought from the father in 1836 by Benjamin J. Cole and two of his brothers, but in a few years Benjamin J. Cole bought the interests of his brothers, conducting the business under the style of B. J. Cole & Co., and the firm soon became widely known throughout northern New Hampshire for the manufacture of parlor and cooking stoves and agricultural implements, being in fact the pioneer in this section in those specialties.

In 1852 Mr. Cole acquired land and water power from the W. L. C. & W. Mfg Co., on which he erected an extensive iron and wood machine shop, and in 1872 the concern was merged into a corporation, the Cole Manufacturing company, which constructed a steam forge, and in 1873 began the manufacture of car axles for steam roads in which they have ever since been constantly engaged and the quality of which is unexcelled in the country.

The concern also makes hosiery, needle, bobbin, and sawmill machinery, forgings, castings of all kinds and iron work generally, including Worrall's friction clutches, shafting, pulleys, and hangers. Benj. J. Cole was from 1836 treasurer and manager until 1883, when he retired from the latter position, being succeeded by his son-in-law, Henry B. Quinby. He retained the treasurership until his death, Mr. Quinby being assistant treasurer. Mr. Quinby is now treasurer and manager, Henry Cole Quinby, President, and A. C. Moore, clerk.

This company has been one of the mainstays and principal industries of this vicinity, having had a continuous activity of seventy-two years.

The Late Hon. Benjamin J. Cole.

Benjamin J. Cole was born in Franconia, N. H., Sept. 28, 1814, and when seven years of age went to Salisbury, where he attended the village school and the Noyes academy, then quite famous, and later went to the school at Sanbornton Bridge, now Tilton.

In 1827 he came with his parents to Batchelder's Mills, now Lakeport, and made it his home until his death which occurred Jan. 15, 1899.

June 17, 1838, he married Mehitable A. Batchelder, whose father, Nathan Batchelder, then owned the water

The Late Hon. Benjamin J. Cole.

power at Batchelder's Mills and from whom the place derived its name.

In 1848 Mr. Cole was an incorporator of the Winnipiseogee Steamboat company and served as its president more than forty years and under his supervision was built the first passenger steamboat, the *Lady of the Lake*, ever launched upon the waters of the beautiful lake from which the company was named.

He was an incorporator and for many years president of the Lake Village Savings Bank, and was also an incorporator of the Laconia National Bank and for a long period one of its directors.

In politics he was a Democrat until the outbreak of the Rebellion, when he became a Republican, and in 1862, '63, and '64 he was a candidate for state senator in the sixth senatorial district.

Mr. Cole was a member of the governor's council in 1866-'67; was a delegate to the National convention which renominated President Lincoln; he was a member of the state constitutional convention in 1876, and represented the town of Gilford in the general court in 1849-'50.

During his seventy-two years of citizenship in Lakeport, Mr. Cole was a prominent factor in its growth and prosperity and chiefly instrumental in bringing the village from a total of seven houses to its present important standing in the state, erecting, himself, more than sixty buildings and was ever public-spirited, benevolent, and mindful of the welfare of his numerous employés, and the citizens generally, by whom he was held in the highest esteem.

He donated the land for a church and a school-house, and gave largely to both edifices. In 1849 he and the late Senator James Bell were chosen a committee to purchase a hand fire-engine for the precinct and bought in Boston, Niagara engine, No. 1, which has from that day to this been ready for efficient service and is cherished with jealous care by the veteran firemen of Lakeport. He also provided at his own expense a house for the engine.

His unfaltering integrity was such that though in 1876, when business declined and values shrank all over the land he was obliged to go through bankruptcy, paying such a per cent. as he and his creditors agreed on, subsequently, when prosperity smiled upon him, he paid with interest every debt, in full, from which he had been legally released ; and that he was able to do this afforded him more pleasure than any other act of his business career.

Col. Henry B. Quinby.

Col. Henry B. Quinby.

Colonel Henry Brewer Quinby, of the Cole Manufacturing Co., at Lakeport, was born in Biddeford, Maine, June 10, 1846, son of Thomas and Jane E. (Brewer) Quinby. Colonel Quinby comes from good old New England stock on both sides of his family. Through his father he is a direct descendant of John Rogers, fifth president of Harvard college, of Major-General Daniel Dennison, the famous colonial officer, of Governor Thomas Dudley of the Massachusetts colony, and of many other colonial celebrities. On his mother's side, Colonel Quinby is descended from Major Charles Frost, the famous Indian fighter, and numbers among his great-great-great-grandmother's two sisters of Sir William Pepperell, the colonial baronet, who won renown at the siege of Louisburg, and is a direct descendant of Reverend Jose Glover, in the ninth generation, at whose charge the first printing press was established in America. He attended Biddeford schools and Nichols' Latin school at Lewiston, as well as Bowdoin college, Brunswick, Me., being graduated from the latter in 1869. He received the degree of A. M. in 1872, and in 1880 was graduated in medicine at the National Medical college, Washington, D. C. He is manager and treasurer of the Cole Manufacturing company at Lakeport, with which he has been connected since 1869. Colonel Quinby was a member of Governor Straw's staff in 1872-'73, a member of the legislature of 1887-'88, state senator in 1889-'90, member of the governor's council in 1891-'92, being chairman of the state prison board, delegate-at-large to the Republican national convention at Minneapolis in 1893, and president of the state Republican convention in 1896. In politics he is a Republican. He was appointed a member of the board of trustees of the New Hampshire Asylum for the Insane in 1897.

He was made a Mason in 1871 in this city, and is junior grand warden of the Grand Lodge of Free and Accepted Masons of New Hampshire, Right Eminent Grand Commander of the Grand Commandery of Knights Templar of New Hampshire, and an active member of the Supreme Council of the Scottish Rite of the Northern Masonic Jurisdiction of the United States of America. He is vice-president of the Laconia National Bank and the City Savings Bank of Laconia.

Colonel Quinby married, on June 22, 1870, Octavia M., daughter of the late Hon. B. J. Cole of Lakeport. He has two children,—Henry Cole Quinby, a lawyer in New York city, and Candace Ellen, wife of Hugh N. Camp, Jr., of New York city.

Henry Cole Quinby.

Henry Cole Quinby.

The president of the Cole Manufacturing company is Henry Cole Quinby, only son of Henry B. Quinby and grandson of the late Hon. Benjamin J. Cole. He was born in Lake Village, now Lakeport, July 9, 1872, and was prepared for college at the Chauncey Hall school in Boston. He was graduated from Harvard college in 1894 with *cum laude*, having completed the four years course in three years, and two years later was graduated from the Harvard Law school, having taken the three years' course in two years; he then passed the examination and was admitted to the Suffolk County bar. After his graduation from the Harvard Law school he entered the office of Evarts, Choate & Beaman, New York city, by whom he was entrusted with the preparation of some important causes; on the motion of Joseph H. Choate, now minister to England, he was admitted to practice in the supreme court of the United States; he began the study of law in the office of the Hon. E. A. Hibbard of this city.

February 1, 1899, he severed his connection with the firm of Evarts, Choate & Beaman, and established an office for himself in the Continental Building, 44 Cedar street, New York city, where he is now located with a large and rapidly increasing clientage.

Mr. Quinby is a member of the New York Bar Association and of the Union League and Harvard clubs of New York.

A Laconia Landmark.

How long the site of the "old corner store," corner of Main and Court Sts., Laconia, now occupied by John Parker Smith, dealer in general merchandise, has been a place of business, is not known, for no record can now be found in regard to it and the oldest inhabitant always has this answer when

The Old Corner Store.

asked any questions concerning its history, "There's been a store there ever since I can remember." Mr. J. T. Coffin (father of Mr. John T. Coffin, now residing on Lyford St., Laconia), and one of the early directors of the old Concord & Montreal railroad, was a clerk here about the year 1812, Daniel Avery being then the proprietor. An old account book of 1813-'14 shows that a tailoring business was being done there by one Starbird. The present store was built about 1834 and was subsequently occupied by Avery & Hazelton, Melcher

& French, French & Avery and H. J. French & Co. In 1859 James H. Tilton, who had entered the employ of French & Avery in 1845, assumed control of the business and was closely identified with it until his death in 1894.

Prominent among those who were associated with him in business and will be remembered by many Laconia people were Frank Keasor and S. S. Wiggin. After the death of Mr. Tilton, the present proprietor, who had entered the store as clerk in 1879, and Mr. R. C. Dickey, bought the business and continued it for a short time when Mr. Dickey sold his interest to his partner, who has since made it his object to maintain the reputation of the store for the variety and good quality of its goods.

Another feature of the old corner store which is of historic interest is the large building on Court street, immediately in the rear, which contains the grain and feed department of the business. This building was the old Gilford academy, an institution of learning which educated hundreds of brilliant and successful men and women and which has a reputation throughout New Hampshire in the old-time academic days. When the Gilford academy was discontinued, the building was occupied for the High school and Grammar school departments of the local public schools, until it was finally purchased by the late James H. Tilton and moved from its former location on Academy square to make room for the present brick High school building.

John Parker Smith.

John Parker Smith, proprietor of the Old Corner Store, is a native of New Hampton, born Feb. 8, 1854. He was educated in the public schools, and completed his studies at the New Hampton Literary Institution, coming to Laconia in 1879. Mr. Smith has been connected with the Old Corner Store since his advent in Laconia, serving as clerk until Mr. Tilton's death, and now being sole proprietor.

John Parker Smith is a member and deacon of the North (Congregational) church and is also superintendent of the Sunday-school at that church. He is a member of Winnipiseogee Lodge of Odd Fellows, and is one of Laconia's most successful merchants, and he deserves the success which he has attained, for he follows his business very closely, and is noted for his square dealing.

Like his predecessor in the same establishment, Mr. Smith takes pride in keeping in stock almost anything and everything which a customer could possibly ask for in a general store, and

John Parker Smith.

the establishment can always respond to a call for anything from gum drops to grindstones or yeast cakes to a bale of hay. Mr. Smith is progressive and up-to-date in his methods, is a liberal advertiser and constantly improving his facilities. He has recently remodeled the interior of the Old Corner Store, and added a modern plate-glass show-window which projects from the front of the building its entire width. The completed improvements in this line afford Mr. Smith an opportunity to boast of one of the largest and best-equipped general stores in New Hampshire.

The Late David Batchelder Nelson.

David Batchelder Nelson was born at Roxbury, N. H., June 7, 1823, his parents being William Nelson and Lucy Batchelder of that town. He acquired the preliminary education leading up to professional life at Newbury, Vt., and the academy at Bradford, Vt., finishing at the Harvard Medical School, from which he graduated in the class of '49. At the age of twenty he began to study medicine with Dr. Fellows of Hill, N. H. After leaving Harvard he began the practice of medicine in Boston, where he remained one year. In 1850 he came to Manchester, N. H., where he was engaged in practice for eleven years. From thence, in 1862, he came to this city and engaged in the practice of medicine, constantly, up to a little over two years ago when he retired from active work and passed the remainder of his life in enjoying the pure air and beautiful scenery with which the city of Laconia is so bountifully supplied.

Few men have been better known or more prominently before the public in this section of the state than has Dr. Nelson for nearly forty years. He was a member of the Harvard Medical Alumni Association, the New Hampshire State Medical Society and a director in the latter. He was town physician for one year, county physician for three years, United States examining surgeon for invalid pensioners, acting alone or as secretary of the board for thirty-two years, member of the local Board of Education for six years, prudential school committee for four years, chaplain, surgeon, and commander of John T. Perley, Jr., Post, No. 37, G. A. R. He was appointed colonel on the staff of Governor Berry in 1861, special transportation agent for the Third regiment, N. H. Vols., during its trip to New York, special mustering officer to raise Troop K, New Hampshire cavalry. Early in the year 1862, the First battalion, N. H. Cav., joined the First R. I. Cav., and Dr. Nelson was made major of the Second battalion. He was appointed captain of Company K, First regiment New England Cavalry, Oct. 9, 1861, and was appointed major of the same regiment in December following. He resigned on June 3, 1862. During his military career he was in command of the advance army, four companies of Rhode Island cavalry at the battle of Front Royal, on May 30, 1862.

The Late David Batchelder Nelson.

He was associated with Dr. William Buck of Boston in 1849, during the epidemic of Asiatic cholera in that city, and was also present in the Massachusetts General Hospital in October, 1846, as a medical student, and witnessed the first surgical operation where ether was used as an anæsthetic.

He was twice married, in the first instance to Cornelia C. Weston in 1851, and secondly to Susan E. Bridges, who survives, together with a son and two daughters, the former being William Nelson, city engineer of Laconia, and the latter, Miss Alice M. and Miss Louise H. Nelson, also of this city.

Dr. Nelson died on July 5, 1898, after a short illness, at his residence on Court street, in this city.

Dr. Edwin P. Hodgdon.

Among the many well-known and skilful physicians of the city on the lakes is Dr. Edwin P. Hodgdon, who has been in practice here about seven years, and who has a large and steadily increasing business in his profession. Dr. Hodgdon was born in Barnstead, May 6, 1867, and was educated at Gilmanton academy, graduating in the classical course, June 10, 1886. He pursued his professional studies at the Burlington (Vermont) Medical School, graduating July 10, 1891. Previous to studying at Burlington, Dr. Hodgdon was for a time connected with the New Hampshire Asylum for the Insane, where he had an opportunity to study and investigate nervous diseases to a considerable extent.

Dr. Hodgdon married Clara E. Hancock of Canterbury. They have no children.

He commenced his medical practice at New Hampton, where he remained about a year, and then came to Laconia, locating in Lakeport in July, 1892.

Dr. Edwin P. Hodgdon.

Dr. Hodgdon takes considerable interest in secret and fraternal organizations. He is an Odd Fellow and a past grand of Chocorua Lodge, No. 51, of Lakeport, and is also at the present time D. D. G. M. of Laconia. He is also a member of Mt. Lebanon Lodge of Masons and is connected with the Masonic Chapter, Council, and Commandery of Knights Templar. He is a member of New Hampton Grange, Patrons of Husbandry, the New England Order of Protection at Lakeport, and Hannah Frances Lodge, Degree of Rebekah, in connection with his Odd Fellowship.

Dr. Hodgdon is one of the board of physicians at the Laconia Cottage Hospital, a member of the New Hampshire Medical Society, and also the Winnipesaukee Academy of Medicine. He was president of the United States board of examining surgeons for pensions at Laconia from 1893 to 1897, during President Cleveland's administration. Dr. Hodgdon is a Democrat in politics and an attendant at the Park Street Free Baptist church.

The Late Noah Lawrence True.

Noah Lawrence True, M. D., only child of Abram and Mary Brown Lawrence True, was born in Meredith, N. H., November 21, 1828.

In early boyhood he was thoughtful and studious, yet full of energy and ambition, often walking several miles over rough and rocky roads, or across fields and pastures to take advantage of extra schooling in neighboring districts. Later he came to Meredith Bridge and was a student at Gilford academy, where he finished his preparatory education.

Having chosen the medical profession he studied medicine with Wm. Leach, M. D., took his first medical degree at Harvard and was graduated from the Eclectic Medical college at Worcester, Mass., June 25, 1851.

Youthful in his appearance and representing an unpopular school of medicine, he began work in Dover, N. H., full of courage and enthusiasm. In a little less than ten years a severe illness necessitated a complete change and he left a large practice, purchased the farm adjoining his boyhood home, and removed there for rest and recuperation. While residing there he represented Meredith in the legislature and served on the board of selectmen.

He came to Laconia in 1865 where he practised his profession until two weeks preceding his death, June 21, 1896. He was a member of the New Hampshire Medical Society, at one time holding the office of president. For several years he served on the board of education, was one of the trustees of the Laconia Savings bank and was a member of Winnipiseogee Lodge, I. O. O. F.

Unassuming in manner, sympathetic, and tender as a woman in the presence of suffering, he possessed keen intuitive perception, great strength of purpose and strong self-reliance, qualities which cheered every sick room he entered, inspired confidence and courage in his patients and won for himself an extensive and successful practice.

He was united in marriage with Mary Elizabeth Tucker of Meredith Bridge, September 22, 1850. They have four children: Emma Frances, wife of Horace Emery Durgin of Laconia; Jennie Alma, wife of Joseph Hector Gingras of Laconia; Walter Harrison, a physician in Laconia; and George Lawrence, a dentist in Cambridge, Mass.

The Late Noah Lawrence True.

Dr. Walter Harrison True.

Walter Harrison True, M.D., was born in Meredith, N.H., July 25, 1866. His parents coming to Laconia the fall of that year, most of his life has been spent in this city. He was a pupil in our public schools until 1882, when he became a student at Gilmanton Academy, where he was graduated, class of '85.

The following two years were spent with Henry Story, pharmacist, of this city. After studying medicine with his father, N. L. True, M. D., he entered Cincinnati Medical college and was graduated in June, 1891, also receiving a special diploma on diseases of the eye and ear under Professor McPheron, M. D., of Cincinnati, O., now of Denver,

Col. While at that college he took two winter courses in clinical medicine and surgery at the Cincinnati City Hospital.

He came to Boston, Mass., and was house surgeon at the Charter Street Hospital, and later having passed the state medical board of examiners at Concord, N. H., he commenced the practice of his profession in company with his father in this city.

He is a member of the New Hampshire Eclectic Medical Society, holding the position of secretary and treasurer at the present time. In the summer of 1894, he took a course of study at the New York Postgraduate school, New York city, receiving a diploma on diseases of the eye, ear, nose, and throat. He was appointed one of the members of the N. H. state board of medical examiners, by Gov. Ramsdell and council, in June, 1897, and is the youngest member on the board. He is a member of the Winnipesaukee Academy of Medicine, also of the N. H. Association of Boards of Health, and has held the office of secretary of the Laconia board of health ever since the city was inaugurated. He is a member of Mt. Belknap Lodge, Knights of Pythias, Laconia, and also of Laconia Grange.

Dr. True was united in marriage with Miss Mabelle Hill of Lakeport, N. H., on March 29, 1899.

Julian Francis Trask.

Julian Francis Trask was born in Beverly, Mass., October 1, 1849. He was educated in the public schools, after which he thoroughly learned the trade of a machinist at the Rhode Island Locomotive Works, in Providence.

Changing his residence to Laconia, he continued his chosen vocation, but gradually drifted into newspaper work, for which he developed a marked adaptation. At first his evenings only were devoted to writing for the press, but subsequently he gave his whole time and attention to journalism, being employed on the *Laconia Democrat*, *Manchester Union*, and representing the Associated Press in the lake region, doing in every assignment and detail, painstaking and commendable work. His generous temperament and cheerful disposition led him to say kindly things, and his indefatigable pen has never been touched in venom. He grew into the good graces of the community, as he did into favor with his employers, and his career as reporter is not marred by any mean act.

Dr. Walter H. True.

Residence of Dr. W. H. True.

When Hon. C. A. Busiel was mentioned for the mayorship and again for the governorship, Mr. Trask's enthusiasm and enterprise knew no limit, and he entered the canvasses at the very outset with an eager devotion that never faltered. He was the governor's choice for messenger to the council, and private secretary to his excellency, positions of confidence and responsibility which he filled with remarkable ability, discretion, and success. His reputation as a conscientious and versatile newspaper man extended throughout the state, and his knowledge of legislation and politics conduced to make him a very considerable factor in public affairs. His appointment as labor commissioner was received with general favor, and his service in that important office during the three years last past won him many valuable friends and acquaintances, and have given him a merited accrediting in popular sentiment that ensures him desirable prominence in whatever field of labor he may now choose.

Whether in the workshop, or on the newspaper, or at the state house, the same prepossessing sunshiny personality has characterized him. He is looking always for the good in humankind, and the saying of charitable things has grown to be a habit with him. Every fiber of his nature is true to the best interests of this community, with which his growth and welfare have been closely associated.

Julian F. Trask.

Mr. Trask married Vicklida E. Anderson of this city December 11, 1875, and they have three children, Helen G., Arthur F., and Marie Louise.

Mr. Trask belongs to the Ancient Order of United Workmen, the Mt. Belknap lodge, Knights of Pythias, and is an active member of the White Mountain Traveller's Association, and is also one of the leading lights of the Coon Club, the state organization of practical newspaper workers. Outspoken honesty is one of the sterling qualities of his manhood. He has availed himself of a wealth of philosophy, softened by a prevailing sense of wit and humor. With distinct ideas of right and wrong, he is, nevertheless, deferential and tolerant of the opinions of others, and his desire is to help and to serve and in all ways possible smooth the rough edges of life. In religion, he is liberal; in politics, a Republican; and in all a public-spirited substantial citizen, worthy of the high respect and fond regard in which he is so widely held.

Dr. A. H. Harriman.

Dr. Alpha Haven Harriman, one of Laconia's leading physicians, was born in Albany, N. H., October 14, 1857, son of Nathaniel G. and Rhoda (Allard) Harriman. He received his preparatory education in the academies at Fryeburg and at Bridgton, Me. His professional studies were pursued at Bowdoin College Medical School, from which he graduated in 1883. He commenced practice in Mercer, Me., but after eight months removed to the town of Sandwich, N. H., where he remained for three years and a half. In November, 1887, he settled in Laconia, and has remained here up to the present time. He has attained a prominent position in his profession, and has been very successful in a business way.

He is a member of the New Hampshire Medical Society and the Winnipesaukee Academy of Medicine, a contributor to periodical medical literature and to "the reference hand-book of medical sciences." He was a member of the board of education of Laconia for four years, and for three years was president of the board. He is a member of Mt. Lebanon Lodge, Ancient Free and Accepted Masons, of Union Chapter, Royal Arch Masons, of which he was high priest in 1897-'99; of Pythagorean Council, Royal and Select Masters, and of Pilgrim Commandery, Knights Templar, Laconia, commander of the latter in 1896-'98.

Dr. Harriman has always been a Democrat, but has never taken an active part in politics. He was married Feb. 10, 1884, to Katherine E. Walker of Lovell, Maine. They have two sons: Haven Walker, born July 26. 1889, and Nathaniel Joy, born Aug. 17, 1892.

Dow & Roberts.

The Dow & Roberts meat and provision market is a first-class up-to-date dispensary of choice meats, vegetables, poultry, canned goods, etc. The establishment was started by E. L. Dow, one of Laconia's veteran market-men and butchers, in 1878, and the present firm of Dow & Roberts took possession in 1894. Herbert E. Dow is a son of E. L. Dow, and Fred S. Roberts is a son of O. N. Roberts of Meredith, and was employed in the grocery business for several years before embarking in business with Mr. Dow.

The Dow & Roberts market is located at No. 605 Main street, and handles everything which would be found in a first class city market. This is the only establishment in the state equipped with an electric plant for grinding bones and sausage meats, and the proprietors are constantly making improve-

Dr. Alpha H. Harriman.

Residence of Dr. A. H. Harriman.

ments in their equipment, and striving to advance the standard of their service.

The market is, of course, provided with ample refrigerator room for the cold storage of fresh meats, of which they purchase the choicest and best, both domestic and Western, which the market affords. Home-made lard, home-cured hams, and home-made sausage are some of the special features of their trade upon which Dow & Roberts pride themselves, and which have proved very popular with the public. In green goods, they always have the earliest peas, dandelions, and other vegetables to be found in Laconia markets. They make another feature of poultry, importing large quantities of Vermont turkeys and chickens, grown and fattened especially for their trade.

Messrs. Dow & Roberts are both young men, enterprising and wide-awake for the increase of their business and the satisfaction of their patrons. They have met with excellent success and keep two delivery teams hustling all the time, in addition to their large store trade.

William Hall Flanders.

Prominent among the rising young legal lights in Belknap county is William Hall Flanders of this city, residing at Lakeport. Mr. Flanders was born in Gilford, in that part known as Lake Village, May 20, 1865; his parents being Charles and Amanda G. (Hall) Flanders of Gilford. His mother was a native of Middletown, Pa., whose ancestry were of Revolutionary stock and among the first settlers of Pennsylvania. On the paternal side, his remote ancestry were among the first settlers of Gilmanton. He was one of a family of four children, three of whom survive.

Mr. Flanders was educated in the public schools at Philadelphia, and Franklin Falls. Later he completed his education in the Quaker city, particularly that relating to business. Al

Dow & Roberts' Meat and Provision Market.

though many years covering the period of his early life have been spent outside of Laconia, chiefly on account of business interests, yet during all these years, he has never renounced his allegiance, love, and kind remembrance for his native heath.

He studied law in the office of Jewell & Stone in this city and was admitted to the bar March 4, 1890, and soon after opened an office at Lakeport.

Previous to this Mr. Flanders spent about two years in the south, where he was associated with mining companies, with headquarters at Staunton, Va. About this time he was admitted to practice in the supreme court in the District of Columbia, October 26, 1892.

Soon after he returned to this city. In 1898 he was admitted to practice in the United States district court of New Hampshire. Since being admitted to the bar in New Hampshire, he has conducted a general law practice, in which he, for a young man, has been eminently successful.

Mr. Flanders is a member of the Mt. Lebanon lodge, No. 32, A. F. and A. M., Union Chapter, No. 7, R. A. M., Pilgrim Commandery, Knights Templar, Mount Washington Chapter, No. 13, Order of the Eastern Star.

He is also in good standing as an Odd Fellow, having become a member of that order in Philadelphia. He is a member of several other secret societies and holds official positions in all of the Masonic bodies. He is a member of the Belknap County Fish and Game League.

In 1898 he was elected a member of the Laconia board of education. His political affiliations are with the Democrats. October 25, 1892, he wedded Miss Carrie Morgan of Milford, Delaware. His religious affiliations are with the Episcopalians.

Mr. Flanders was a resident of Prince William county, Virginia, for about six years, subsequently he resided in Philadelphia, later at Franklin Falls, N. H. In all Mr. Flanders has resided in this city about twenty years.

Socially he is ever at his best, in consequence of which he is possessed of numerous friends local and elsewhere. Though modest in temperament he has a keen appreciation of the eternal fitness of all his environments. As a counselor he is conservative yet decided, seldom vouchsafing an opinion without imparting the most careful scrutiny and deliberate consideration.

In domestic life he is much attached to the home circle. He resides at 973 Union avenue, where he is surrounded by home comforts such as are dictated by liberal tastes for enjoyment and other auxiliaries conducive to happiness.

William H. Flanders.

Fred B. Rowe.

Fred B. Rowe, hosiery manufacturer, is a native of Laconia, and one of our younger manufacturers who has made a success in this line. He was born January 13, 1872, and received his education in the public schools of this city. In 1888 he commenced as book-keeper for the Laconia Manufacturing Company, and continued with this concern for three years. In 1891 he started in the hosiery business for himself in a small way, and two years later formed a partnership with M. R. Marshall.

The partnership continued for four years, and then Mr. Marshall retired from the firm, and Mr. Rowe has since carried on the business alone with excellent success. He now employs about one hundred hands in the operation of his industry, and has a production of two hundred and twenty

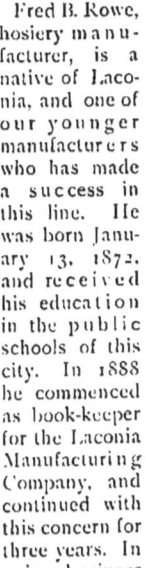

five dozen hosiery per day. His factory is located on Meredith Court. He manufactures hosiery for ladies, gents, misses, and infants, and makes a specialty of medium and high-class goods. Mr. Rowe disposes of his product mostly to the jobbers and direct trade.

Mr. Rowe was married in 1893 to Miss Annie R. Woodburn, and they have two children, Elmer W., six years old; and Charles M., aged three years.

In politics, Mr. Rowe is a Democrat, and in the secret orders he is a member of Winnipiseogee Lodge of Odd Fellows.

Laconia has always taken pride in her hustling young business men and manufacturers, and to this class Mr. Rowe undoubtedly belongs. He is wide-awake and up-to-date in his methods, and deserves the success which he is meeting in his business.

Fred B. Rowe.

Col. Benjamin F. Drake.

Although now a resident of Norfolk, Virginia, where he conducts a large grocery business, Col. B. Frank Drake still claims Laconia as his home, still owns property in the City on the Lakes and will undoubtedly return here for a permanent residence some time.

Benjamin F. Drake was born in New Hampton, Oct. 8, 1844. When he was two years old his parents removed to Lakeport, where young Drake was educated in the public schools and French's select school. At the opening of the Civil War he entered the government employ at the Springfield armory, where he learned the machinist trade. He was afterwards superintendent of two manufactories in Massachusetts, and later was master mechanic of the Mount Washington railway. In 1878, returning to Lakeport he became a member of the firm of J. S. Crane & Co., retiring in 1885 to assume charge of the construction of the Lakeport & Laconia Water Works, resuming the partnership at the completion of the contract, this time organizing the Crane Manufacturing Co., builders of knitting machinery. Of this corporation, Colonel Drake was the treasurer, a director, and a moving spirit. A year or two ago he sold out his interest in the Crane Co., purchased a large farm and mill property in Massachusetts, but soon afterwards sold out and went South, to Virginia, where he is now located and conducting a very successful business.

Colonel Drake has not limited his attention to his private interests solely, but has been much in public and corporate service. He was aide-de-camp, with the rank of colonel, on the staff of Gov. John B. Smith, has served his town as selectman, represented Gilford in the legislature in 1883, and was a member of the constitutional convention in 1889. He is now a director of the Laconia Water Works, has been a director of the National bank of Lakeport, of the Lake Village Savings bank, president of the Mutual Building & Loan association, a trustee of the public library, and a member of the local board of trade. In 1887 he was appointed steamboat inspector by Governor Sawyer, a position which he held until he left New Hampshire. Colonel Drake is a member of the New Hampshire club, of the Lincoln club, of the Home Market, and of the White Mountain Travellers' association. In secret society life, Colonel Drake has always been much interested and quite prominent. He is a Mason, Knight Templar, and has reached the thirty-second degree, he is an Odd Fellow, a Patriarch Militant, a Red Man, a Knight of Pythias, a Knight of Honor, and has received honors in all of these fraternities. Colonel Drake is a Republican in politics and was a member of the first city council of the city of Laconia.

Few Laconia men have been better known throughout the state of New Hampshire than Col. Frank Drake, and he is popular and esteemed wherever known, for he is always genial and agreeable, and a good companion as well as a good business man.

Col. Benjamin F. Drake.

Hon. Charles F. Stone.

Probably no member of the legal profession in New Hampshire is more widely and favorably known than Hon. Charles F. Stone, of Laconia, ex-naval officer of the port of Boston, Mass. Mr. Stone's ancestors were among the early settlers of Vermont, emigrating to Cabot, in the northern part of the state as early as 1794. Lawyer Stone was born May 21, 1843, son of Levi H. and Clarissa (Osgood) Stone. His boyhood was passed upon a farm, where he acquired a vigorous physique, and at the age of twenty years started out to secure an education to enter a profession. He attended the academy at Barre, Vermont, for two years, and fitted for college, entering Middlebury in 1865, and graduating in the class of '69. He paid his own way both in academy and college by teaching the district schools and also as instructor in singing-schools. He was a natural musician and from the time he was nineteen years of age, until his voice was weakened by an attack of pneumonia, he was most of the time director of a church choir.

After Mr. Stone's graduation from college, he read law for a year in the office of ex-Governor J. W. Stewart in Middlebury, Vt., and at the same time served as principal of a graded school. In 1870 Mr. Stone came to Laconia and entered the office of Judge E. A. Hibbard, where he continued his studies until admitted to the practice of his profession in 1872. He then formed a partnership with the late Col. George W. Stevens, which continued for one year. For the next seven years Mr.

Stone practised alone, devoting himself entirely to his professional labors and meeting with much success. In 1880, a partnership was formed with Lawyer E. P. Jewell, which was continued with some changes in membership, until 1898, when Mr. Stone withdrew from the firm and formed a new partnership with Lawyer Edwin H. Shannon.

Mr. Stone was reared a Republican in politics, but about twenty years ago he became dissatisfied with the Republican policy on financial and revenue matters, and at the opening of the campaign in 1880, he took the stump for Hancock and English. He is one of the most effective campaign speakers in New Hampshire, and he has been several times chairman of the Democratic state committee, the Democratic candidate for governor and also for congress. He was a member of the state legislature from Laconia in 1883-'84 and again in 1887-'88. He was commissioned naval officer of Boston, July 3, 1894. and at the expiration of his term, returned to the practice of his profession in Laconia and also opened a branch office in Manchester.

Mr. Stone has been a member of the Masonic fraternity since attaining his majority, and is also a member of Laconia grange and the Belknap Pomona grange.

He married July 7, 1870, Minnie A. Nichols of Sudbury, Vt., who died September 22, 1875, leaving one daughter, Flora M. Stone. Mr. Stone married September 12, 1896, Mrs. Isabel Smith Munsey of Laconia. In religious matters Mr. Stone is of the progressive and liberal type and has long been actively connected with the Laconia Unitarian church.

Edwin H. Shannon.

Edwin Howe Shannon, of the law firm of Stone & Shannon, was born in Gilmanton, March 8, 1858, son of James C. and Judith W. (Batchelder) Shannon. He traces his descent in the paternal line from an early settler of Portsmouth, his grandfather, George Shannon, having been born in that place. In the maternal line he comes of the family which was related to that of the famous statesman, Daniel Webster, his great-grandmother having been a cousin of the statesman. Mr. Shannon received his education in the public schools of his native town, and at Gilmanton Academy. He studied law with Hon. Thomas Cogswell of Gilmanton, and was admitted to the bar in 1881.

Mr. Shannon then became a partner of Colonel Cogswell, remaining such for about a year, when the partnership was dissolved by mutual consent, Mr. Shannon seeking a wider field for practice than was afforded him in Gilmanton. He thereafter practised his profession alone until 1893, having offices in Farmington and Pittsfield, where he soon acquired more than a local fame for his ability in the trial of causes, and gained

Hon. Charles F. Stone.

for himself a considerable clientage. In 1893, Mr. Shannon came to Laconia and entered into partnership with Lawyer W. S. Peaslee, the firm subsequently becoming Shannon, Peaslee & Blackstone. In 1894, he withdrew from this firm and practised alone until 1898, when the law firm of Stone & Shannon was established.

Mr. Shannon is counsel for a number of large and prosperous corporations and has devoted considerable study to this especial branch of the law. He is also considered an authority upon the Law of Personal Injuries, has a large practice in that branch of his profession, where he has been successful in winning some of the most important cases which have ever been instituted in Belknap county. Mr. Shannon is a man of strong personality, is quick to determine and prompt to execute. Fearless in thought and action, with strong common sense as a guide, he does not hesitate to carve a way where none appears.

Precedents have no terrors for Mr. Shannon. If they appear to be right he follows them, but if wrong he fearlessly attacks them, and some at least, have gone down before the logic of his reasoning. As a counselor, wise and prudent, in the trial of causes, strong and tactful, and as an advocate, earnest and eloquent, he has acquired a large and lucrative practice. In politics he is a Republican. He was married Oct. 18, 1882, to Myra E., daughter of Ira L. and Lavina E. (Drew) Berry, of Barnstead. They have three children : Ella C., Mildred, and Edwin H. Shannon, Jr.

The Oberon Ladies Quartette.

The Oberon Ladies Quartette was organized by Mrs. O. M. Prescott in 1891, and they have won a reputation as a musical organization in all sections of New England. The personnel of the quartette is as follows: First soprano, Mrs. O. M. Prescott; second soprano, Miss Minnie O. Woodhouse; first alto, Mrs. C. K. Sanborn; second alto, Mrs. George B. Cox.

The following will indicate to some extent the popular favor with which the Oberon Ladies Quartette has everywhere been received:

"It has been my good fortune to be present on two occasions when the Oberon Quartette were the vocalists of the evening. They have exquisite voices which harmonize admirably. They sing with expression and distinct enunciation, and win the favor of the audience from the start. They have a charming *repertoire*, which they rendered with grace and melody. I found it easy to lecture after being stirred by their inspiring music."— *Mary A. Livermore*.

"The Oberon Ladies Quartette of Laconia made its first appearance in Concord at this concert, but it is safe to say it will not be the last. In all the five numbers given the combination was at its best, and the result was the highest satisfaction of an audience

Edwin H. Shannon.

composed of those who are never satisfied with anything less than excellent work in this line. Two numbers were encored and the responses were equally pleasing. Each member of the quartette has a fine, well-trained voice, and they all blend harmoniously together. The young city of Laconia may well be proud of the Oberon Ladies Quartette. —*Concord People and Patriot.*

"The Oberon Ladies Quartette made quite a hit at the banquet of the Massachusetts State Board of Agriculture at Dalton, Mass., last evening. Governor Greenhalge and many other high dignitaries were present and had only words of praise for Laconia's fair vocalists."

"At the evening concert of the N. H. Music Teachers association the Oberon Ladies Quartette rendered selections. The quartette did very fine work, their voices blending perfectly,—singing in good style. In fact they were an agreeable surprise."—*Prof. Henri G. Blaisdell in Granite Monthly.*

The Late Hon. John Carroll Moulton.

From the year 1836 until the date of his death, July 23, 1894, the late Hon. John Carroll Moulton was one of the most prominent and active business men and manufacturers in this section of New Hampshire. He was born at Centre Harbor, N. H., December 24, 1810, son of Jonathan Smith and Deborah (Neal) Moulton. The Moultons trace their ancestry back to the Normans, and some of them accompanied William the Conqueror in his invasion and conquest of England in 1066. As many as seven Moultons were in America at a very early date, one in the settlement at Jamestown, Virginia. Two of the Moultons came to New Hampshire in 1638. Gen. Jonathan Moulton,

The Oberon Ladies Quartette.

grandfather of the subject of this sketch, was one of the leading men in the state in the old colonial days. In 1736, the town of Moultonborough was granted to him and sixty-one others by the Masonian proprietors. Governor Wentworth granted to General Moulton "a small gore of land adjoining Moultonboro," which was named New Hampton in honor of his native town and which contained nearly twenty thousand acres, and now constitutes a part of the town of Centre Harbor. General Moulton distinguished himself in the Revolutionary War, and did much to build up the early settlements around the lake, actually creating the three towns of Moultonborough, Centre Harbor, and New Hampton.

John Carroll Moulton was educated in the district schools in his native town and afterwards attended Holmes academy at Plymouth, N. H. Master Dudley Leavitt, the world-famous astronomer and mathematician, was one of his instructors in his boyhood days.

Mr. Moulton commenced his business life at Sandwich, where he entered into trade but after a few months removed to Centre Harbor, where he continued as a merchant and also opened a hotel, which was the pioneer of the numerous and elegant summer resort hotels which now abound in the lake region.

In 1836 he changed his residence to Lake Village, and engaged in merchandizing and manufacturing. In the year 1841 he came to Meredith Bridge, now Laconia, and from that time until his death was one of the formative and directing forces in the growth and development of the town. He was first landlord of the popular Belknap Hotel, next a bookseller and druggist, then postmaster of the village, appointed by President Tyler. He continued as postmaster for about six years, being reappointed by President Polk, but was removed under President Taylor's Whig administration, as an offensive partisan. He was again reappointed by President Franklin Pierce, and continued in office by President Buchanan, but during President Lincoln's term was succeeded by a Republican, after sixteen years of service in the post-office.

In 1861, Mr. Moulton became interested in the Laconia Car manufactory, which had been conducted by Charles Ranlet & Co., until Mr. Ranlet's death in 1860. Mr. Moulton gave his personal attention to the car building business and rapidly developed a large and profitable industry. The works were frequently enlarged, extensive buildings put up, and the quality of work advanced, until passenger cars of the finest style were manufactured here and the Laconia Car Company had a national reputation. This gave employment to hundreds of workmen, and the pay-rolls amounted to eight thousand dollars a month. The entire plant was destroyed by fire in 1881, but with characteristic energy Mr. Moulton began work on new buildings before the ruins were cold and work was resumed in the new factory in less than a month. This was done by Mr. Moulton when most men of his advanced years and ample fortune would have retired from active life and its cares and responsibilities.

In 1865 Mr. Moulton turned his energies to the establishment of a national bank to accommodate the financial needs of the business interests of Laconia, which were so rapidly increasing. His efforts for a charter were finally successful, and he founded the Laconia

The Late Hon. John Carroll Moulton.

National bank, of which he was the first president, a position which he held until his death. Other local enterprises in which Mr. Moulton engaged included the Gilford Hosiery Mills, of which he became sole owner in 1868, and conducted successfully for many years, furnishing employment to hundreds of operatives and having an annual production valued as high as one hundred and twenty-five thousand dollars. In company with the late Benjamin E. Thurston, Mr. Moulton owned and conducted the Laconia grist-mill, and in other and various ways he was interested and contributed greatly to the improvement, growth, and prosperity of Laconia. He was beyond all doubt one of the ablest financiers in this section of New Hampshire.

In politics Mr. Moulton was always a sterling Democrat. He represented the sixth district in the state senate in 1871 and in 1872, and was a member of the governor's council in 1874. He was a delegate to the Democratic national convention in 1876, and a candidate for presidential elector on the Tilden ticket.

In religious affairs, Mr. Moulton was a liberal Christian, and he was one of the organizers and principal supporters of the First Unitarian church in Laconia. Mr. Moulton was one of the charter members of Winnipiseogee lodge of Odd Fellows which was founded at Laconia in 1842, and was also connected with the Uniformed Patriarchs of that order.

Mr. Moulton married, July 15, 1833, Nellie B. Senter of Centre Harbor, whose ancestors were among the early settlers of that town. They had five children, Edwin C., Samuel M. S., and William H., all three deceased, and Horatio F., now located in Los Angeles, California, and Ida L., who married Hon. Joshua B. Holden of Boston, Mass.

Mrs. Moulton died November 18, 1860, and in August, 1866, Mr. Moulton married Sarah A. McDougall, whose death took place May 10, 1894, a few weeks before the death of the subject of this sketch.

The Late William Clow.

William Clow, for nearly twenty years a citizen of Lakeport, was one of the pioneer hosiery manufacturers of the United States. He was born in Leicester, Eng., but came to this country at the age of fifteen years. Mr. Clow was located at Portsmouth, N. H., where he first engaged in the hosiery business, and he manufactured about the first full-fashioned hose made in America. His goods took high rank among similar productions, and were awarded all the prizes at the exhibitions and fairs.

Mr. Clow was located in Portsmouth for about twenty-five years, and then went to Manchester, where he continued in the hosiery business, until he

The Late William Clow.

came to Lakeport, which was about 1880. At this time, Mr. Clow, with his son, Henry B. Clow, formed the firm of Wm. Clow & Son, and reëngaged in the hosiery manufacture in Lakeport. Mr. Clow died in January, 1899, and is survived by a widow and six children,—three sons and three daughters.

Wm. Clow & Son.

The firm of Wm. Clow & Son, located at No. 44 Bayside court, Lakeport, is one of the successful hosiery concerns of Laconia. The business was established about twelve years ago by the late William Clow and his son, Henry B. Clow. The industry employs about one hundred and twenty operatives, and produces between four and five hundred dozen hosiery per day. Henry B. Clow

Henry B. Clow.

Henry B. Clow, manager of the establishment of Wm. Clow & Son, was born September 30, 1863, in Portsmouth, N. H. He was educated in the public schools of that city, and came to Lakeport when a young man, about eighteen years ago. Mr. Clow was married to Cora B. Lane of Lakeport in 1882, and has five children, three daughters and two sons. Mrs. Clow died about five years ago, and in June, 1898, Mr. Clow married Nellie E. Judd, also of Lakeport. Mr. and Mrs. Clow reside on a magnificent farm on Lake street, leading to The Weirs. This farm was formerly the stock farm of Dr. Joseph C. Moore, and is one of the finest country places in New Hampshire, situated upon a commanding eminence, with broad fields, fenced with

Residence of Henry B. Clow.

is the manager of the business, and the firm manufactures ladies', misses', boys' and infants' hosiery, in wool and worsted.

substantial split stone walls, and the scenery is unsurpassed, embracing a most charming and magnificent view of lakes, mountains, and farming country.

with the city of Laconia in the background.

Mr. Clow is connected with several of the secret fraternal orders. He is a member of the Odd Fellows, Knights of Pythias, Rebekahs, and Patrons of Husbandry. In politics Mr. Clow is a Republican.

Joseph H. Gingras.

Joseph H. Gingras, proprietor of the "Gingras Shoe Store," was born in St. Paul, P.Q., September 15, 1863. A little later his parents removed to Stanstead, P. Q., where he attended the public schools, coming to Laconia at the age of seventeen. Naturally ambitious, he perseveringly applied himself to procure the means for a course at the New Hampton Literary Institution, upon the completion of which he entered the employ of O'Shea Bros., where for many years he had charge of the boot and shoe department. In 1888 he opened a shoe store in Berlin, but soon, having an advantageous opportunity to sell, he returned to Laconia and resumed his former position. April 18, 1893, he married Jennie A., daughter of Dr. and Mrs. N. L. True, of Laconia.

In 1896 he resigned his position at O'Shea Bros. to take a course of study at the Klein Optical school in Boston, Mass. The following two years he devoted exclusively to the optical business, traveling chiefly in northern New Hampshire. In April, 1898, he established the boot and shoe business at 548 Main street and has since then limited his optical profession to home practice. Having a large experience in public trade with characteristic enterprise, Mr Gingras has supplied the demand for finer lines of footwear than have ever before been shown in this city. His shelves are filled with the latest and most noted makes of boots and shoes for men, women, and children, which cannot be found elsewhere outside the largest cities. He also carries medium and low-priced goods. Honorable in all his transactions, always on the alert to please his customers, success was assured from the first and in a little more than a year the Gingras shoe store has become the leading store of its kind in northern New Hampshire. Mr. Gingras is a member of Mt. Lebanon Lodge, Free and Accepted Masons and also of Granite Lodge, A. O. U. W., of this city.

Joseph H. Gingras.

Joseph P. Morin.

Among the enterprising young hosiery manufacturers of Laconia is Joseph P. Morin, whose establishment is located in a portion of the old Belknap Mills property. Mr. Morin employs about sixty people in his industry and his mill has a capacity of two hundred dozen hosiery per day. He makes a specialty of misses' and infants' medium and high-grade goods.

Mr. Morin has a beautiful residence on Gilford avenue. He married Georgia M. Jacques in 1880, and has a family of four children, two boys and two girls. In religion, Mr. Morin is a Catholic and an active member of the society, at the Church of the Sacred Heart.

Mr. Morin was born in Ham Nord, P. Q., June 26, 1860. He came to Laconia in early life and attended our public schools, completing his education at the New Hampton Literary Institution. He is a practical hosiery manufacturer, and is familiar with every detail of the industry.

Mr. Morin, although not an active politician, has been honored by an election as one of the board of supervisors of the city of Laconia, several times, having held this position for about ten years, up to the present time.

Mr. Morin has also been quite prominent in the order of Catholic Foresters, and at the present time is state secretary of New Hampshire for this order. He is also a member of the Ancient Order of United Workmen of Laconia.

The Pepper Manufacturing Co.

The Pepper Manufacturing Co. was incorporated in May, 1890. The business dates back to 1857, being one of the oldest industries, in the line of manufacture of knitting machinery, in the United States. The first machines built by the founder of the business, Mr. William H. Pepper, were of the class known as the circular rib frame, which were constructed and intended to produce a tubular ribbed fabric which was cut to the required length for the legs of stockings. Subsequently the flat heeler and footer was built, on which the feet of the stockings were knit. Later, the Pepper flat frame was invented, with patent welt and slack course device for the production of shirt cuffs and drawer bottoms with finished ends. From year to year improvements were made and new devices were perfected and patented, and the business enlarged to meet the increasing demand for the machines, which are to be found to-day in nearly all the principal knit goods business towns in the United States, Canada, and the Provinces. From a limited business, it soon acquired more than a local reputation, and it was necessary to enlarge and broaden the industry, and from the comparatively few kinds of machines built the company are now producing machinery for the production of all sizes of tubular, plain, and ribbed fabrics, from the size of infants' mitts, to men's jackets, and sweater bodies, including the different gauges of fabric, and patterns for stripes, blocks, diamonds, etc., many of the devices for

Joseph P. Morin.

producing these patterns being secured by letters patent.

In 1887, A. T. L. Davis and G. A. Sanders were admitted as partners in the business, the style of the concern being W. H. Pepper & Co.

Three years later the Pepper Manufacturing Co. was incorporated with W. H. Pepper, president, A. T. L. Davis, treasurer, and G. A. Sanders, secretary. In August, 1897, Mr. Davis disposed of his interest in the company, retiring from the business. The present officers are president, W. H. Pepper; secretary and treasurer, G. A. Sanders.

The works and office of the company are at No. 25 Quinby street, Lakeport, N. H.

William H. Pepper.

William H. Pepper, an esteemed resident of Lakeport, and the founder and president of the Pepper Manufacturing Co., was born in the year 1830 in Nottingham, Nottingham county, England, son of Daniel and Mary (Parkins) Pepper. The father was a lace maker by trade. Of his five children, four sons and a daughter, William H., is the sole survivor. Both parents are also deceased.

Having come to this country in his early boyhood, William H. Pepper received his education in the common and high schools of Portsmouth, N. H., where his father was engaged in the manufacture of hosiery. After leaving school, he entered his father's shop and operated a hand loom until he was seventeen years old. He was next, for a short time, employed in the hosiery mill of Warren & Sanford at Portsmouth. On leaving there he worked in a machine shop in Lowell, Mass. While at the last named place, Hosea Crane sent him to Philadelphia in charge of a knitting machine to be placed on exhibition. After this he returned to Portsmouth, but subsequently went to work in the Henry Marchant mills at Pawtucket, R. I. Later he was employed in Valley Falls in a rubber lining establishment. He next secured a position as overseer in the John Nesmith mills at Franklin, N. H., with which he had been connected four years when the plant was destroyed by fire in the spring of 1857. Going then to Lake Village, he became superintendent in the Thomas Appleton mill, where he remained between two and three years. On leaving that employment he formed a co-partnership with his brother and engaged in the hosiery business, which they conducted under the firm name of J. & W. H. Pepper. Later on he was associated with J. S Crane, forming the firm of Crane & Pepper in the manufacture of knitting machines for his brother John. John afterward joined him in the

William H. Pepper.

enterprise, once more forming the firm of J. & W. H. Pepper, which lasted for several years. After separating from his brother he carried on the business alone until 1886 when he admitted two of his workmen to partnership, and the style of the firm became W. H. Pepper & Co. In 1890, the Pepper Manufacturing Co. was formed with William H. Pepper as president, G. A. Sanders as secretary, and A. T. L. Davis for treasurer, Mr. Pepper being also a director. He has also served as a director of the Lake Village savings bank, and was for a number of years a director of the Lakeport National bank, also a member of its financial committee. Mr. Pepper has been married three times. His first marriage was contracted with Ellen A. Jackson of Corinth, Me.; his second with Mrs. Addie Cheney, of Lakeport; and his third, with Nellie S. Moulton, daughter of William P. Moulton of Lake Village. His daughter, Emma M., by his first marriage, married George A. Sanders. Mr. Pepper is a Republican, and has always taken considerable interest in political matters. In 1890 he was elected to the state legislature, where he served on the manufacturing committee and gave his support to the passage of the bill for providing buoys for the lake, and for the lighting of the Weirs channel. Previous to entering the legislature he was chairman of the board of supervisors for two years. He is a member of Chocorua lodge, No. 51, I. O. O. F., being a P. G., also P. C. P. of Laconia Encampment, and a member of Canton Osgood, P. M.

George A. Sanders.

George A. Sanders, secretary and treasurer of the Pepper Manufacturing Co., was born in Gilford, N. H., October 4th, 1851, son of George W. and Sarah (Smith) Sanders. He received his education at the schools in Gilford and New Hampton.

On leaving school he entered the office of his father, who, in connection with his farming interests, operated the "Lake Co's" sawmill at Lake Village, the product of the mill being dimension lumber, shook, hosiery cases, etc. After about two years he gave up this position, going to Boston, where he secured employment as salesman in the retail dry goods house of Jordan, Marsh & Co., remaining there one and one half years, subsequently returning to Gilford and was engaged for one season as express and mail agent on the steamer "Lady of the Lake," Capt. S. B. Cole, commanding. In the fall of 1875 he entered the machine shop of W. H. Pepper to learn the trade.

In the year 1887 Mr. Sanders se-

George A. Sanders.

cured an interest in the business of kniting machine building, at which time the firm of W. H. Pepper & Co. was formed. In 1899, when the Pepper Manufacturing Co., was incorporated, he was chosen as secretary of the company, which position he still holds. On the retirement from the business of Mr. Davis, the treasurer, in August, 1897, Mr. Sanders was chosen to fill the vacancy. He was married in November, 1875, to Emma M., daughter of W. H. Pepper. Mrs. Sanders died in March, 1879, leaving one daughter, Ethelyn M. In 1884 he was married to Ella E., daughter of Palmer A. Wood, of Lakeport.

In political views and affiliations Mr. Sanders is a Republican. For twenty-seven years he has held membership in Chocorua lodge, No. 51, I. O. O. F.,

F. Geo. H. Osgood.

Osgood & Co., jewelers, succeeded to the business of S. E. Young & Co., on August 6, 1888, and although Mr. Osgood is one of Laconia's youngest business men, he is at the head of a long-established and successful business, the store having been conducted by the late Samuel E. Young for nearly thirty years before Mr. Osgood took possession. F. George H. Osgood, the present proprietor, was born on the Gilford side of the river, which is now part of the city of Laconia, August 6, 1865, and was educated in the public schools of Laconia, including the Laconia High school. He was married July 21, 1896, to Miss Mary A. Sanders. He has always been interested in secret fraternities.

F. George H. Osgood.

Jewelry Store of F. George H. Osgood.

also being a member of Laconia encampment, and Canton Osgood, No. 5, P. M., having passed the chairs in the three branches of the order named.

ties, and is a member of the Masons, Knights Templar, Odd Fellows, Knights of Pythias and Ancient Order of United Workmen.

Osgood & Co. always carry a large stock of watches, clocks, silverware, chains, optical goods, and trinkets of all kinds in the jewelry line. They handle reliable goods and only ask a fair profit. Watch repairing and engraving are departments of their business and square-dealing is the motto in every department. In these days of cheap watches, gold bricks and paste diamonds, it is pleasant to deal with reliable merchants, and people who trade with Osgood & Co. may depend on getting their money's worth, whether they invest in solid silver and gold jewelry or in the plated goods.

Walter H. Pitman.

Walter H. Pitman, youngest son of the late Joseph P. Pitman, is a native course at Tilton seminary. Almost before he left his studies he was a clerk in the general store of his father, the firm then being Pitman & Tilton. Most of Mr. Pitman's life has been spent in this store, which is now conducted by his brother, Joseph W. Pitman, and himself, under the firm name of J. P. Pitman & Co., carrying a large line of hardware, mill supplies, cutlery, small wares, paints, oils, bicycles, field and garden seeds, etc.

Mr. Pitman is also interested in the manufacturing business, being a stockholder and director in the well-known Pitman Manufacturing Co., one of the largest and oldest hosiery manufacturing concerns in New Hampshire. He also has a considerable real estate interest in this city, owning numerous cottages for rental.

Walter H. Pitman.

Residence of Walter H. Pitman.

Laconian and has always resided in this city. He was born August 28, 1856, and received his education in the public schools of Laconia, supplemented by a In religious affairs, Mr. Pitman is a Congregationalist, being a member of the North church, and quite active in all the affairs of the church and society. Mr.

Pitman married Flora E. Jackman, and they have two children at their elegant and pleasant home on Pleasant street, Florence Ruth Pitman and Joseph Prescott Pitman. An older daughter, Helen Elizabeth Pitman, aged 7 years, died February 27, 1898.

The Huse Machine Shops.

The Huse machine shops, under the ownership and management of Warren to six men being employed at the start. The industry has grown and prospered during the twenty years of its existence, and now employs from thirty-five to forty men.

In 1896 the old shops became inadequate to handle the increasing business, and consequently a new three-story building was erected and connected with the former establishment, giving over ten thousand square feet of floor space. The establishment is a model

The Huse Machine Shops.

D. Huse, at No. 117 Union avenue, is not only one of the important industries of the city of Laconia, but is also an establishment which has acquired much more than a local fame, being well-known in all parts of the United States, where knitting machinery is used to any extent.

Mr. Huse is a manufacturer of circular rib knitting machines, yarn winders, and other knitting mill machinery. The business was established in 1878 by Mr. Huse, in a small way, only from four machine shop, fitted with all the modern improvements, up-to-date machinery, etc., and divided into separate departments for drawing, pattern and model making, experimental work, blacksmithing, etc., and equipped with much machinery especially adapted to produce the fine machinery for which the Huse shops have a well-earned reputation, wherever their inventions have been introduced, and the Huse machines are well and favorably known among the knitting mills throughout this country.

Mr. Huse has been actively engaged in the manufacture and operation of knitting machines for over thirty years, and has invented quite a good many improved devices, which have made his machines especially desirable. He has associated with him his two sons, who have both taken an active part in the management of the business for over ten years, Leon C. Huse taking part in the construction and improvement of the machines, and Walter L. Huse takes charge of the office affairs and business end of the industry. Nearly all of the men employed in the Huse shops are skilled mechanics and among the best workmen to be found in this section of the country.

In addition to the knitting machinery business, which was the foundation, perhaps, of this industry, the concern is also engaged extensively in general job work in their line, which includes the construction and repairs of all kinds of machinery, building of engines, the furnishing and erection of steam and hot water heating apparatus, in both private and public buildings. Up-to-date plumbing is a special branch of the Huse shops which receives much attention, and this concern is the recognized headquarters for work in this line in this section. The advent of the bicycle has created an important branch of business at the Huse shops, special attention being paid to repairs of all kinds in this line.

Warren D. Huse.

In politics Mr. Huse is a Republican, and he has served as a member of the Laconia city council, but he is not an active politician, preferring to spend all the time he can spare from his business interests, in the enjoyment of life on the shores of our lakes, he and his sons having a handsome and convenient cottage on Lake Winnipesaukee.

The Late George Alvin Sanders.

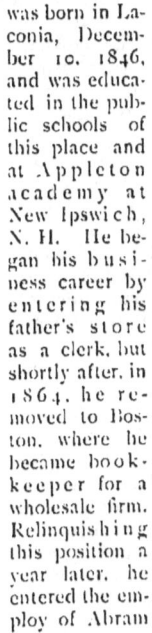

The late Col. George Alvin Sanders was born in Laconia, December 10, 1846, and was educated in the public schools of this place and at Appleton academy at New Ipswich, N. H. He began his business career by entering his father's store as a clerk, but shortly after, in 1864, he removed to Boston, where he became bookkeeper for a wholesale firm. Relinquishing this position a year later, he entered the employ of Abram French & Co., by whom for twenty-one years he was employed as a traveling salesman, canvassing almost the entire New England states in his routes.

In 1886, his father's failing health drew him back to his old home in Laconia, where in company with his brothers he assumed the management of his father's business, under the firm name of Sanders Bros., a partnership which terminated in 1892, when Colonel Sanders assumed sole charge.

As a Republican, Colonel Sanders

has been prominent. In the legislature of 1889-'90 he headed a successful legislative ticket in Laconia. In 1891 he was made an aide-de-camp on the staff of Governor Tuttle, with the rank of colonel. In 1892 he was chosen a commissioner of Belknap county. Colonel Sanders was active in the formation of the White Mountain Travelers' association, and served as its secretary and treasurer. In the new city government of Laconia he held the position of chief engineer of the fire department. He was a trustee of the Belknap Savings Bank, and a director in the Laconia Gas Co.

In secret society circles he ranked as a thirty-second degree Mason, Past Eminent Commander of Pilgrim Commandery of Knights Templar, a Knight of Pythias, and a Red Man. At the time of his death he was Senior Grand Warden of the Grand Commandery of Knights Templar, of New Hampshire.

Colonel Sanders possessed a wide circle of friends and acquaintances. He was generous to a fault, it being a prominent trait of his life never to let the needy depart wanting any of the comforts of life which he could supply. He was faithful to every trust imposed, either public or private, and everywhere he ranked as a whole-souled, genial, companionable, active man, the best of friends, the truest of comrades.

Colonel Sanders was twice married, his first wife being Miss Addie E. Currier of Cambridge, Mass., and his second wife, Miss Ida M. Chase of New Hampton. He left a widow and three children, Frank Currier Sanders, Emma Louise Sanders, and Serena Gertrude Sanders.

Colonel Sanders died December 2, 1898, of Bright's disease, and his death took from Laconia one of our most active and popular citizens, a man who was always promptly interested in every enterprise and movement of a public nature. But few men have been so prominent in Laconia social and business life, and but few men would be more missed by the general community.

The Late George Alvin Sanders.

Dr. Charles S Gilman.

Dr. Charles S. Gilman, now located at Suncook, N. H., where he enjoys a large and lucrative practice, was born at Lake Village, when the territory was a part of the old town of Gilford, October 23, 1871. He is the son of Noah C. and Mary (Sleeper) Gilman of 54 Clinton Street, Lakeport, and is a descendant in his paternal line from Edward Gilman, who came from Norfolk county, England, in May, 1670. Dr. Gilman attended the public schools of Lakeport and Laconia, and then went to Tilton seminary at Tilton, N. H. After graduating from Tilton seminary he did reportorial work on the Manchester *Union* and the *New Hampshire Republican*, and worked at Cram's grocery, Hubbard's shoe store, and Collins' pharmacy at Lakeport, to secure funds to enable him to pursue a course of study in medicine. Dr. Gilman studied medicine at the University of Vermont, Burlington, and at Tufts College Medical school at Boston, and finally at the Baltimore Medical college at Baltimore, Maryland. Dr. Gilman graduated from the Baltimore Medical college April 22, 1896. He studied the practical side of his profession at the Boston Dispensary with Dr. W. T. Slayton of Boston; at the Maryland General and Lying-in Hospital at Baltimore, and at the Baltimore Medical College Dispensary.

After taking his degrees, Dr. Gilman practised his profession at Lakeport for a few months, and then removed to Suncook in February, 1897, taking the office of the late Dr. G. H. Larabee, where he has been unusually successful, and where he has a steadily-increasing general practice.

While at Tufts college, Dr. Gilman was editor from the medical school of the "Brown and Blue," Tufts junior class annual, a member of Gamma Chapter Alpha Kappa Kappa, a Greek letter medical college fraternity. He is also member of the Winnipesaukee Academy of Medicine, the New Hampshire Medical society, and of Pembroke grange, Patrons of Husbandry.

Edwin D. Ward.

One of the most active and prominent citizens of the Lakeport end of Laconia is Edwin D. Ward, who at the present time carries on a successful undertaking business, and also carries a complete assortment of mouldings and fixtures. For the past twenty-seven years he has been a photographer, a part of that time in partnership with George B. Munsey, but he now leases the photograph studio, though still devoting some time to that branch of business. As a photographer, Mr. Ward's rooms have always had a good reputation, and there is hardly a photographer in New Hampshire who has made as many pictures as Mr. Ward.

Mr. Ward is a native of Bradford, N. H., where he still loves to spend a portion of his time. Mr. Ward was a great friend and admirer of the late Mason W. Tappan, of Bradford, attorney-general of New Hampshire.

In secret societies Mr. Ward is "a joiner." He is a member of Chocorua Lodge, No. 51, I. O. O. F., and of Laconia encampment, No. 9, and Esther Rebekah Lodge, No. 7, of the same order. He served as the grand master of the order in New Hampshire in the years 1894 and 1895, and was elected as grand representative from this state to the Sovereign Grand lodge for the years 1896 and 1897. These bodies met in Dallas, Texas, and Springfield, Ill., and at both sessions Mr. Ward served on important committees. He is a P. C. C. of Endicott Rock lodge, Knights of Pythias, a member of J. A. Greene division, No. 12, Uniform rank, K. of P. Mr. Ward is

Dr. Charles S. Gilman.

also a member of Mount Lebanon lodge, Free and Accepted Masons.

In politics Mr. Ward is a firm Republican, and he has been honored by numerous positions of responsibility and trust by his fellow-townsmen. In the old town of Gilford he was for five consecutive years chosen as treasurer of the town, and was a member of the New Hampshire legislature in the session of 1891. At the present time he is a member of the Laconia city council, from Lakeport, elected in 1897 and re-elected for two years in 1899. In the council he has served upon the committee on accounts and claims, and other of the more important committees. In 1898 Mr. Ward was appointed by Governor Ramsdell one of the New Hampshire ballot law commissioners for two years.

Mr. Ward has not only been successful in his business, but as a public servant he has proved himself faithful, efficient, and conscientious. His public spirit has never been found wanting, and his efforts on all occasions for the best welfare of the community have gained for him the confidence of the people of the whole city.

Edwin D. Ward.

Dr. George H. Saltmarsh.

Dr. George Harrison Saltmarsh of the Lakeport end of Laconia, is one of the best-known physicians throughout New Hampshire of any who are located in this city. He was born in Gilford March 3, 1859, the son of Thomas and Sallie (Gilman) Saltmarsh. Dr. Saltmarsh obtained his preparatory education in the public schools of his native town, and also attended the New Hampton Literary Institution. After completing his course of studies at New Hampton, he commenced to read medicine in 1879 with Dr. William H. Rand of that town, and then attended three courses of medical lectures at Dartmouth Medical College, where he graduated M. D. November 3, 1883. Dr. Saltmarsh has been in practice in Laconia since May, 1884, and is one of the busiest men in his profession. He is a member of the New Hampshire Medical society, and was honored by an election as president of this organization for the years 1898-'99. He is also a member of the Winnipesaukee Academy of Medicine, and served as secretary of this society from its incorporation, July, 1895, until 1898, and is now the vice-president of the society. He is president of the New Hampshire pension board of examining surgeons at Laconia, and is on the surgical staff of the Laconia cottage hospital. He is also surgeon for the Boston & Maine Railroad corporation, and attends to cases in which the railroad is interested in this section of New Hampshire.

Dr. Saltmarsh is a Republican in

politics, and was a member of the New Hampshire legislature in 1895-'96.

In secret societies Dr. Saltmarsh is a member of the Independent Order of Odd Fellows, the Knights of Pythias, and the New England Order of Protection.

In addition to his professional duties and the official positions which he has held in political and medical circles, Dr. Saltmarsh has found time to contribute some to the medical press.

He was married July 23, 1891 to Miss Mima, daughter of Leonard R. and Mary C. Avery of Portland, Maine. They have two children, Robert C., and Arthur Avery Saltmarsh.

John F. Merrill.

John Franklin Merrill, general manager of the Laconia Electric Lighting Co., has been a prominent business man and leading citizen of Laconia for half a century. He was born in Holderness, N. H., Oct. 31, 1833, son of William and Hannah C. (Batchelder) Merrill. He traces his ancestry back to the first settlers of Newbury, Mass. Later on the members of this family took active parts in the French and Indian and Revolutionary Wars. Mr. Merrill was educated in the public schools of Laconia and at old Gilford academy. He then learned the marble and granite business with the late Albert G. Hull, for whom he worked a year after completing his apprenticeship. In 1856, Mr. Merrill was taken into partnership in the business, the firm name being changed to Hull &

Dr. George H. Saltmarsh.

Merrill. This connection continued for twelve years and then Mr. Merrill purchased his partner's interest in the industry and carried on the business alone until January, 1892, when he sold out.

When the Laconia Electric Lighting Company was organized in 1884, Mr. Merrill became associated with the corporation as one of its directors, which position he still holds, and since 1893 he has also been general manager of the business.

When Union Cemetery association was formed in 1860, Mr. Merrill was elected a director and the treasurer of the association. These positions he has held now for almost forty years, and it is largely to his careful attention and wise management that Laconia takes pride today in the beautiful burial grounds which this association owns and controls.

Mr. Merrill is a staunch Republican and he has been honored by an election to the city council, and has served several times as a selectman of Ward 4.

Mr. Merrill has always been prominent in the Masonic and Odd Fellows' fraternities. He is a member of Mt. Lebanon lodge, Union chapter, Pythagorean council, and Pilgrim commandery, Knights Templar. In the Odd Fellows, he is a member of Winnipiseogee lodge, and has filled all of the officers' chairs in both lodge and encampment.

Nearly half a century ago Mr. Merrill became a member of the Free Baptist society, and he has been treasurer and secretary of this society for over forty years.

Mr. Merrill married Miss Flora Abby Rowe, Dec. 7, 1865, daughter of Morrison and Sarah (James) Rowe of Belmont, N. H. They are the parents of three sons and a daughter: Albert R., is junior partner in the firm of Hilliard & Merrill, wholesale dealers in cut soles at Lynn, Mass.; Frank Carleton is a piano tuner; Frederick Dimock is employed in the leather business with his brother in Lynn, Mass.; and Eva Lillian, is the wife of Eugene N. Best, a prominent lawyer of Minneapolis, Minn.

nia, which was formerly Lake Village, born May 15, 1841, and died May 12, 1895. He was educated in the public schools of Lake Village, a pattern-maker by trade and a very skilful workman. April 21, 1866, he was married to Alice M. Randlett of Belmont, who survives her husband, with one son, E. Roscoe Davis. Mr. Davis was a veteran of the civil war. He enlisted as a private in the Fourth regiment of New Hampshire

John F. Merrill.

Volunteers on July 12, 1861, and was discharged Nov. 13, 1864, as first lieutenant of his company. Mr. Davis was a Republican in politics and attended the Free Baptist church. He was a member of the Independent Order of Odd Fellows, Chocorua lodge. Mr. Davis received numerous political honors at the hands of his fellow-townsmen, serving as selectman in 1877, and as a

The Late Francis H. Davis.

The late Francis H. Davis was a native of that part of the city of Laco-

member of the board of education in 1881, 1882, and 1883. When Laconia was made a city, Mr. Davis was elected a member of the first city council, representing Ward two, and served so acceptably that he was re-elected for a second term in 1894 and 1895. In the council chamber, Mr. Davis always acted for what seemed to him the best interests of the city, and was always ready to give sound reason for the position he took upon any issue under discussion in the city government. Other councilmen might sometimes forget the taxpayers and vote to indulge in extravagances, but Mr. Davis always spoke and voted in the interests of the men who pay the bills, and he well earned the title of the "watchdog of the city treasury." Modest and unassuming, always genial and social, interested in every movement for the development and welfare of Laconia, he was a good citizen and the City on the Lakes lost a true Laconian when Francis H. Davis passed away.

Hampton Literary Institution at New Hampton. He married Alice Reed Sawin, June 15, 1882, and resides in a handsome residence on Gilford avenue. Mr. Chase is a member of the Knights of Pythias and the Uniform Rank, and is an attendant of the First Baptist church. For twelve years Mr. Chase conducted the well-known Round Bay Farm, a couple of miles from the centre of the city, and then for about three years was engaged in the carriage business.

At the present time, Mr. Chase is conducting a sporting resort and lunch room, in the Chase building, on the corner of Main street and Railroad square. The ground floor of this block has been handsomely fitted up for the purpose, with billiard and pool tables, sporting publications, etc., making a cosy and comfortable resort for citizens who desire to pass a pleasant hour handling the cue, or discussing sporting events. The premises are neat and clean, and there is no necessity for any movement in the direction of maintaining good order, for the establishment is patronized by the best of people, and is as clean in this respect as a private club room.

In addition to the attractions in the sporting line, Mr. Chase has provided a neat lunch counter, where sandwiches, doughnuts, tea, coffee, soda water, ginger ale, and other similar light drinks can be obtained, or a more substantial

The Late Francis H. Davis.

Chase's Sporting Resort.

Ethan Allen Chase, proprietor and manager of Chase's Sporting Resort and Lunch Rooms, is a native of Meredith, N. H., born January 7, 1856. He was educated in the Meredith public schools and also attended the New

repast can be ordered if desired. The location of the establishment near the Boston & Maine passenger station makes this a convenience for the traveling public as well as the citizens of the community. There is no restaurant in connection with the railroad station, and hungry passengers who alight from the trains or who go to the station to take a train can have their wants in the luncheon line supplied at short notice, with the choicest food, neatly served, and at reasonable prices.

Chase's Sporting Resort has been recently opened, but it is receiving a liberal patronage, and will evidently be a permanent institution and a success in every direction under Mr. Chase's careful management.

three daughters, Lillian M., Ethel W., and Grace L., at his pleasant residence on Gilford avenue.

Mr. Moore is a Republican in politics and was a very active and efficient member of the first city council of Laconia. He has been for eight years a member of the Laconia board of education, and with exception of one year served as secretary of the board. Mr. Moore was tendered the position of city clerk of Laconia, by mutual consent of both political parties, but declined the honor.

In secret societies, Mr. Moore is connected with the local branches of the Masonic fraternity and is a thirty-second degree Mason. He is also a Knight of Pythias, and a member of the United Order of Pilgrim Fathers, and New England Order of Protection.

Chase's Sporting Resort.

Albert C. Moore.

Albert C. Moore, clerk at the Cole Manufacturing Company shops, and secretary of the Laconia Building and Loan Association, was born in Boston, Mass., September 8, 1858. He was educated in the public schools of Boston and at Abbott academy (Little Blue) at Farmington, Me. He married Clara A. Edgerly, formerly of Tilton, N. H., and has a charming family of

Mr. Moore is an accomplished elocutionist and takes great interest in theatrical affairs. He is, himself, an amateur actor of much more than ordinary talent, and if he had chosen this profession would undoubtedly have scored a success. Mr. Moore and the famous Harry Dixey were boy friends and companions in Boston and made their first appearance upon the stage together in that city, in their juvenile days. Mr. Moore is acknowledged one of the most efficient book-keepers in Laconia, and in addition to his duties as clerk for the Cole Manufacturing company is secretary of the Laconia Building and Loan Association, a position which he has filled since the association was started in 1888. Probably no man in New Hampshire is better posted upon building and loan matters than Mr. Moore, and it is due to his skill and care that the books of the Laconia association are frequently cited as a model by the bank commissioners of the state.

Albert C. Moore.

Superintendent Blaisdell of the City Schools.

Joseph H. Blaisdell, superintendent of the Laconia public schools, is a native of Meredith, N. H., the only child of Daniel S. and Sarah (Potter) Blaisdell, but removed to Gilford at a very early age.

He attended the district school until he was about 16 years of age. It was the desire of his parents that he be given as good an education as was in his power to acquire, and with this end in view he studied Latin and Greek with a private teacher, and entered Gilmanton academy in the autumn of 1878, and graduated from the classical course two years later, fitted for college. During the following year he taught three terms of school, and entered Dartmouth college in the fall of 1881, graduating in the class of '85, with the degree of A. B., and receiving the degree of A. M. three years later. During his Sophomore and Junior years he taught short terms of school. While at college he was connected with the K. K. K. society, of which he was a prominent member.

After graduation he was elected principal of the Hamilton (N. Y.) Union school. Here he had under his supervision four hundred pupils and ten teachers. As Hamilton is the seat of Colgate university, it was a very important position, and called for the best efforts of any teacher. After two years' successful work, wishing to give attention to teaching the classical rather than the elementary branches, he became principal of an academy at

Residence of Albert C. Moore.

Lincoln, Maine. In two years more he became principal of the Whitcomb High school, Bethel, Vt., where he remained five years, fitting boys for college, and girls to become teachers. It was here that as principal of a small high school he taught Latin, Greek, German, English, history, mathematics, and science daily as necessity demanded. In 1894 he became principal of the Pepperell (Mass.) High school, and for three years taught the Latin, Greek, and mathematics. In 1897 he was elected superintendent of the public schools of Laconia, which position he now holds.

Mr. Blaisdell's experience as a teacher has been varied, having taught in every state in New England, except Rhode Island, with the additional state of New York. During the fourteen years since graduating at Dartmouth he has either taught or supervised every grade from primary to college preparatory.

He was married in 1888 to Clara L. Britton, and has no children. He is a member of Beacon Lodge, No. 175, I. O. O. F., Pepperell, Mass., Mount Lebanon lodge, No. 32, A. F. and A. M., and Union Chapter, No. 7, of Laconia.

Joseph H. Blaisdell, Superintendent of Schools.

Principal Hoyt H. Tucker.

Hoyt H. Tucker, principal of the Laconia High school, is a native of Athens, Maine, born October 6, 1858. He was educated in the public schools, and at Somerset academy, Nichols Latin school, and Bates college. Mr. Tucker first taught school in Maine at the Free High school at Gray. He then went to Wolfeborough, and was located there for three years, after which he returned to Maine, and was principal of the Hartland academy for two years. He was at Fairhaven, Mass., one year; at Holbrook, Mass., four years, and came to Laconia in 1894, as principal of the Laconia High school, succeeding Mr. W. N. Cragin. Mr. Tucker is a member of the New Hampshire Teachers' association, and is vice-president of this organization at the present time. He is president of the Winnipesaukee Teachers' Association, and also president of the Laconia Teachers' club, and a member of the New England History Teachers' Association.

When Mr. Tucker came to Laconia he entirely revised the course of study, and introduced one course founded on the report of the committee of ten. By this means the standard of the school was raised and its work made equal to that in many of the larger and better schools of New England.

Mr. Tucker takes great interest in his profession as a teacher. He has been very successful in our Laconia schools in arousing an interest among the students for a higher education than is afforded by our common schools. In years past a very large proportion of the pupils of Laconia have been content to drop their studies before graduating even from the high school, but during the past few years the graduating classes have been larger, and many of the graduates have continued their education in higher schools and colleges.

Mr. Tucker takes considerable interest in school athletics, and has endeavored to instill some of his enthusiasm into the students under his charge. He was prominent in the organization of the Laconia Education Society, largely composed of citizens of this city who are interested in our schools and in education generally, and the formation of this society cannot fail to be beneficial to the public schools of Laconia.

Mr. Tucker was united in marriage to Villette Maud Parker of Wolfeborough, in 1893, and they have two daughters, Bethania, aged five years, and Sara Josephine, aged three years.

Fred A. Young.

F. A. Young, tax-collector of the city of Laconia, and manager of Young's insurance and real estate agency, is a native of Barnstead, N. H., born August 4, 1866. He came to Laconia when a child, and was educated in the public schools here, and at New Hampton Literary Institution and Commercial College.

Mr. Young was employed for about a year as bookkeeper for George W. Riley, and afterwards entered the employ of the Melcher & Prescott Insurance Agency, with which he was connected for about six years, and then engaged in the insurance business for himself, afterwards adding a department for the handling of real estate transfer and renting of property.

In politics, Mr. Young is a Republican, and he has held several positions of political honor and trust. He was register of probate for Belknap county four years, being elected in 1892, and held the position for two terms. He was elected tax collector of the city of Laconia in 1897, 1898, and 1899, and his record of tax gathering is the best which has been made by any collector since Laconia became a city.

In secret orders, Mr. Young is a member of Mt. Lebanon Lodge of Masons, and also of Winnesquam colony, No. 34, United Order of Pilgrim Fathers. In religious affairs, Mr. Young affiliates with the Free Baptists, and he is president of the society at the South church, and a member of the committee on finance and church debt. He represents an excellent line of strong and reliable insurance companies, and places risks against fire, accident, loss of life, damage to steam boiler by explosion, etc. He is not only active in the interests of the companies which he represents, but also is energetic and enterprising in the interest of the patrons who purchase insurance. Mr. Young also handles investment bonds, securities, and mortgages. By careful management and close attention to business, he has succeeded in building

Hoyt H. Tucker, Principal of High School.

up a good line of patronage in Laconia and surrounding towns.

Mr. Young also makes a special feature of handling real estate for his clients, and always has a good line of farms and village and city property for sale. In this department, Mr. Young also attends to the renting and collecting of rents for landlords of tenement property in this city and vicinity. He has met with good success in this branch of his business, and now has upon his books a larger list of rental property than can be found elsewhere in this vicinity.

Mr. Young was married in 1891 to Miss Carrie B. Andrews. They have no children.

The Late D. A. Tilton.

Prominent among the business men of this city, ever contributing to its substantial prosperity covering a period of nearly a half century, was Daniel Atkinson Tilton. Mr. Tilton was one of a family of nine children, five sons and four daughters. These were children of John and Eunice Jacques Tilton, of Sanbornton. The subject of this sketch was born in the part of that town near what is now East Tilton, November 16, 1823. His early boyhood days were spent in Sanbornton, Tilton, East Tilton, Meredith, and at Pembroke, and it was from the latter town that the family came to this city in 1842, taking up its residence at what is now known as the Willard Hotel. The son, Daniel A., came a year later, having secured a position as clerk with the firm of H. J. French & Co., at that time conducting a general store located at the corner of Main and Court streets, the same being now occupied by John Parker Smith. At that time the firm consisted of Henry J. French and Woodbury Melcher, the latter the father of Hon. Woodbury L. Melcher of this city. Here Daniel A. remained until the spring of 1845, when he secured a similar position with the late Joseph P. Pitman, who conducted a hardware and grocery business on Main street, in the store now occupied by J. P. Pitman & Co. A few years later he formed a partnership with his employer, the style of the firm being J. P. Pitman & Co. With this union of interests, combining zeal with business tact, the firm soon entered upon an era of eminent success and prosperity. About 1868 the firm engaged in the manufacture of hosiery, and the business was continued up to the year 1875, when the firm of J. P. Pitman & Co. merged into the Pitman Mfg. Co., having been incorporated as a stock company. Mr. Tilton was made its treasurer, holding the position of treasurer at the time of his death, Nov. 25, 1889.

As previously indicated, Mr. Tilton, from the time of his first coming to Laconia, had been prominently identified with the business interests of the town, being one of the board of directors of

Fred A. Young.

the Laconia Savings Bank, and also one of the board of directors of the Laconia and Lake Village Street Railway Company. His political career began in his election as one of the board of selectmen of the town of Gilford, which he held for several terms, and also two successive terms as representative in the legislature from Gilford, at the time when that part of this village south and east of the Winnipesaukee river was a portion of Gilford. At the biennial election in 1888 he was elected as one of the board of county commissioners for Belknap county, but was obliged to decline the honor conferred, on account of ill health.

March 8, 1855, Mr. Tilton married Mary Ann, daughter of the late David and Margaret Ann Swazey Bowman, of Laconia. The result of the union proved to be a most happy one, covering many years of mutual devotion and one in which peace and happiness was no divided condition of their domestic life, but a unit. The wife of General William F. Knight, residing on Main street in this city, is a niece of Mr. Tilton.

To those who were accustomed to the every-day routine life of Mr. Tilton, he was known at his best. He was of a decided philanthropic nature, constantly developing a sentiment in "the greatest good to the greatest number," and on that account it was the cause of remark that his enemies were few. Socially he was always genial and courteous, greeting one and all with a happy smile of assurance that all was well, and these conditions prevailed as well within the domestic circle and financial board and the threaded thoroughfare of business life.

His religious sentiments were liberal, yet his affiliations were with the Congregationalists (the North church), toward whom it was his wont to bestow charity liberally in its support.

The late Daniel A. Tilton.

The Late Dr. Oliver Goss.

Dr. Oliver Goss, who died April 12, 1896, was for many years one of the best known and most successful physi-

Residence of the late Daniel A. Tilton.

cians and surgeons in this section of the state. He was born in Rye, Oct. 26, 1819, son of Jonathan Goss and Olive (Adams) Goss. His father removed his family to Moultonborough in 1822, where the subject of this sketch grew to manhood. His education was completed at Sandwich, Meriden, and Gilmanton academies, and he taught school for a time in the rural districts of Moultonborough and Gilmanton. He decided to adopt the medical profession, and first studied with the late Dr. W. H. H. Mason, of Moultonborough, in 1843, then in 1844 went to Boston, where he studied under the late professors, Oliver Wendell Holmes, Jacob Bigelow, and Henry J. Bigelow, of the Harvard Medical School.

der of his life. He was an active member of the New Hampshire Medical Society, joining in 1853. He was a member of the Winnipesaukee Academy of Medicine, and was the first president of this association. He was for years a prominent Odd Fellow, ever striving to exemplify in his daily life its teachings of "Friendship, Love, and Truth." He was always interested in agriculture, and was a valuable member of Laconia grange, Patrons of Husbandry. In politics Dr. Goss was a Democrat. He served for years as a member of the pension bureau.

The late Dr. Oliver Goss.

The late Elizabeth Honor (Flanders) Goss.

He returned to New Hampshire, and in 1845 graduated M. D. from Dartmouth Medical College. He commenced to practice at Melvin Village, on the shore of Lake Winnipiseogee, but in 1852 settled in Lakeport, where he continued in practice until his death, a continuous practice of over fifty years. In 1846 he was married to Elizabeth H. Flanders, who died June 2, 1891, daughter of Joseph Flanders of Gilmanton. Four children were born to them, three of whom are dead ; one son, Dr. O. W. Goss, survives them.

Soon after coming to Lakeport, Dr. Goss became a member of the Park Street Free Baptist church, of which he remained a worthy member the remain-

Dr. Goss as a youth was amiable and steadfast in high moral principles. He was possessed of rare mental faculties, he was temperate, frugal, and steadfast, immovable as the granite hills in his sense of right, ever quick to respond to the call of charity, and to render aid in cases of destitution and suffering. During the war Dr. Goss attended the soldiers free of charge, accepting no recompense, deeming this service a sacred duty he owed to them. Both in public and private life Dr. Goss was an exponent of high moral sentiments, and in his death the medical profession lost a valuable member, and the general public will long miss his smiling countenance, ripe judgment, and professional skill.

The late Elizabeth H. (Flanders) Goss.

Elizabeth Honor (Flanders) Goss, the estimable wife of Dr. Oliver Goss, died at the family residence on Elm street, June 2, 1891, at the age of seventy-four years and twenty-eight days. Interment was made in the family tomb in the Hillside cemetery. She was one of a family of six children. Her father, the late Joseph Flanders, was born in Belmont, January 15, 1790, and died May 6, 1871, in Laconia. Her mother, Sophia (Hall) Flanders, was born in Exeter, N. H., March 7, 1793, and died in Sanbornton, October 31, 1862. Mrs. Goss was born in Gilmanton, May 16, 1817. She was educated in the public schools and Gilmanton academy. April 1, 1845, she was united in marriage to Dr. Oliver Goss, which union was blessed with four children, two girls and two boys, all deceased except Dr. O. W. Goss.

Mrs. Goss joined the church in Upper Gilmanton, and after coming to Lakeport to live she became a member of the Free Baptist church, in which she was a willing worker and ardent supporter.

Dr. O. W. Goss.

Ossian Wilber Goss, M. D., one of Laconia's best known and most successful physicians, is a son of the late Dr. Oliver Goss and Elizabeth Honor (Flanders) Goss, and grandson of Jonathan Goss, was born March 21, 1856, in Laconia. He attended the common and the select schools until 1873, was a student for one year in the New Hampton Institution, and was graduated from the New Hampshire Conference Seminary and Female College at Tilton, at the close of a two years' classical

Dr. Ossian W. Goss.

Residence of Dr. O. W. Goss.

course in 1876. Having completed his preparatory education, he entered Bates college, Lewiston, Maine, in 1876. In 1880, he matriculated in the medical school of Harvard university, and was graduated M. D., in June, 1882.

In 1886 he entered the Post-Graduate Medical School of New York for special courses in medicine and surgery, also taking up at various times special studies at Harvard Post-Graduate and Boston Polyclinic.

Dr. Goss is a member of the New Hampshire Medical Society, the Winnipesaukee Academy of Medicine, and the American Medical Association. He has been in the practice of medicine and surgery since June, 1882, in Laconia, and has a large and lucrative practice. In the literary line, Dr. Goss has contributed various articles pertaining to medicine and surgery, that have met approval in the medical profession.

Dr. Goss was married in 1882 to Miss Mary P. Weeks of Sanbornton. Their only child died in infancy August 15, 1883.

Dr. Goss is prominent in the secret and fraternal orders, being a member of the Odd Fellows, Masons, Pilgrim Commandery, K. T., Knights of Pythias, Red Men, Elks, Royal Arcanum, Pilgrim Fathers, New England Order of Protection, Masonic Relief Association, etc.

Morgia Porter Wilson.

Morgia Porter Wilson

Morgia Porter Wilson, so well and favorably known in Laconia as a leading vocalist and teacher, is a native of Manchester, N. H., and the daughter of Charles C. P. and Caroline (Patch) Porter. Her voice in childhood was noted for its purity and compass.

At the age of sixteen she had sung the leading rôles in several operettas with marked success, and soon after began her career as a choir singer in the cities of Concord, Manchester, and Lawrence, continuing in that capacity for several years. Meantime, while on a concert tour in the West, her voice attracted the attention of the late John B. Gough, and through his generous assistance she began to study under Madam J. H. Long, of Boston, subsequently taking the Rudersdorff method of other teachers. With five years careful study, she attained a high musical reputation as a vocalist throughout New England. She married, in 1873, Mr. Julius E. Wilson, now of Lakeport, where they have resided for the past thirteen years. She is the only recognized vocal teacher in Laconia, and her ability as such is attested by the rapid progress of her pupils.

Charles L. Simpson.

Charles L. Simpson, who was one of the representatives of Ward six (Lakeport), city of Laconia, in the state legislature of 1898-'99, is a native of Canterbury, N. H., born May 25, 1874. He was educated in the public schools of Lakeport, and for a young man has been very prominent in social and fraternal affairs. He is assistant superintendent of the Park Street Free Baptist Sunday-school, and is on the executive committee of the society. He is also an ex-president of the Young People's Society of Christian Endeavor, connected with the church.

Mr. Simpson is a Democrat in politics, but was elected representative to the legislature from a strong Republican ward. He is employed as a clerk in the grocery business.

Mr. Simpson is a past grand of Chocorua lodge, No. 51, I. O. O. F., and a member of Hannah Frances Rebekah lodge, No. 41. He is also a member of Belknap lodge, No. 48, New England Order of Protection, and treasurer of the Odd Fellows' Mutual Relief Association. He served as business manager of the *New Hampshire Philatelist* during its publication in this city, and is a director in the Lakeport Building and Loan association.

Mr. Simpson married Miss Clara Cyrilla Sargent.

Wellington L. Woodworth.

Wellington L. Woodworth, cashier of the Lakeport National bank, has been called the youngest national bank cashier in New Hampshire, and we think the claim has never yet been disputed. He is a native of Lake Village, born May 18, 1873. He attended the public schools at Lakeport and later Tilton seminary. Mr. Woodworth was at one time public librarian of Lakeport, and for several years served as assistant postmaster of Lakeport under his father. He is a member of Chocorua lodge, No. 51, I. O. O. F., and is a past grand of this lodge.

Mr. Woodworth married Edith M. Hull, May 18, 1898.

He is a member of the Freewill Baptist church. Although a young man to hold so responsible a place as cashier of a national bank, Mr. Woodworth has proved himself equal to the position and not only discharges his duties with efficiency and fidelity, but is very popular with all the patrons of the bank.

Charles L. Simpson.

Wellington L. Woodworth.

The Laconia Lumber Works.

Down at the lower end of Water street, on the banks of the Winnipesaukee river and the shores of Lake Winnisquam, is located one of this city's most prosperous and thriving industries, the Laconia Lumber works, of which George W. Riley is president, manager, and proprietor.

The Laconia Lumber works is a model plant of the kind, and covers seven acres of land, including the sawmill, sash, door, and blind factory, office-building, lumber yard, and numerous the lumber-yards affords facilities for loading the sawed and finished product of the concern.

The wood-working factory buildings are all equipped with the latest machinery and labor-saving devices. The boilers are supplied with fuel from the sawdust made in the various departments, which is sucked up into pipes by fans and blown into the boiler-room, while the exhaust steam, after operating the big engine for making the power which propels the machinery, is run through immense coils of steam pipes, heating the air to warm the work-shops

The Laconia Lumber Works.

storehouses for sawed and finished lumber. The concern carries an immense stock of material in the lumber line, the amount of logs in the river, awaiting the sawyers at the sawmill, being reckoned by the million feet, while the various sheds and storehouses around the lumber-yard are always filled with the finished product of the mills, besides large stocks of sawed lumber imported from the Southern states, etc.

A substantial elevated railroad track enables the car-loads of timber from the north country to be dumped directly into the river close to the sawmill slip, while another line of track down into and dry the lumber, the heated air being also distributed around the premises by powerful fans.

The shops are lighted by electricity, the concern having its own dynamo, which requires little or no attention and produces incandescent lights at very small expense.

It is something of a conundrum where all the lumber and other material goes which is turned out every day at the Laconia Lumber works, but the concern manufactures everything in the woodworking line from dimension lumber down to shingles, and has a steady run of work in sash, blinds, packing-cases, etc., and is constantly shipping large orders of building materials to down-country customers. During the past season, also, considerable lumber has been sawed out for the Laconia car-shops.

George W. Riley.

Mr. George W. Riley, the proprietor and manager of the Laconia Lumber works, has been a citizen of Laconia since 1883, and is one of our most active and enterprising manufacturers. He was born in the eastern part of the town of Northfield, N. H., Feb. 9, 1848. He was educated in the public schools near his home, and when seventeen years old started in to learn the carpenter's trade. Before he was old enough to vote, Mr. Riley was in business for himself, in Belmont, as a contractor and builder. He remained in Belmont until 1883, at which time he came to Laconia and continued in the same line of business, also taking the wood-working shops formerly conducted by Ralph Merrill, near the Abel machine shops. The business was not a success under Mr. Merrill's management, but it increased rapidly and prospered with Mr. Riley, and in a few years the industry had outgrown its quarters. Then Mr. Riley and several associates leased the property of the Laconia Lumber works, in 1890, which he purchased outright about two years ago, having bought out all of his

George W. Riley.

partners in the concern during the past few years.

Mr. Riley married Emma F. Elkins, in 1874, and they have one son, Phil M. Riley. They reside in their elegant residence on Church street, and are attendants at the Congregational church.

Mr. Riley is a man whom Laconia takes pride in claiming as an adopted citizen. He is quiet, unassuming, and easy of approach, on business or any other matters. He carries the entire business of the Laconia Lumber works in his mind, and is the recognized head and director of every department of the large establishment. His word is as good as his bond, and he has built up his large and successful industry by square dealing, enterprise, hard work, and strict attention to business.

He is public-spirited, and ready to lend a helping hand in any public movement for the benefit of Laconia.

Residence of George W. Riley.

Winnipesaukee Gas and Electric Company.

The Winnipesaukee Gas and Electric Company was incorporated March, 1897, and was at that time the successor of the old Laconia Gas Company, a corporation which had been in operation for many years, and had perhaps outlived its usefulness, as the plant was old and out of date, and the quality of gas produced was not satisfactory.

The Winnipesaukee Gas and Electric Company have a plant which was put in entirely new in 1894, at an expense of $65,000, and which is one of the finest and best-equipped gas plants in New England. The factory is a brick building of ornamental design, located on Messer street, and equipped with all new and up-to-date machinery, while a side track from the adjacent railroad affords facilities for unloading materials for the manufacture of gas, directly from the freight cars into the gas factory. During the past two years two hundred and sixty new consumers have been added, and the number is rapidly increasing. About twelve miles of street mains have been laid up to the present time, covering almost the entire city; but extensions are constantly being made in every direction, both at Laconia and Lakeport. to reach new consumers and thereby extend the service. The corporation furnishes gas for lighting, cooking, heating, and power purposes.

The use of gas in Laconia for heating and cooking purposes is comparatively a new idea, but for both these purposes there is a constantly increasing demand for gas; and these features of the company's business are proving very popular, both on the ground of convenience and cheapness. There are now in use in this city over one hundred and fifty two-oven four-burner gas ranges, besides many smaller gas stoves, both for cooking and heating.

The officers of the corporation are: President, Charles A. Busiel; superin

Winnipesaukee Gas and Electric Company.

tendent, J. H. Bledsoe; treasurer, Nathaniel J. Edgerly; directors, Chas. A. Busiel, Albert G. Folsom, John T. Busiel, Samuel B. Smith, Henry J. Odell, Edwin F. Burleigh, Charles L. Pulsifer.

Under this strong board of management the Winnipesaukee Gas and Electric Company has succeeded in supplying a first-class gas, of very high illuminating quality, in place of the old-time dim, smoky, and offensive-smelling product, and the innovation has met with the approval of the citizens of Laconia, and resulted in building up a profitable business which promises to be more successful and popular from year to year.

Herbert S. Sanborn.

Herbert S. Sanborn, familiarly known as "Doc" Sanborn, proprietor of Sanborn's drug store, is a native of Concord, N. H., born July 27, 1869. He was educated in the common schools of the capital city, and learned the drug trade with H. F. Wyatt at Plymouth. N. H. Later, he came to Laconia as a drug clerk for George A. Hatch, and then managed H. F. Wyatt's Laconia drug store for one year. In 1891 he purchased Mr. Wyatt's interest in the drug business in this city and embarked in trade for himself.

April 28, 1893, Mr. Sanborn married Miss Lottie A. Chandler, and they have a bright little daughter of four years and a son of two years.

Amoskeag Veterans of Manchester, and a Red Man.

Mr. Sanborn prides himself upon the complete stock of goods which he carries in his drug store, including the freshest and purest drugs and chemicals, articles for the toilet, fancy goods, soaps and perfumes of domestic and foreign manufacture, cigars, and druggists' sundries, etc.

In the "patent medicine" line, Sanborn's drug store aims to carry every reliable concoction which is placed upon the market, and it is difficult to ask for any remedy which he cannot immediately produce from his extensive stock.

A specialty is made of compounding family recipes and physicians' prescriptions with accuracy and care, only the purest drugs being used for this pur-

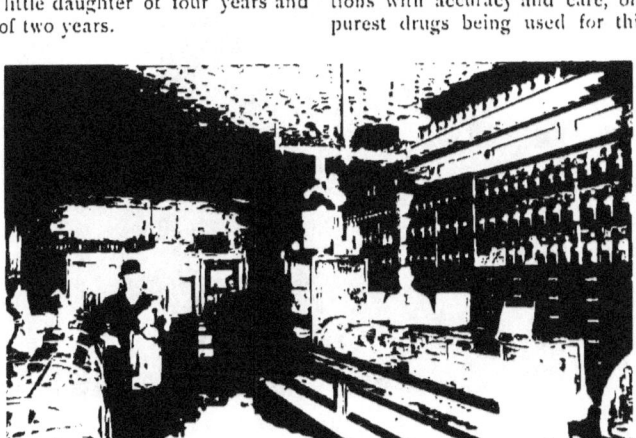

Herbert S. Sanborn.

Drug Store of Herbert S. Sanborn.

Mr. Sanborn attends the Episcopal church, is a Democrat in politics, is a member of the Masonic fraternity, and is also a member of the celebrated

pose. Pure soda and mineral waters are dispensed, all syrups being the choicest the market affords.

Mr. Sanborn himself is a thoroughly

expert pharmacist and always employs skilful assistants.

Mr. Sanborn is comparatively a young man, but the Sanborn drug store is an old-established pharmacy, and its reputation for carrying a complete stock of every known drug and every patent remedy that is known in the market is is constantly in mind and ever on the increase.

City Marshal Scott.

City Marshal Henry K. W. Scott was born in Lebanon, on September 6, 1866, and was educated in the "little red schoolhouse" of Scytheville, a suburb of that town. After leaving school he served an apprenticeship with the Baxter Machine Co., of Lebanon, and after several unsuccessful attempts to find steady employment at his trade, in Massachusetts and in New York, he came to Laconia, where he was employed with the American Twist Drill Co., the Crane Manufacturing Co., and the Eastman Freight Car Heater Co. Later for a short time he was employed by the Eastman Heater Co., in Boston, but soon returned to Laconia, and was with the Abel Machine Co., in 1893, when Laconia became a city. At that time he was elected city marshal and has held the position continuously ever since. March 8, 1890, he married Miss Nellie I. Shackley of Laconia, and has a family of two promising sons.

City Marshal Scott is a past chancellor of Mt. Belknap Lodge, No. 20, of Knights of Pythias, and also a member of the order of United Workmen. He was a promoter and organizer of the New Hampshire Chiefs of Police Union of which he is now the vice-president. As a public servant, Marshal Scott is not only efficient, but faithful and conscientious, and enjoys the hearty good-will of the community. His reputation for spotting crooks and dealing with all habitual criminals is recognized and thoroughly appreciated by this class of people and consequently Laconia is remarkably free from pickpockets, bunco men, and professional crooks of all kinds.

The Laconia police department is admitted to be a model organization, and much credit is due to Marshal Scott.

City Marshal Henry K. W. Scott.

The Late Levi B. Brown.

The late Levi B. Brown, who died September 2, 1898, was one of the best known hotel landlords in New Hampshire. He was born in Hartford, Vt.,

The late Levi B. Brown.

Sept. 21, 1822, and during his early life was a stagecoach driver. He afterwards engaged in the wholesale and retail hardware business at Claremont, N. H., for a long time, and then went to Providence, R. I., where he was again interested in the staging business.
In 1873, Mr. Brown came to Laconia and from that date until the time of his death was engaged in the hotel business. He was proprietor of the Mt. Belknap House at Lakeport for about twelve years, and under his management this house was generally admitted to be one of the most popular and best patronized establishments in New Hampshire north of Concord. When the Eagle Hotel was remodeled at the Laconia end of the city, landlord Brown was its first proprietor and was again successful in building up a large business and winning an excellent reputation for the hotel. After selling out the Eagle Hotel, Mr. Brown retired from business for a time, but afterwards purchased the City Hotel which he conducted successfully until failing health compelled him to retire from business a short time before his death.

The Late Orison Twombly.

The fame of Laconia as a hosiery town and as a centre for the manufacture of knitting machinery of all kinds, is largely due to the inventive genius of some of the Laconia men who grew up in the hosiery and knitting machine industries of the city. Among these men was the late Orison Twombly, a native of Portsmouth, N. H., born Oct. 12, 1828. He was educated in the common schools, and early in life developed a genius for mechanical inventions. He was for many years an overseer in the Ashland knitting mills at Ashland, N. H., and later came to Laconia about the year 1870. After coming to this city, Mr. Twombly devoted most of his attention to the invention and development of numerous devices for the improvement of knitting machinery, and he held letters patent on various inventions in this line, some of which were very successful machines and quite valuable. He was located in Boston a

The late Orison Twombly.

large part of the time during his residence in Laconia, having his general headquarters and business office in that city. Mr. Twombly died Nov. 9, 1897.

The Waverly Shoe Company.

The Waverly Shoe Co. was started in 1883, under the name of Waverly School Shoe Co., Bemis & Fletcher, proprietors, in Crompton's block, 13 Mechanic street, Worcester, Mass.

At the end of two years the business had increased to such an extent that it was necessary to secure larger quarters, and the concern moved to Taylor's building, 154 Front street. Three years later it was necessary to occupy a part of the adjoining block, as the business was still increasing rapidly. In 1891

The Waverly Shoe Company.

it again became necessary to have a still larger factory, which was secured in the Rice building, Franklin square, a five-story building, where the business was carried on until the company removed to Laconia, in February, 1897.

The Waverly School Shoe Co. confined themselves entirely to school shoes until they moved to the Rice building, when they added new lines and changed the name to Waverly Shoe Company.

The reputation of the Waverly shoe has always been of the very highest, as it has been the aim of the company to use only the best of leather and material, and to make a shoe that would give the best of satisfaction.

The shoes are sold direct to the retail dealer, and in almost every state and territory of the Union.

The demand for the Waverly shoes still continues to increase, and the company have had a steady call for them all through the hard times, doing a larger amount of business at the start in Laconia than they did in Worcester.

The Waverly Shoe Co. shops in Laconia were erected especially for this concern and are generally admitted to be as good as can be found in New England, all things considered, for the purpose. The shops are equipped with electric power, elevator, fire sprinklers, and all the modern improvements and conveniences. The business is under the management of the head of the concern, Mr. Gilbert C. Bemis, who is permanently located in Laconia and a welcome addition to our enterprising business men.

John L. Roberts.

John L. Roberts conducts the largest wood, coal, ice, and brick business in the city of Laconia. His headquarters and office is located at No. 19 Canal court, his wood and coal yards are at the lower end of Water street, and his ice pond and ice houses are located on Durkee brook, near the Marsh hill springs. The ice, wood, and coal business was comparatively new in Laconia a few years ago, and at first was limited for various reasons. Ice was a luxury a few years ago, but is to-day almost an absolute necessity, and must be pure and clean to meet with public approval. A few years ago, wood was nearly all purchased of farmers who hauled the cordwood into town during the winter, and waited in the streets for customers. To-day a telephone message to Mr. Roberts will bring the desired quantity of wood at short notice, either hard or soft, sawed by machinery any required length, and also split by machinery if so ordered. The coal business is also an industry of recent growth, and the amount consumed in Laconia still increases steadily from year to year. In all of these departments, Mr. Roberts has good facilities for supplying the public promptly, and with any quality desired. He employs nine horses, and about fifteen men in his business, and handles more wood, coal, and ice than any other concern in the city. Some three years ago Mr. Roberts constructed one of the best ice houses in New Hampshire, near the Marsh Hill springs in Belmont, near the city, where he also built an artificial pond by damming the stream, and his present plant for cutting and handling ice cannot be surpassed in New England, for the waters of the Marsh hill spring are widely famous for their purity and medicinal qualities, and there can be no better ice in the world than Mr. Roberts delivers to his patrons.

Mr. John L. Roberts, the proprietor of this business, was born in Belmont, September 11, 1858, and was educated in the common schools. He started in the milk business in Gilford in 1879, and continued for about ten years. He came to Laconia in 1889, and started in the wood, coal, and grain business alone. In April, 1892, Mr. Roberts, with C. A. Dunn, and Frank M. Sanborn, formed the Laconia Ice, Coal, and Wood Co., and continued until October 22, 1896, when Mr. Roberts bought the entire business, which he still continues.

Mr. Roberts married Ada F. Randlett of Belmont, Oct. 3, 1880, and they have one son, aged fourteen years. He is a member of the Free Baptist church, and in secret orders is connected with the Ancient Order of United Workmen.

The traditional jokes regarding the short weights of the average coal dealer, and the small cakes of the ordinary iceman, which melt before they can be stored in the housewife's refrigerator, do not apply to Mr. Roberts, for he is square and upright in all his transac-

John L. Roberts.

tions, honest to the last cent, and gives good weight and measure every time. These principles have been recognized by the public and have resulted in a successful and steadily-increasing business.

George B. Munsey.

George B. Munsey, of the Depot square clothing and furnishing goods store, was born in Gilford, N. H., Oct. 9, 1861, and resided there until about seven years of age, when his parents, the Rev. and Mrs. J. G. Munsey, removed to the town of Gilmanton, and lived there four years. They then removed to East Tilton, where they remained five years, and during a portion of this time the subject of this sketch attended the Tilton seminary. His parents then went to West Lebanon, Maine, and from there to Andover, N. H., and while residing in the latter town, Mr. Munsey completed his education at New Hampton Literary Institution.

After completing his education he first engaged in the printing business at Tilton, which he conducted successfully for some time. Later he sold out the printing business and came to Lakeport, where he took up the photographer's profession, some twelve years ago, in company with Edwin D. Ward, forming the partnership of Ward & Munsey.

Mr. Munsey was also senior member of the firm of Munsey & Heath, the well-known bicycle dealers.

About a year ago Mr. Munsey disposed of his interest in both the photograph and bicycle business, and at that time purchased the clothing and gentlemen's furnishing store, previously conducted by R. P. Babbitt & Co., in Depot square. Mr. Munsey has built up a good trade at this stand, and carries a large stock of reliable goods, including all the latest novelties and popular styles in gentlemen's clothing and furnishings of all kinds.

The great advance made in the manufacture of ready-made clothing during the past few years, enables Mr. Munsey to carry a line of goods which will compare favorably with custom-made goods, both as to style, quality, and perfection of fit; while in the matter of price, of course the ready-to-wear suits are much more popular with all classes of customers. He has a line of goods which cannot be excelled by any similar establishment outside of the largest cities, and his business is very prosperous and steadily increasing.

Mr. Munsey is an attendant at the Park Street Free Baptist church, and in secret societies is connected with the order of Pilgrim Fathers.

He was married in 1883 to Miss Mary A. Rollins, and they reside in a handsome home on Union avenue.

George B. Munsey.

George B. Cox.

George B. Cox was born in Ashland, Grafton county, N. H., July 16, 1860, son of Benjamin Franklin and Ann (Currier) Cox. His paternal ancestors were among the first settlers of Holderness (now Ashland), N. H., and his mother's family was of Scotch descent.

He was educated in the public schools of Ashland, a private school at Plymouth, the New Hampton Literary Institution, and Wesleyan university. Previous to beginning his professional studies he taught school at Candia, N. H., during one year, and was twice chosen as superintendent of schools in the town of Ashland. In 1885 he began the study of law with Judge E. A. Hibbard, and two years later entered the Boston University Law school, where he was graduated in 1888, with the degree of bachelor of law. He was admitted to the New Hampshire bar in July of the same year, and has since practised law in Laconia.

In politics Mr. Cox is a Democrat, and has in several campaigns stumped the state in the interests of his party. For three consecutive years he served as a member of the board of education of Laconia, being chairman of the board during the last year.

In 1890 the Citizens' Temperance union was formed in Laconia, and for four years he was retained as its counsel. In January, 1894, he was elected a member of the executive committee of the Law and Order league of New Hampshire, a strong temperance organization, supported by many of the most influential citizens of the state. In 1895 he was retained as counsel for the league, but in 1897 he severed his connection with that organization that he might devote his entire time to his private law practice.

Mr. Cox was married February 10, 1897, to Nellie M. Hoyt of Laconia. The *Bristol Weekly Enterprise* of Jan. 30, 1896, makes the following analysis of Mr. Cox's ability as an orator: "Mr. Cox is a young man who uses sense, reason, and treats fairly and squarely from every standpoint his subject. He is logical, clear, and emphatic, takes his points well, and argues his case in a manner that carries conviction to his listeners. He does not rant, but puts cold facts in pointed sentences with practical illustrations and a generous spirit that recommends him to the consideration of those who do not endorse his theories or accept his doctrines. He indulges in sarcasm only when necessary to expose the fallacy of some of his opposer's claims, and bombards men and matters only when he deems it necessary for the welfare of the public."

The Laconia *Democrat* of March 19, 1899, says: "Mr. Cox fully maintained his invincible position as one of the best public speakers among the lawyers."

George B. Cox.

Laconia Savings Bank.

The handsome engraving of the Laconia Savings Bank accompanying this sketch of its history shows that it is not behind in progress of financial stability.

This bank has been in existence since 1831. It was organized under the name of the Meredith Bridge Savings Bank, by John T. Coffin, Daniel Tucker, John Sanborn, George L. Sibley, George P. Avery, James Molineux, and Benjamin Jewett, 3d, the original incorporarors. Its charter was signed by Samuel Dinsmoor, governor; Samuel Cartland, president of the senate; Franklin Pierce, speaker of the house of representatives; and approved July 2, 1831.

The original list of officers was as follows: George L. Sibley, president; Stephen C. Lyford, treasurer; George L. Sibley, John T. Coffin, Woodbury Melcher, Daniel Tucker, James Molineux, F. W. Boynton, John L. Perley, John Sanborn, and Stephen L. Greeley, trustees.

The first deposit was received in March, 1832, and since that time it has paid 134 consecutive semi-annual dividends, amounting to about one million three hundred and fifty thousand dollars.

None of the original incorporators or officers is now living, and since its foundation nearly seventy years ago it has had five presidents and five treasurers, an average term of service of nearly fourteen years each.

In 1869 its name was changed to the Laconia Savings Bank, and its financial soundness has been maintained through all these years.

In 1884 its quarters were remodeled and a new vault put in which sufficed for the needs of the institution until 1895, when the banking rooms were enlarged to twice their former size, a new safety deposit vault and bankers' safe added, till now it has fine and conveniently-appointed banking rooms.

The present officers of the institution are A. G. Folsom, president, and Edmund Little, treasurer. The board of trustees is composed of the following well-known men: Albert G. Folsom, Ellery A. Hibbard, Almon C. Leavitt, Samuel B. Smith, W. L. Melcher, Gardner Cook, Frank H. Lougee, George A. Hatch, Alburtis S. Gordon, Alfred W. Abbott.

The appended statement of the condition of the bank's affairs speaks for itself:

ASSETS.

Loans,	$425,257.15
State, county, city, and district bonds,	521,150.00
Bank stock,	34,950.00
Railroad bonds and stock,	101,425.00
Miscellaneous bonds,	160,357.00
Real estate,	83,642.00
Bank fixtures,	11,000.00
Deposits in national banks,	40,215.76
Cash on hand,	7,067.64
	$1,385,364.55

LIABILITIES.

Deposits,	$1,277,937.20
Guaranty fund and surplus,	107,427.35
	$1,385,364.55

This old reliable savings bank has always been noted for its conservative investments, preferring security of principal and moderate rate of interest rather than large interest return with proportionate risk.

Its present list of assets is composed of first-class securities consisting of home investments and gilt-edge bonds.

People's National Bank.

This bank, which occupies rooms with the Laconia Savings bank, as shown on opposite page, was organized in 1889, and has already passed its tenth milestone.

It has enjoyed a liberal patronage and a prosperous and increasing business from its organization to the present time; it aims especially to accommodate its patrons, furnishing unexcelled facilities for the transaction of every branch of the banking business.

The People's National bank quarters are very handsomely fitted with tile floors, elegant directors' room, and modern safety deposit vaults, and in all its appointments and business transactions the establishment is a model of the kind.

The officers are Albert G. Folsom, president; John T. Busiel, vice-president; Edmund Little, cashier; Albert G. Folsom, Gardner Cook, John T. Busiel, Samuel B. Smith, Edwin F. Burleigh, Frank H. Lougee, Frank E. Busiel, directors, and the following report of its condition at the present time indicates a well managed and successful institution:

Story's Drug Store.

Story's drug store, established in 1880, is recognized as one of the most reliable and best conducted establishments in the pharmacy line in Laconia. Mr. J. Henry Story, the proprietor, is himself a skilful pharmacist, and he employs thoroughly competent assistants in his establishment. The Story drug store carries a large and complete stock of the purest and freshest drugs which the market affords, supplemented by

Story's Drug Store.

RESOURCES.

Loans and discounts,	$111,730.07
Overdrafts,	169.60
U. S. bonds,	25,000.00
Premiums,	1,500.00
Stocks and bonds,	5,672.50
Real estate and mortgages,	5,715.76
Due from National bank redemption,	25,113.19
Redemption fund with U. S. treasurer,	1,125.00
Cash,	9,702.83
	$185,749.34

LIABILITIES.

Capital stock,	$50,000.00
Surplus,	6,000.00
Undivided profits,	2,610.49
National bank notes outstanding,	22,500.00
Deposits,	104,638.85
	$185,749.34

patent medicines of almost every kind and nature, including, of course, all of the standard prepared remedies.

In addition to the compounding of physicians' prescriptions and the sale of drugs, herbs, and barks, the Story drug store always carries a well-selected line of toilet articles, surgical appliances, and, in fact, all of the small wares which are usually found in a well-equipped and properly-conducted metropolitan drug store. A choice line of cigars and the usual line of summer drinks from a soda fountain are features of the business at this establishment which receive proper attention from the proprietor and a liberal appreciation from the public.

Mr. J. Henry Story, the proprietor of the Story drug store, was born in Hopkinton, N. H., Nov. 8, 1857. He was educated in the public schools, and learned the druggists' business at the establishment of George F. Mallard, entering this store in 1876. In 1880 he established himself in business, and has been very successful in building up a first-class trade in his line. Mr. Story was married in 1884, to Miss Idella J. Bean, of Laconia.

In politics Mr. Story affiliates with the Democrats, and he served as deputy sheriff of Belknap county from the year 1886 until 1890. He is a member of the Knights of Pythias, the Masonic bodies, and Pilgrim commandery, Knights Templar. In religious affairs Mr. Story is inclined to liberal views, and is an attendant at the First Unitarian church.

business. Since coming to Laconia he has handled numerous large contracts, including most of the new brick buildings and the immense brick chimneys at the Laconia car works, the magnificent Gordon-Nash library at New Hampton, etc.

In politics Mr. Wallace is a Republican, and while at New Hampton received many political honors from the hands of his fellow-townsmen. He served as tax collector, was selectman for two years and also represented the town in the New Hampshire legislature. He married Fannie G. Huckins of New Hampton and has one daughter, Miss Clara Bessie Wallace.

Mr. Wallace takes considerable interest in secret fraternal organizations. He is a member of the Odd Fellows, Knights of Pythias, Uniform Rank, and the Patrons of Husbandry.

Wm. Wallace.

William Wallace, the brickmason and contractor, came to Laconia from New Hampton about five years ago and by square dealing, faithful work, and attention to business, has built up a profitable and steadily-increasing patronage.

He was born in Epsom, New Hampshire, August 1, 1858. When four years of age he went to New Hampton with his parents, and was educated at the New Hampton Literary Institution.

In New Hampton he followed the occupation of a farmer in connection with the brick-mason and contracting

William Wallace.

Cottrell's.

Laconia has one establishment which actually runs "full time" the year around, twenty-four hours in the day, from one end of the year to the other. Cottrell's lunch-room, on Bank square, Main street, is always open, day and night; it is, perhaps, the handsomest-fitted establishment in the city on the lakes, and is as neat and clean as my lady's parlor. Cottrell's lunch-room is so up-to-date and inviting that people go there and eat who are not even hungry, and whether the patron invests in merely a sandwich, a cup of coffee or tea, the food served is wholesome and appetizing, and the prices are all right. Cottrell's is comparatively a new institution in Laconia, but its genuine merit made the establishment a success from the start, and the place is patronized by our best business men and a host of strangers within our gates.

Irving M. Cottrell is a native of Belfast, Me., and was born April 8, 1864, but is wide-awake and enterprising enough to be easily mistaken for a genuine Laconian. He was educated in the public schools of Belfast, is married and has one child, a daughter of about three and one half years. Mr. Cottrell is manager of the Moulton opera house, proprietor of Cottrell's lunch-room, manager of the ice skating rink, and for the past two seasons has managed the Pearl Street baseball grounds, besides running a night-lunch cart, erecting a neat little business block on Main street for rental purposes, and officiating as bill-poster. Incidentally, when Mr. Cottrell isn't doing anything else he caters for public and private parties, excursions, etc., and his efforts in this line also have met with the hearty approval of the public in Laconia.

As a rule, it is said that a jack at all trades is master of none, but there are exceptions to all rules, and Mr. Cottrell has not yet made a failure of anything he has undertaken in Laconia.

He finds time to enjoy membership in the fraternal orders, and is a Mason, Odd Fellow, Knight of Pythias, Red Man, and a member of the Ancient Order of United Workmen.

Interior of Cottrell's Lunch Room.

John B. Moore.

The old established firm of J. L. Moore & Son, at 532 Main street, is one of the stand-bys in Laconia, for the undertaking and wall paper business of this concern was founded many years ago. The establishment is now conducted by Mr. John B. Moore, and in addition to the undertaking business and stock of caskets and burial supplies, wall papers, picture mouldings, etc., the store now handles the complete line of bicycles manufactured by the Pope

Manufacturing Co. of Boston and Hartford, and also has the agency of the Standard Rotary Sewing machine, both bicycles and sewing machines being generally admitted the best in the world.

Mr. John Brackett Moore, the manager of the business, was born in Laconia on the Gilford side of the river, July 27, 1853. His parents were Jonathan L. and Lucy Sanborn Moore of Sanbornton. He received his education in our public schools and at New Hampton Institution. Mr. Moore was engaged in the hotel business for twelve years in his early manhood, serving as clerk and cashier in hotels in New York city and other places. He was also a traveling salesman for a Chicago firm for seven years, previous to his return to Laconia to engage in his present business. He was married to Julia M. Redington at Cleveland, Ohio, Jan. 12, 1882, and they have three children, two daughters aged fifteen and ten years, and a son of four years. Mr. Moore is a member of Mt. Lebanon lodge of Masons, Granite lodge, A. O. U. W., and Cyprus council, Royal Arcanum. He is a Republican in politics, and was the first city clerk of Laconia.

The late Maj. N. B. Gale.

The late Maj. Napoleon Bonaparte Gale will be remembered and honored for years to come in Laconia, not only from the fact that the Gale family have always been strong men and prominent citizens, almost from the first settlement of this region, but because the late Major Gale made provision in his last will and testament for a permanent monument to his memory, in the shape of a memorial building and public park. Major Gale left the bulk of his large estate, estimated at $150,000, to the city of Laconia, for the pur-

John B. Moore.

Residence of John B. Moore.

poses indicated, and this magnificent bequest will provide this city with a handsome and substantial memorial building, which will be utilized as public library and as a historical museum. The large property of the late Hon. John C. Moulton, located at the corner of Main and Church streets, has already been purchased as a site for both the park and memorial structure, and in the near future the trustees and building committee will be ready to procure plans and go ahead with the beautifying of the grounds and the erection of the building, which will undoubtedly be one of the handsomest and most suitable structures of the kind in New Hampshire. The Gale bequest will not only complete the work of erection, but will provide a fund for its care and maintenance. The whole matter is in the hands of Messrs. John T. Busiel, Edwin F. Burleigh, and Charles F. Pitman, who are executors and trustees under the Gale will, and also trustees and building committee for the city.

Napoleon Bonaparte Gale was born in Gilmanton (now Belmont), March 3 1815, son of Daniel and Abigail (Page) Gale. His grandfather was Stephen Gale, who was born in Exeter, in 1739, who figured prominently in the French and Indian wars, and who settled in Gilmanton in 1780. Both Stephen and Daniel Gale were influential men in the colonial days, the latter being a selectman for twenty years, justice of the peace, representative, and an associate judge of the Court of Sessions.

Napoleon Gale passed his early years on the Gale farm, attended the common schools and also the Sanbornton and Gilmanton academies. When eighteen years of age, he became a clerk in the store of his brother, Daniel M. Gale, at Lakeport, where he remained for a short time. In August, 1835, he went to Boston and was a clerk in a grocery store there for four years, then went to Meredith and engaged in business with Joshua R. Smith, but in 1840 he removed to his father's home on account of ill health, and after the death of his father, in 1845, he carried on the home farm. In August, 1852, his health was reestablished, and he entered the Belknap county bank, as a substitute cashier for his brother, Daniel M., who was ill. From that date Major Gale was ever afterwards connected with the bank, being elected cashier in 1853, and holding the position when the charter expired, in 1866. In 1868 Major Gale was one of the incorporators of the Belknap Savings bank, and was one of its trustees. He was elected president of the bank, at the retirement of Dr. Perley, and held the presidency until his decease, Dec. 21, 1894. Politically, Major Gale was a Democrat, and he represented both Belmont and Laconia in the legislature. He was a man of unblemished integrity

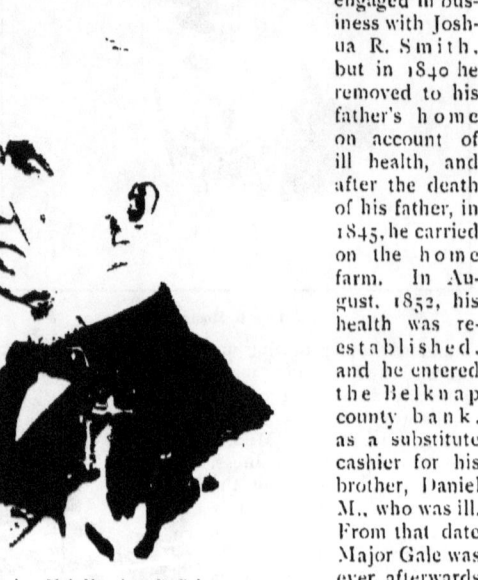

The late Maj. Napoleon B. Gale.

and conscientious uprightness. He was a man of great strength of character, kind-hearted and generous, public-spirited and enterprising,—in short, one of the most honored and respected of Laconia's citizens.

Dr. J. N. Letourneau.

Dr. J. N. Letourneau, physician and surgeon, is the proprietor of the Pharmacie Cannadien, and also has an extensive practice of his profession in this city.

He was born in St. Dominique, Canada, May 12, 1861, and was educated at Jacques Cartier Normal school of Montreal, and Laval university of the same city.

Dr. Letourneau left Canada in 1867, and went to the state of Maine, where he resided until 1880, then returned to Canada and remained there until he came to Laconia and opened his drug-store in July, 1893.

Dr. Letourneau has held the office of county physician, and is a Knight of Pythias, a member of the Foresters of America, Catholic Foresters, Elks, Red Men and the Amoskeag Veterans. In religion he is a Catholic.

He married Clarisse Valois, August 28, 1893, and they have one child.

Dr. Letourneau is not only a successful and skilful physician, but he conducts the Pharmacie Cannadien, a popular drug store,where pure drugs and all the standard patent medicines and remedies are on sale. Physicians' prescriptions are carefully and correctly compounded, and a full line of toilet articles, cigars, etc., are always in stock.

Dr. Letourneau first opened his establishment on Mill street, but his business increased rapidly and he soon found it necessary to procure the more convenient and commodious store in his present location at No. 519 Main street.

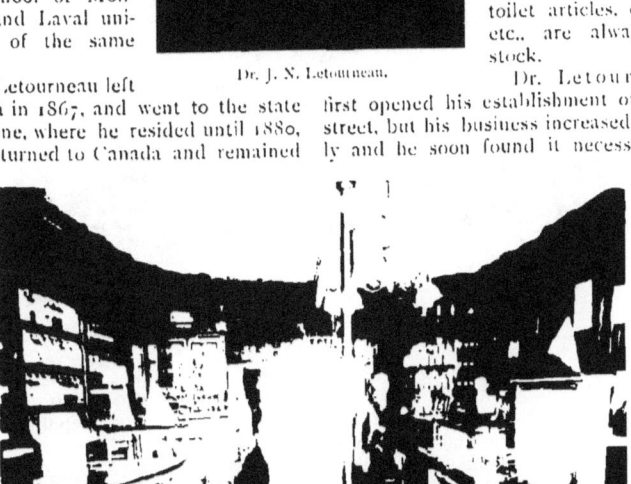

Interior of Dr. J. N. Letourneau's Drug Store.

Daniel Kellogg.

Probably many Laconia people who never visited the carriage shops of Daniel Kellogg on Union avenue have but a faint idea of the size and importance of this business, which has been built up by Mr. Kellogg during the past ten years. He carries one of the largest stocks of carriages and sleighs to be found in New Hampshire, and can supply almost any variety of vehicle called for, from a costly turn-out, with all the modern conveniences and improvements, down to a cheap road-wagon or a dump-cart.

until he now has a mammoth establishment, well filled at all times with a well selected and thoroughly reliable stock.

Mr. Kellogg was born in Westville, Conn., in 1851, but removed to New Haven, Conn., when very young. He learned the trade of carriage painting, and went to Vermont in 1872, and while a resident of that state was united in marriage to Miss Mary T. Dearing, at West Randolph. In 1883, Mr. Kellogg came to this city, first locating at Lakeport, but he soon decided there was an opening here for a first-class carriage shop, and he has since proved that his conclusions were correct.

Kellogg's Carriage Manufactory.

Mr. Kellogg located at 269 Union avenue, on Casino square, in 1889, and is not only a dealer in carriages and sleighs, but also manufactures these vehicles to order. Of course, repairing and repainting is a special feature of this business, and Mr. Kellogg also deals in harnesses, robes, whips, halters, and, in fact, in supplies of all kinds in this line. The original building in which Mr. Kellogg embarked in business proved inadequate for his rapidly increased trade, and he has erected additions and other buildings

In secret orders, Mr. Kellogg is a member of the Masonic fraternity, and in politics he is a Republican. He was elected to the Laconia city council from ward two in 1884, and also represented his ward in the last session of the New Hampshire legislature.

Mr. Kellogg has just completed a handsome new residence on Gilford avenue, and he deserves the success with which he has met in Laconia, for he is honorable and upright in all his transactions, and enterprising and energetic in his business methods.

Ex-Mayor Charles L. Pulsifer.

Ex-Mayor Charles Leroy Pulsifer, at the present time a member of the Board of Assessors, is a native of Lakeport, and has been constantly in public life for the past twenty years. He was born Jan. 1, 1849, son of Lyman B. and Sarah (Sawyer) Pulsifer. His father was for many years a manufacturer of yarns at Lakeport, and was a native of Gilmanton, whither his grandfather removed from Brentwood in March, 1795. The Pulsifers are of Scotch-Irish descent, and came to this country in 1766.

Mr. Pulsifer attended the public schools of Lakeport, and the Tilton seminary, and was graduated from Colby academy, New London, in 1874. He graduated from Brown university in 1878. From 1879 to 1894 he was principal of the Lakeport High school and superintendent of the graded schools of Lakeport. In 1895 he resigned this position and entered the Lakeport Savings bank as assistant treasurer, and was recently chosen treasurer. He has been a member of the Board of Education for Laconia and Lakeport almost constantly since 1879, his present term running to 1901. From 1886 to 1892 he was a selectman of Gilford, which then included Lakeport. He was a representative in the New Hampshire legislature in 1890-'91. He is a director in the Lakeport National bank, Lakeport Savings bank, Mutual Building and Loan association, and Winnipesaukee Gas and Electric Co.

When the city of Laconia was inaugurated, Mr. Pulsifer was elected a member of the first city council and served until March 9, 1897, when he was elected mayor unanimously, having been nominated by the Republicans and endorsed by the Democrats. He was re-elected the following March by a heavy majority, and served the city so faithfully and conscientiously that he won the approval of all classes of citizens in both parties. Upon retiring from the mayorship in March, 1899, Mr. Pulsifer was elected a member of the Board of Assessors, which position he now holds.

Ex-Mayor Charles L. Pulsifer.

Fraternally, Mr. Pulsifer is a past officer in Chocorua lodge, No. 51, I. O. O. F., and of Laconia encampment, also a member of Canton Osgood, Patriarchs Militant. He is a member of the several branches of the Masonic fraternity in this city, including Pilgrim commandery, Knights Templar, and Mt. Washington chapter, Order of Eastern Star, and he is also a thirty-second degree Mason, a member of Edward A. Raymond Consistory at Nashua. He is an attendant at the Union Avenue Baptist church, Laconia. He was married July 30, 1885, to Susan E. Smiley, daughter of Dr. J. R. Smiley of Sutton, N. H., who died April 2, 1890.

Ex-Mayor Pulsifer is probably more familiar with Laconia's financial and other municipal affairs than any other citizen in the city. He is a man of the strictest integrity, fair-minded, and progressive, and has the good-will and esteem of the entire community, a fact which perhaps his long-continued public service fully demonstrates.

Knight & Huntress.

The dry goods establishment now conducted by Messrs. Knight & Huntress (William F. Knight and Hamlin Huntress) is one of the oldest mercantile establishments in Laconia. In the old Meredith Bridge days this store was conducted as a general store, handling dry goods, groceries, etc., by Messrs. Rufus K. and Charles Parker, both now deceased. William F. Knight, the senior member of the present firm, entered the store as a clerk for Parker Bros. in June, 1864, and in 1867 he was practically in control of the business. He eventually bought out the original firm and in company with the late Mrs. Mary T. Hull, under the firm name of W. F. Knight & Co., conducted a flourishing trade for ten years. During the following ten years Mr. Knight was sole proprietor, and then Mr. George Tetreau became his associate, the firm name becoming W. F. Knight & Tetreau. Mr. Tetreau was succeeded by Mr. Hamlin Huntress, and the style of the firm was changed to Knight & Huntress, the present firm.

In addition to the dry goods business, Mr. Knight is also interested in the furniture business in the same block. In 1873 Mr. Knight was a member of the firm of Mansur & Knight, one of the oldest concerns in the furniture trade in this place. In 1887 the furniture firm was changed to Knight & Robinson (William F. Knight and Mark M. Robinson).

Located at the corner of Main and Mill streets, one of the busiest spots in the city, the establishment of Mr. Knight has always been a thriving and prosperous concern. Strictly reliable goods and moderate profits has always been the motto at this store, and has resulted in a constantly increasing trade

Knight & Huntress's Dry-Goods Store.

during the last half century. The Knight & Huntress establishment today carries a larger stock and does a larger business than at any time in its history.

William Franklin Knight, the senior member of the firm, was born in Hanover, N. H., Oct. 13, 1847, son of Edwin Perry and Elizabeth W. T. (Vaughan) Knight. Mr. Knight comes of patriotic stock, and numbers among his ancestors several of the early colonists of New Hampshire. His great-grandfather, William Knight, and a brother were Revolutionary soldiers, and the latter received a captain's commission for conspicuous gallantry on the bloody field

William F. Knight.

of Bennington Capt. Jabez Vaughan, the great-grandfather on the mother's side, was also a Revolutionary soldier, and promoted from the ranks for long and meritorious service.

Mr. Knight was educated in the common schools of Hanover and at West Randolph academy He came to Laconia in 1864, and has been prominent since that time in mercantile, financial, political, and social life. He is a director in the Laconia National bank, a director in the Laconia Building and Loan Association, and a trustee of the Belknap Savings bank. He is a member of the Laconia Board of Trade, and has been secretary and treasurer of the trustees of the Laconia public library for the past fifteen years.

Mr. Knight has been a stanch Republican all his life, casting his first presidential ballot for the late U. S. Grant in 1868. He was elected town clerk of Laconia in 1875, and served two years. He was elected treasurer of Belknap county in 1883, and reëlected in 1885. He was in the New Hampshire legislature in 1889, serving on the railroad committee, and also the committee on national affairs. He was elected state senator from district No. 6, in 1894, for the term of two years, and in 1896 was quartermaster-general on the staff of Governor C. A. Busiel.

He is a thirty-second degree Mason, and a member of all the various branches of the order in this city, as well as the Scottish Rite at Concord, and the Consistory at Nashua. He attends the Unitarian church and is active in the management of this society and advancement of liberal religion.

Mr. Knight was married in 1872 to Fannie E., daughter of James Taylor, of Franklin, N. H. They have no children.

Hamlin Huntress, of the firm of Knight & Huntress, is a native of Sandwich, New Hampshire, born August 19, 1861. He was educated in the town schools of Moultonborough,

Hamlin Huntress.

S

and when he first embarked in business conducted a general store at Moultonborough for eight years. He came to Laconia in 1893, and two years later he formed the partnership with William F. Knight in the dry goods business.

Mr. Huntress is a member of Chocorua lodge, No. 51, I. O. O. F., at Lakeport, and in religious affairs is a Methodist, being quite active and much interested in church work.

Politically Mr. Huntress is a Republican. He served as town clerk of Moultonborough from 1883 to 1890, was postmaster of the town for eight years, and represented Moultonborough in the legislature of 1893. Mr. Huntress married Amy L. Rollins of Moultonborough, and they have one son, — Ernest Hamlin Huntress.

Court House.

Belknap County Farm.

Edwin P. Thompson.

William Thompson, great-grandfather of Edwin P. Thompson, clerk of the supreme court for Belknap county, came to Gilmanton among the early settlers and located on a farm near the centre of the present town. He died in 1827, leaving a family of eight children, one of whom, William Thompson, was the grandfather of the subject of this sketch. He settled in Gilmanton, where he devoted his life to farming, at one time having the care and management of Captain Salter's farm in Barnstead. In 1836 he purchased the farm adjoining the homestead where his boyhood had been spent, where he lived until his death, Dec. 6, 1855. He married, first, Lydia Sanborn of Gilford, a sister of the late Dea. Levi Sanborn of Laconia, by whom he had ten children, among them being Albert G., at one time landlord of the Willard Hotel in Laconia, for about three years, and later steward of the Fifth Avenue Hotel in New York city, from its opening July 15, 1859, to his death August 12, 1889. Another son was John S. Thompson, at one time connected with the Cerro Gordo and the Willard hotels in Laconia, the Pemigewasset Hotel at Plymouth, the Proctor House at Andover, and the Phenix at Concord; he was also a deputy under Sheriff Hanson Bedee from May 31, 1862, to the end of the term, January, 1866. Asa T., another son, was a member of Co. A, Twelfth regiment, N. H. Volunteers in the Civil War, and station-agent at Alton from the time of his return from the army in 1863 to the spring of 1872. Another son, William B. Thompson, was the father of the subject of this sketch, who was born in Gilmanton, July 28, 1852, his mother being Luezer J. Thompson. Edwin P. was the eldest child and has one brother, Albert W. Thompson of Concord.

He spent his early years on the farm in Gilmanton and attended the district schools near his home, and later Gilmanton academy. At the age of twenty, in September, 1872, he commenced the study of law with Hon. Thos. Cogswell of Gilmanton, with whom he studied three years, and in November, 1875, came to Laconia and studied with E. P. Jewell until his admission to the Belknap County bar, April 1, 1876, when he immediately returned to Gilmanton Iron Works and commenced the practice of his profession in company with Colonel Cogswell, with whom he remained for a year and then practised alone until the fall of 1879, at which time he removed to Belmont where he has since claimed a legal residence.

Edwin P. Thompson.

He has served as treasurer of the town, and in March, 1884, he was elected moderator of Belmont and has since served the town in that capacity except when prevented by sickness, a part of the time being the choice of both parties.

In January, 1885, he was appointed clerk of the supreme court for Belknap county, which office he still holds.

Upon the organization of the City

Savings bank in Laconia, in the spring of 1897, he was elected one of the trustees and has been re-elected since. He is also secretary of the Belknap County Bar association. In politics he is a Republican.

December 9th, 1896, he married Minnie E. James, daughter of Orrin F. and Dora James of Campton. They have no children.

Judge True W. Thompson.

The subject of this sketch, True William Thompson, was born in the town of Durham, New Hampshire, on Aug. 15, 1841, in that part of the town known as "Lovingland." His parents were Jacob Burleigh and Ann Carr Stilson Thompson, natives and lifelong residents of that town. His parents are now deceased. Judge Thompson was reared on a farm. He was educated in the public schools of his native town and at Newmarket, N. H., closing his school days at the Cartland academy, Lee, N. H., under the tutorship of that well-known, practical educator, Moses A. Cartland.

Both on the paternal and maternal sides Judge Thompson's ancestry were Revolutionary stock, both of his great grandfathers serving side by side in the War of the Revolution at Bunker Hill. His paternal ancestry were Scotch-Irish, while those of his mother were English. Her less remote ancestry were the Lord family of Somersworth, N. H. Immediately after ending his school days he engaged in teaching suburban schools for four years, for which the trend of his efforts was always in the direction of that to impart knowledge most likely to be the most practical in future years. In this he was successful. He was a member of the board of education in his native town in 1868 and '69 for a term of two years. In March, 1872, he became a student at law in the office of Charles H. Smith at Newmarket, where he remained for nearly three and a half years. He never made application to be admitted to the bar, preferring to take journalism as a profession, he having been engaged in that calling to some extent for about fifteen years previous, and for which he still retained a great liking. He is one of a family of two sons and a daughter; the latter resides at Concord, N. H. Judge Thompson is not married, although possessed of a son and two daughters, all of whom are married. He came to this city from Newmarket in May, 1882, having secured a situation as city editor on the *Belknap Daily Tocsin*, the first daily newspaper to be established in Laconia. Since, from time to time, he has been employed in every newspaper office in the city. During the past dozen years he has also acted as local correspondent for the Boston *Globe*, and Manchester *Union* for several years. May 11, 1897, he was ap-

Judge True W. Thompson.

pointed associate justice of the Laconia police court by Governor Ramsdell. At the biennial election in 1898, he was elected register of probate for Belknap county for a term of two years. In politics he is an ardent Republican, having held the position of president of the Republican club in Ward 4 since the city was incorporated in 1893.

Judge Thompson is widely and favorably known as a newspaper man. During all the years of his extensive literary work he has served the public with conscientious fidelity. No journalist ever had greater respect for private right than has Judge Thompson. He has never rudely trespassed upon purely personal matters to gratify a depraved appetite for scandal or sensation, always working along a line of legitimate journalism, incurring the respect and confidence of the people. Nothing was ever contributed by his pen to poison and inflame the public mind; on the contrary his newspaper work has ever been clean and praiseworthy. Judge Thompson is liberal, fair-minded, companionable, and unselfish. His purpose as a man and as a judge is to do right. While his judgments are all tempered with mercy, no real offender can hope to escape.

Herman C. Weymouth.

Herman C. Weymouth, superintendent of the Belknap county farm and jailer of the county jail, is a native of that part of old Gilmanton which is now Belmont, and was born Feb. 9, 1846. He attended the district schools and also the academies at Gilmanton and New Hampton. When at the age of twenty years he engaged in the meat and provision business at Boston, where he remained about three years and then returned to Belmont. In 1871 he married Miss Abbie L. Smith, youngest daughter of Mr. Daniel P. Smith of Meredith. His family consists of two daughters, Misses Maude and Blanche Weymouth of this city. When in Belmont Mr. Weymouth was interested in the Free-will Baptist church and worked hard for the support of music, which was highly appreciated. In 1880 he removed to Meredith where he engaged in the summer boarding-house business. He later engaged with Prof. G. H. Brown in extensive farming and summer boarding. In 1885 he purchased a large place in Andover, N. H., where he carried on a prosperous dairy business in connection with a large boarding-house for summer guests.

Herman C. Weymouth.

In 1896 he bought and built a residence in Laconia, where he has since lived. In 1898 he was appointed superintendent of the Belknap county farm. While residing in Belmont he was elected superintendent of schools and also filled the offices of selectman and road agent in Andover. He is a member of the Knights of Honor, Aurora lodge, No.

708, of this city, and was a prominent member of Highland Lake grange at East Andover. He has never aspired to political fame, but has rather preferred to attend to his own business which he believes to be more profitable. He has a large circle of friends in Belknap and Merrimack counties whom he has won by fair and honest dealing and attending strictly to his own business. As superintendent of the Belknap farm he is not only well liked by the inmates of the establishment but is efficient and faithful as a public servant in the rather trying duties of this position.

Sheriff Charles W. Baldwin.

Sheriff Charles W. Baldwin.

Charles W. Baldwin, sheriff of Belknap county, and more familiarly known as "Warren" Baldwin, is a native of Hillsboro, born April 3, 1838. He came to Meredith Bridge, now Laconia, when a mere boy, and was educated in our public schools. Mr. Baldwin is a joiner by trade, and was for nearly thirty years employed by the Laconia Car company in this city.

When less than seventeen years old he left Laconia and went West, where he enlisted in the First Illinois Light Artillery, Jan. 4, 1862. He was discharged in April, 1864, but re-enlisted March, 1865, in A Co. of the Seventh Illinois Cavalry, and was mustered out Nov. 20, 1865, at Springfield, Ill., and immediately took the train for Laconia, where his family had preceded him. He arrived here Nov. 23, and has been a resident of Laconia since that date. Mr. Baldwin was engaged in but two battles during his service in the army, but they were both engagements of considerable importance, Donaldson and Shiloh. He is a charter member of John L. Perley, Jr., Post, G. A. R., and also a charter member of Pontauhum Tribe, No. 18, Improved Order of Red Men.

Mr. Baldwin married Mary E. Bentley, of Mt. Vernon, Ill., and has three children, Charles G., Media B., and James S., the two former born in Mt. Vernon, and the latter first saw the light of day in Laconia.

Mr. Baldwin has always been a strong Republican, and has been honored by his party by election as supervisor of check-lists under the old town government, chairman of supervisors for two years under the city government, selectman of Ward three for three years, and in 1898 was elected sheriff of Belknap county, which office he assumed April 1, 1899.

Mr. Baldwin is not a member of any church, but believes with the Unitarians, in one God.

Martin B. Plummer.

Martin Bartlett Plummer, register of deeds for Belknap county since 1892, was born at Meredith on the 11th day of October, 1844, and was educated in the public schools of that town. In 1863 he came to Lakeport to learn the machinist trade in the shops of B. J. Cole, and worked there until April 14th, 1864, when he went to Concord and enlisted in Co. A, First New Hampshire cavalry for three years. Mr. Plummer went to the front with his regiment and first served under Gen. Wilson. The regiment went on the "Wilson raid," and was then sent into the Shenandoah valley under Gen. Sheridan and served until the close of the war.

After being mustered out of the United States service, Mr. Plummer lived in Gilmanton Iron Works until the fall of 1868, when he removed to Meredith where he remained with the exception of one year in Waterville until 1872, at which time he came to Laconia and has resided here since that date.

Mr. Plummer was employed for some years at the shops of Gardner Cook & Son, also at the Laconia car shops and the shops of George W. Riley. In May, 1892, he was appointed clerk of the Laconia police court, which office he holds at the present time. In the November election of 1892, Mr. Plummer was elected register of deeds for the county of Belknap and he has been reelected to the same office by large majorities at every election since 1892. Mr. Plummer is a Republican in politics.

Mr. Plummer is a member of John L. Perley, Jr., Post, G. A. R., having served as its commander, and also served in the department on the council of administration, and was in 1895 elected by the department a delegate to the National Encampment which was held at Louisville, Kentucky. He is also a member of the Pilgrim Fathers and the Belknap County Fish and Game League.

Mr. Plummer married Ellen L. Cook, daughter of Danford Cook of Gilmanton Iron Works, Nov. 29, 1866. Four children have been born to Mr. and Mrs. Plummer, two of whom died while quite young; Mabel E. married Amber R. Connor, and is now clerk in the register of deeds office of Belknap county, and Fred D. is a student in the Pernin Shorthand school in Boston, Mass.

Belknap county has been remarkably fortunate in having careful and popular officials in the register of deeds office, and "Mart" Plummer is surely no exception to this rule. He receives many votes from the opposition political party and always leads all other candidates on his party ticket. Belknap county people are evidently satisfied to retain Mr. Plummer as their register of deeds and he can undoubtedly hold the position as long as he desires to retain it.

Martin B. Plummer.

Judge Frank M. Beckford.

Judge Frank M. Beckford, one of the best-known members of Laconia's legal fraternity, is a native of Salem, New Hampshire, born Oct. 13, 1851. He was educated at Tilton seminary and New Hampton Literary Institution, and before he engaged in the practice of the legal profession, was connected with various mercantile pursuits and the hotel business. He first entered the dry goods house of Brooks Bros., at Haverhill, Mass., where he remained six years, and then went to Boston, where he was head salesman in the large carpet house of Judkins & Muccullough, afterwards with the well-known firm of Jordan & Marsh. Later he went to the town of Bristol, New Hampshire, and engaged in the manufacture of woolen goods. It was here that he began the study of law in the office of George A. Emerson, Esq.

Judge Beckford came to Laconia in the year 1884, and purchased the Laconia hotel business, as it was then called. He changed the name of the house, Hotel Wonolancet, and conducted the establishment successfully for a few years.

He resumed the study of law in the office of the late Col. Thomas J. Whipple, and after being admitted to practice, became the partner of this widely-known attorney, and upon Colonel Whipple's decease in 1889, Judge Beckford succeeded to the large practice.

Judge Beckford has always been an active Republican, and has generally been upon the stump during most of the political campaigns since attaining his majority.

He represented Laconia as a member of the last constitutional convention for the state of New Hampshire, was appointed justice of the Laconia police court in 1892, and held the position until 1895, when he resigned; elected solicitor of Belknap county in 1896, and re-elected in the fall of 1898, which office he now holds.

Judge Beckford is prominent and takes great interest in the various fraternal societies. He is a member of Mt. Belknap lodge, Knights of Pythias of Laconia, and is also a member of the Supreme lodge, and holds the position of supreme representative for this state in that order; he is a member of Chocorua lodge, I. O. O. F., of Laconia, and Pontahaum Tribe of Red Men, being a member of the Great Council for New Hampshire, and is a member of Laconia Commandery, U. O. G. C., Laconia grange, Patrons of Husbandry, and a member of the State and National Grange. He is also an active member of the military branch in the Knights of Pythias, and to his efforts is largely due the fact that New Hampshire has a brigade formation of the Uniform Rank. He holds the position

Judge Frank M. Beckford.

of assistant judge advocate-general upon General Hoyt's staff; also an active member of the Laconia Board of Trade, and is interested in nearly all the local enterprises of a public nature.

Judge Beckford's law practice is a large and lucrative one, he being an able pleader, and one of our most successful lawyers.

Judge Beckford is married and has one son, Dr. Henry S. Beckford.

Mark M. Robinson.

Mark M. Robinson, of the well-known furniture establishment of Knight & Robinson, and the treasurer of Belknap county since 1892, was born in Meredith, N. H., on August 22d, 1853. He was educated in the public schools and at Tilton seminary. In his early manhood, Mr. Robinson learned the jeweler's trade with the old firm of S. F. Young & Co., and he afterwards carried on the jewelry business for himself, for a period of about eight years, both at Lakeport and Laconia.

About twelve years ago, Mr. Robinson bought out the interest of the late Franklin Mansur in the furniture establishment then conducted under the firm name of Mansur & Knight, one of the oldest furniture concerns in this section of New Hampshire. He formed a partnership with Mr. William F. Knight, under the style of Knight & Robinson, which partnership still continues. Carpetings and upholstery departments have been added to the business in recent years, and the firm carry one of the largest stocks to be found in their line in this vicinity, and have always enjoyed a most successful and prosperous business.

Mr. Robinson was married May 13, 1880, to Charlotte L. Moore. They have no children.

He is a member of the Odd Fellows, Masons, and Royal Arcanum, having held numerous offices in all of these orders, being a Past Master of Mt. Lebanon lodge, No. 32, F. & A. M., a Past High Priest of Union chapter, No. 7, R. A. M., and T. I. Master of Pythagorean council, No. 6, R. & S. M.

In politics, Mr. Robinson is a Republican. He was elected treasurer of Belknap county in the year 1892, and has been re-elected to the same office at every subsequent election since that date.

Mark M. Robinson.

County Commissioner J. F. Smith.

Although a legal resident of the neighboring village of Meredith Centre, County Commissioner Joseph F. Smith is one of our Belknap county officials who makes his business headquarters in this city, and he has been a familiar figure on our streets for several years past, and will continue to be, since he is again chairman of the board of commissioners for 1899 and 1900.

Joseph Frank Smith, the youngest son of Daniel P. and Abigail (Dolloff) Smith, was born on the same spot where his residence now stands, in the year 1848, Sept. 12. He was the ninth in a family of ten children, five of whom are now living, one dying in infancy, and one brother, Gilman Smith, was killed in the battle of Chancellorsville. The father, Daniel P. Smith, is still living, at the age of ninety years, and is remarkably well preserved, and appears to enjoy life.

Joseph F. Smith left home at the age of sixteen years, and attended school at New Hampton, and in 1867 went to work at the New Hampshire Insane Asylum, under the late Jesse P. Bancroft, to whom he is indebted for a great deal of good advice. In 1872, Mr. Smith went to Nashua, and was employed as a clerk in a store. The following year he entered the employ of Bridgeman & Co., 48 Bedford street, Boston, dealers in woolen goods, and in a few weeks was sent out on the road by the firm to solicit orders. He remained with this firm one year, and then connected himself with the Franklin Woolen Co., of Franklin Falls, N. H., with headquarters in Boston, continuing with this concern until April, 1893. During the time he was connected with the Franklin Woolen Co., he had full control of the selling end of their business, and personally sold nearly all their goods in the New England states.

He was married in 1881 to C. Isabel Robinson, youngest daughter of Thomas J. and Eliza (Glidden) Robinson of Laconia. Mr. and Mrs. Smith have been the parents of eight children: Rachel Gertrude, Daniel Thomas (who died in infancy), Joseph Frank, Jr., Mary Eriline, Barbara Eloise, Robinson Wayland, Frederick, and Maurice Preston.

In politics, Mr. Smith is a strong Republican, and he has received numerous political honors. He represented the town of Meredith in the legislature in 1889, was selectman of Meredith in 1893 and 1894, was elected a commissioner of Belknap county in November, 1894, was re-elected in 1896, and elected for the third time in 1898. He has served as chairman of the board since 1896, and is chairman of the present board.

Joseph F. Smith.

In secret societies, Mr. Smith is a member of Chocorua lodge of Masons at Meredith and Union chapter of Laconia. He is also a Knight of Pythias, and a member of the Odd Fellows fraternity. He is a member of Winnipesaukee grange at Meredith and of Belknap County Pomona grange.

Mr. Smith resides on the Smith farm on the shores of Wickwas lake, one of the most beautiful of the small lakes of New Hampshire.

As a public official, Mr. Smith has

evidently given satisfaction to the people of Belknap county, as is indicated by his re-election for a third term, an honor which has been rarely if ever bestowed upon any candidate. He is a strong man in all business affairs and an officer of unusual executive ability.

Commissioner Oscar Foss.

County Commissioner Oscar Foss, of Barnstead, one of the most wide-awake and prosperous business men of Belknap county, was born in Barnstead, N. H., Nov. 17, 1845, and was a son of Eli H. and Mary A. (Furber) Foss.

Eli H. Foss, who was born in Barnstead, July 16, 1819, married, in 1843, Mary A. Furber, of Alton, N. H. She was the daughter of Edmund Furber, a well-known farmer and business man, and a leader in church work, and who lived to be ninety-five years old. She died in 1888, at the age of seventy. Eli H. Foss, now living in Barnstead, learned the blacksmith trade of Asa Garland, of North Barnstead, and followed that business most of the time for fifty years.

Oscar Foss was the only son and the oldest of four children. He received his education in the common schools of Barnstead and at Pittsfield academy. He attended the latter institution in the winter season, spending the remainder of the year in his father's blacksmith shop, learning the trade.

Oscar Foss.

On Nov. 5, 1871, Mr. Foss was joined in marriage with Miss Sarah U. Young, a daughter of Oliver H. P. and Emily J. (Tuttle) Young. Mr. Young was a carpenter by trade, and was born on Beauty hill. He afterwards moved to Centre Barnstead. He enlisted in the 12th N. H. regiment, and served three years in the Civil War.

At the age of twenty-one Mr. Foss purchased a half interest in a water-power sawmill at Centre Barnstead, N. H., in company with Nathaniel Blaisdell. At the end of one year his partner died, and Mr. Foss bought the other half, and has since carried on the business alone, receiving the greater part of the trade from the locality. Not confining his attention to this particular mill, however, he has been quite extensively engaged in buying lots and putting in temporary mills, and preparing the lumber for the market and shipping it to different large cities. His first trial in this direction was the purchase of a timber lot in Northwood. Since then the business has greatly increased.

In 1895, '96, '97, '98 he had five mills in operation most of the time. He handles large amounts of cord wood, bark, pulp wood, and lumber. When he started in the mill business he was obliged to go into debt for the most of his contracts and real estate purchases. At the time the Barnstead shoe factory was built, he was one of the leading promoters of the enterprise, and he is now the owner of the plant. When the question of bringing new business into town arises, he is the one chosen to confer with and to influence desirable parties to locate here. He was one of the prime movers in getting the railroad and telephone. As an individual he has done much for the welfare of the town. He has never forgotten his struggle for prosperity, and is ever ready to assist any ambitious young man who is deserving of help.

Mr. Foss has from the first been a staunch Republican, and a very active worker for the principles of his party. When he became a voter the vote of the town was three to one Democratic, and for the first time, in 1896, the Republicans had a majority. Mr. Foss has been town treasurer, and in 1896 was elected supervisor, and in 1898 was elected one of the county commissioners of Belknap county, having the largest vote of the board. As a justice of the peace, he writes deeds and mortgages and does other legal duties.

Commissioner Jonathan C. Shannon.

Jonathan Coffin Shannon, the Democratic member of the Board of Belknap County Commissioners, and the only Democratic official who now holds office in this county, was born in Barnstead, N. H., Nov. 29, 1842, the son of Stephen and Ann P. (Chase) Shannon. He removed to Gilmanton with his parents when five years old, and was educated in the public schools of Gilmanton and at Gilmanton academy. When nineteen years of age, Mr. Shannon came to Laconia and entered the employ of Folsom & Smith, general merchants. He went into business for himself in 1865 in the grocery trade, and continued under various partnerships until about 1894. For the past few years Mr. Shannon has devoted himself to the auctioneering business, with excellent success, and has won a wide reputation for his efficiency in this line. He also conducts a second-hand furniture store and auction rooms, being located in Masonic Temple at the present time.

Politically, Mr. Shannon is a Democrat, and he was elected overseer of the poor for seven years. In 1890 he was elected to the board of county commissioners, and served one term, being reëlected in 1898, at which time he was the only successful candidate on his party ticket.

He is a member of the Masonic fraternity, including Pilgrim commandery, Knights Templar, and is also a member of the Ancient Order of United Workmen. He is a member of the Congregational church. He was married Jan. 28, 1866, to Miss Ella A. Jewett of Gilford, daughter of Samuel S. and Edith A. Jewett.

Jonathan C. Shannon.

As a county official, Mr. Shannon has always been popular with all classes of people, and at the same time he has been a faithful and conscientious public servant, always acting as seemed in his judgment to be for the best interests of the taxpayers and community.

Dr. Henry C. Wells.

One of the most public-spirited and busiest of Laconia's medical profession is Dr. Henry C. Wells, a native of Bristol, N. H., born Feb. 24, 1856. Dr. Wells obtained his preparatory education in the public schools, and then attended New Hampton Literary Institution, Tilton seminary, and Kimball Union Academy at Meriden, N. H., graduating from Meriden in 1874. He read medicine with Dr. J. M. Bishop of Bristol, and graduated M. D. at St. Louis Hahnemann Medical College, of St. Louis, Mo., in 1876. He came to Laconia in 1879, and has been here ever since, enjoying a large practice not only in Laconia but in nearly all the surrounding territory. He is a Republican in politics, and was elected county physician for Belknap county in 1890, and has held the position with the exception of one term since that time. He was city physician in 1896 and again in 1898. In secret orders Dr. Wells is an Odd Fellow and a Red Man, a member of the Patriarchs Militant in connection with his Odd Fellowship, and also a member of Ridgely Association, of Worcester, Mass., and N. E. O. P.

During his twenty years' residence in Laconia, Dr. Wells has won a reputation as a skilful physician and surgeon, and has made a special study of children's cases, which has brought him much practice in this line.

He is an active worker in the Republican ranks, taking great interest in all political events, both local and national. He is also interested in all movements of a public nature for the growth and development of Laconia, and generally finds time from his professional duties to lend a helping hand in any enterprise of this nature in which he is interested.

Dr. Henry C. Wells.

Laconia Electric Lighting Co.

Laconia has always kept pace with the outside world in the speedy adoption of all the modern inventions and conveniences which have been introduced with such rapidity during the past fifty years, including the telegraph, telephone, electric cars, gas, and electric lights. The Laconia Electric Lighting Company established the first central electric lighting station in the state of New Hampshire. This company was organized December 26, 1884, with Dennis O'Shea as president and treasurer; Frank H. Champlin, clerk and general manager. The capital stock at that time was but $4,000, and the central station was in the basement of the brick Belknap mill. The electric lights were introduced in this city both for public street lighting and for commercial lighting, and proved popular from the very start. The central station remained in the Belknap mills until October, 1889, when the business increased so as to outgrow the accommodations, and the plant was removed to the lumber works of Gardner Cook & Son, where it was operated until January, 1893, at which time the dynamos and other machinery were removed to the new power station, fitted up by the corporation at Lakeport. The power station at Lakeport is one of the best arranged and most convenient for the electric lighting business to be found in New Hampshire. The power

Laconia Electric Lighting Station.

is obtained by powerful water-wheels which are located at the outlet of Lake Winnipesaukee, and which furnishes the most reliable motive power possible to be obtained anywhere. The increase of business has, of course, made it necessary to invest in new machinery from time to time, and the corporation has always responded promptly to all demands for increased service. They now furnish nearly one hundred arc street lights of 2,000 candle-power for lighting the streets of the city of Laconia, besides many commercial arc lights, and a large number of incandescent lights for the illumination of stores, public buildings, and private residences.

The corporation has always made a point of furnishing lights of standard quality and it can be truthfully stated that no city in New England has better electric lights than the city on the lakes.

The corporation has increased its capital stock from time to time, until from the small beginning with only $4,000 capital, it now has a capital of $45,000.

The present officers of the concern are: Directors, Dennis O'Shea, John F. Merrill, Jefferson Gilbert, Frank P. Holt, Addison G. Cook, Gardner Cook, and Albert G. Folsom; president, Dennis O'Shea; clerk and treasurer, Charles W. Tyler; general manager, John F. Merrill. The office of the corporation is at No. 523 Main street.

Albert G. Folsom.

For the past fifty years, no citizen of Laconia has been more prominent in financial, real estate, and business enterprises of all kinds than Albert Gallatin Folsom, who has been president of the Laconia Savings bank for over a quarter of a century, and president of the People's National bank since its incorporation in May, 1889, and who is, also, the oldest Odd Fellow in Laconia. Mr. Folsom was born in Laconia, Oct. 12, 1816, son of Jonathan and Sarah (Rowe) Folsom, and he comes of an old New Hampshire family. His father was a native of Dover, N. H., and a carpenter by trade, but he was one of the early settlers in Meredith Bridge, and opened a way-side tavern here on Pleasant street as early as 1813, which he conducted successfully for a number of years. This house is now known as the Atkinson residence. He owned the land on Main and Pleasant streets above the present railroad tracks, and was a prominent and popular citizen. He represented the town in the legislature in 1832. He died, in his ninety-fourth year, in 1872. He and his wife, who was a native of Gilford, were the parents of eleven children, of whom the subject of this sketch is the only survivor.

Albert G. Folsom was born in the Pleasant street home, and was educated in the common schools of this town. He was not robust as a boy, and was unable to attend school regularly, and when about eleven years old his parents sent him to Portsmouth to enter a store kept by an older brother, in the hope that the change would benefit his health. Commercial life aroused his ambitions and improved his health, and his brother eventually went West, leaving him in charge of the store. In 1836 he returned to Laconia, and entered the store on Mill street, kept by James Molineaux, which he purchased about three years later. He afterwards took in Geo. F. Bosher as a partner, and this partnership continued until 1860. In 1857 he purchased and moved into the Gove block on Main street, and subsequently had a clothing store at Cerro Gordo place. In 1861 ex-Mayor S. B. Smith became his partner, and eight years later Mr. Folsom sold out his interest in the business and retired from mercantile life.

Mr. Folsom has a well-earned reputation as a sagacious and prudent business man, and a wise financier. He has been identified with many of Laconia's more important enterprises. He built Folsom block in 1861, and was associated with Mr. Smith in erecting the Smith block on the opposite side of the street. He opened the Folsom opera house in 1862, and was one of the organizers and prime movers of the Laconia street railway corporation. He has been identified with the Laconia Savings bank nearly sixty years, being a member of the board of trustees about 1841.

Mr. Folsom has been twice married. His first wife was Olive B. Robinson of Gilford, and of four children only one now survives, Mrs. Samuel B. Smith. His second wife was Miss Imogene F. Harris of Franconia, and they have one daughter, Miss Alberta. In secret societies, Mr. Folsom has been quite prominent. He is a thirty-second degree Mason, a member of Pilgrim commandery of Knights Templar, and Edward A. Raymond Consistory, the latter at Nashua. He has filled all the chairs in Winnipiseogee lodge of Odd Fellows, and is a member of the Laconia encampment.

Although in poor health until he was about twenty years old, Mr. Folsom now enjoys excellent health for a man of his years, appearing much younger than he actually is, and attending personally to his large busness interests.

Albert G. Folsom.

The Crane Manufacturing Co.

The Crane Manufacturing Co., of Lakeport, is known in every city and town in the United States where hosiery, underwear, and web goods are manufactured, and the numerous knitting machines furnished by this concern have aided materially in developing and promoting the knit-goods industry in this country. The production of nearly every one of the most familiar articles of everyday use involves the assistance of mechanical contrivances of which the grandparents of the present generation were entirely ignorant, and the manufacture of stockinet, eiderdown, jersey cloth, shirts, drawers, or hosiery, affords a good illustration of this fact.

The Crane Manufacturing Co. was incorporated in 1890, but was originally established in 1870, as J. S. Crane & Co., and the concern has won a widespread reputation in knit-goods circles for furnishing such machines and improvements as would most readily accomplish the desired object in the manufacture of the goods mentioned.

The commodious and well-arranged factory of the Crane Manufacturing Co. consists of a main building whose dimensions are 36 by 80 feet, with two wings, one 22 feet by 26 feet, the other 18 feet by 20 feet, of two stories each, with cemented basement, and operated by a steam engine built by Payne of Elmira, N. Y. Everything that skill and attention to detail can devise is to be found in this machine shop, which has a Thomson-Houston electric plant, from which all the departments are lighted, the capacity being one hundred incandescent lights.

The concern manufactures circular spring-needle knitting machines for underwear, jersey cloth, rubber linings,

The Crane Manufacturing Company.

stockinets, etc., also circular spring needle knitting machines for hosiery, latest improved stockinet feeds, of the W. & J. H. Osborne patents, which are owned by the Crane Co., also removable hardened-blade burr wheels, with self-oiling brackets. The Crane machines are constructed of any gauge and diameter desired, fitted and put to work in their shops before they are delivered to customers.

To those interested who may be unacquainted with the firm it might be said, that the Crane Manufacturing Co.'s business is conducted upon the broadest basis of fairness and good faith.

John S. Crane.

Mr. John S. Crane, the head of the concern, is one of the pioneer manufacturers of knitting machinery, having devoted over thirty-five years to manufacturing and perfecting this class of machinery, and his experience is certainly worthy of consideration by manufacturers of knit goods and valuable to the establishment. The officers of the company are: President, John S. Crane; secretary and treasurer, M. L. Crane.

John Summerfield Crane, the founder and president of the Crane Manufacturing Co., was born in Springfield, Mass., Feb. 3, 1834, son of Luther and Rebecca (Manter) Crane. Mr. Crane is a direct descendant of Governor Bradford of the Massachusetts colony. He received a common school education, and attended the Berwick academy, in Maine. As a young man he possessed a craving for a life at sea, and after leaving school he shipped on a clipper bound for India. The voyage lasted twenty-two months, and gave young Crane a trip around the world and at the same time cured him of any further desires in this direction. For a year he was busy learning the machinist's trade at Salmon Falls, and then removed to Lawrence and afterwards to Lowell, where he had charge of a sewing-machine factory.

Subsequently he resided in Manchester for a time, and then went West in search of a promising business opening, but returned and finally located in Lakeport in 1857, where he was employed by Thomas Appleton in the hosiery business. In 1862 he formed a partnership with William Pepper to build knitting machines. In 1864 he became superintendent of the Winnipesaukee Hosiery Co., in which he was part owner, and in 1865, having bought out his partners he sold this business to R. M. Bailey. In 1879 he was connected with the late Walter Aiken of Franklin in the proprietorship of the Gilmore revolving diamond stone dressing machine. In 1872 Mr. Crane engaged in the manufacture of

Mazellah L. Crane.

circular knitting machines, the firm being Crane & Peaslee. The following year he patented a machine for making shirts and underwear, and this industry was added to the business. In 1878 the firm became J. S. Crane & Company, and in 1890 the Crane Manufacturing Co. of to-day was incorporated.

Mr. Crane represented Laconia in the New Hampshire legislature in 1875, and Gilford in the legislature of 1878. He was one of the incorporators of the Lake Village Savings bank, is vice-tution, after which he entered the machine shops of his father and acquired a thorough knowledge of the machinist's trade and a familiarity with the business by labor in the various departments. In 1885 he became associated in the business of manufacturing knitting machines with his father, under the firm name of Crane Manufacturing Co. Both John S. Crane and Mazellah L. Crane are men of recognized commercial ability, who have built up a large industry and are upon a sound

Residence of J. S. Crane.

president and a director in the Lakeport National bank. In politics he is a Republican. He is a thirty-second degree Mason. Mr. Crane married in 1856, Clara J. Smith of Nashua. He has one son, Mazellah L. Crane, who is associated with him in business.

Mazellah L. Crane, secretary and treasurer of the Crane Manufacturing Co., was born in Lakeport, April 27, 1858, son of John S. and Clara (Smith) Crane, the only child of his parents. He attended the public schools of Lakeport and New Hampton Literary Insti-and successful financial basis. On February 5, 1896, Mr. Crane was united in marriage with Fannie E. Taylor of Laconia. There are two daughters by a previous marriage. Mr. Crane is a member of Endicott Rock lodge, No. 20, Knights of Pythias, of Lakeport.

The Melcher & Prescott Insurance Agency.

The Melcher & Prescott Insurance Agency of Laconia, with offices at Smith block, rooms 6 and 7, Main street, and Morgan block, 766 Union avenue, is one of the largest and oldest established insurance agencies in this section of New Hampshire. This agency was founded in 1862 by Hon. Woodbury L. Melcher, who at that time represented the Phœnix Fire Insurance company of Hartford, Conn. The insurance business rapidly increased, and in 1886 Mr. True E. Prescott was taken into the concern as a partner, since which time it has been known as the Melcher & Prescott Agency. In 1891 Mr. Melcher's private business inter-

following list of well-known insurance companies:

Aachen & Munich Fire Ins. Co. of Germany.
Ætna Ins. Co. of Hartford, Conn.
Agricultural Ins. Co. of Watertown, N. Y.
Commercial Union Assurance Co. of London, England.
Continental Insurance Co. of New York.
Insurance Co. of North America of Philadelphia.
Lancashire Insurance Co. of Manchester, England.
Magdeburg Fire Insurance Co. of Germany.
National Fire Ins. Co. of Hartford, Conn.
Niagara Fire Ins. Co. of New York.
Palatine Ins. Co. of Manchester, England.
Phœnix Assurance Co. of London, England.

Residence of M. L. Crane.

ests became so great that it was necessary for him to be away most of the time, and consequently the entire business and management of the insurance agency was turned over to Mr. Prescott who has since conducted the affairs of the concern. This agency does not mix any other line of business with insurance, but devotes entire attention to this branch alone.

From the one insurance company with which Mr. Melcher started in 1862 the agency has gradually and carefully increased its facilities until the Melcher & Prescott Agency now represents the

Phœnix Ins. Co. of Hartford, Conn.
Phenix Insurance Co. of Brooklyn, N. Y.
Queen Insurance Co. of New York.
Springfield Fire & Marine Ins. Co. of Springfield, Mass.
Williamsburg City Fire Ins. Co. of New York.
Boston Insurance Co. of Boston, Mass.
Greenwich Ins. Co. of New York.
Traders and Mechanics of Lowell, Mass.
Merchants' and Farmers' Ins. Co. of Worcester, Mass.
Concord Mutual Insurance of Concord, N. H.
Manufacturers' and Merchants' Mutual Ins. Co. of Concord, N. H.
Capital Fire Insurance Co. of Concord, N. H.
Fire Underwriters' Association of Concord, N. H.
Granite State Fire Insurance Co. of Portsmouth, N. H.

New Hampshire Fire Ins. Co. of Manchester, N. H.
Lloyd's Plate Glass Ins. Co. of New York.
Fidelity and Deposit Co. of Baltimore, Md.
Maryland Casualty Co. of Baltimore, Md.
Employers' Liability Assurance Corporation of London, England.
Northwestern Mutual Life Insurance Co. of Milwaukee, Wis.

This long list of strong companies enables the agency to place $200,000 or more insurance on any one risk, facilities which are unsurpassed by any other agency in New Hampshire. Their vative methods of the Northwestern Mutual have won the admiration of everyone seeking this line of insurance, and has enabled the Melcher & Prescott Agency to establish a very good business in this line.

The accident and liability department, which was hardly known a few years ago, is now one of the leading features of this agency, which represents the Employers' Liability Assurance company of London, and the Maryland Casualty Co. of Baltimore, Md., which

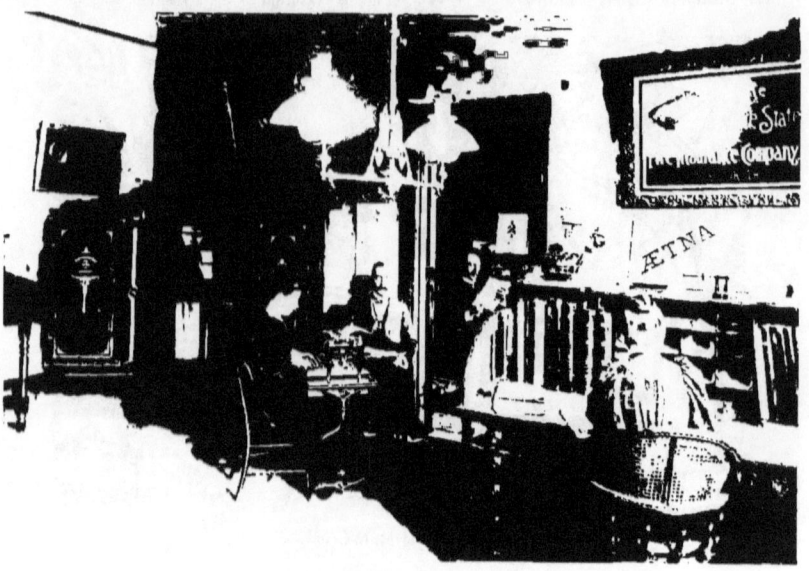

Melcher & Prescott's Insurance Office.

business is not confined to Laconia and vicinity, as their arrangements with their companies allow them the entire state, and their largest lines of insurance are carried outside of Belknap county.

The business of the Melcher & Prescott Agency is divided into five departments, viz.: Fire, life, accident and liability, plate glass, fidelity and bond.

In the life insurance department, the Northwestern Mutual Life Insurance company of Milwaukee, Wisconsin, is the company represented. The conser- issued policies for employers, public landlords, elevator, horse, and vehicle liability, and individual accident. The agency has paid many losses, and relieved some of our citizens from lawsuits which they would have had forced upon them if it had not been for this line of insurance.

In the plate glass insurance department the Melcher & Prescott Agency represents the Lloyd's Plate Glass Insurance company of New York, the oldest institution in America doing this line of insurance. This company has adjusted every loss sustained since its organization, without a single lawsuit.

In the fidelity insurance line this agency represents the Fidelity and Deposit Co. of Baltimore, Md., and this branch of their business includes the furnishing of bonds for salesmen, agents, secretaries, treasurers, officers of beneficial and building and loan associations, appointees and employees of the United States government, contractors for building or other operations, clerks of courts, sheriffs, cashiers, administrators, guardians, in fact every position of trust.

The Melcher & Prescott agency represents besides their other fire insurance companies many of the leading mutual fire insurance concerns, thus giving their patrons who are partial to this kind of insurance an opportunity to select from the best, which is a very important consideration in a mutual insurance company.

The Melcher & Prescott agency is not only one of the oldest insurance agencies in this part of the state, but it has a well-deserved reputation for settling losses, which reflects unlimited credit upon its management. During all its years of business the agency has never been known to falter; not a single loss has ever occurred but the company insuring has been able to pay one hundred cents on the dollar. No agency can have a better record for fair and honorable dealing than the Melcher & Prescott concern.

Col. S. S. Jewett.

Col. Stephen S. Jewett, of the law firm of Jewett & Plummer, has not only won a reputation throughout New Hampshire as a successful lawyer but probably no man of his age is better or more widely known in Republican political circles. He is the son of John G. and Carrie E. (Shannon) Jewett, born in that part of Gilford which is now included in the city of Laconia, September 18, 1858. He comes of English stock, and his great-grandfather, Samuel Jewett, who was one of the Revolutionary patriots at Bunker Hill, resided for some time in Hollis, N. H., whence he removed to Laconia, he and his brother being practically the first settlers of this place.

Stephen Shannon Jewett acquired his early education in the public schools of Laconia and under private tuition by his father, who was for some years a schoolmaster. At the age of seventeen years, Mr. Jewett entered the law office of Hon. Charles F. Stone and was prepared for examination to practice law in 1879, but being under age was compelled to wait a year. He was admitted to practice in March, 1880, and at once commenced to practice his profession in Laconia, conducting an independent business until 1889, when Lawyer William A. Plummer became his partner. During his twenty years of legal practice, but few important cases have ap-

True E. Prescott.

peared on the Belknap court docket without his name in connection, either for plaintiff or defendant. In 1884, he accepted the position of clerk of the supreme court for Belknap county, as an accommodation for the convenience of the court, and served for a short time. He drafted and secured the passage of Laconia's city charter, was the first city solicitor and has held the position ever since.

Colonel Jewett is actively interested in numerous local enterprises outside of his professional duties. He is a director in the Laconia National bank, in the Laconia Building and Loan Association, in the Laconia Land and Improvement company, the Standard Electric Time company, the Masonic Temple association, etc.

Mr. Jewett has a wide reputation as a successful manager and leader in political campaigns. He first actively engaged in politics in 1876, when a youth of seventeen, and was soon recognized as a leader in political matters. He conducted the affairs of the Republican town committee from 1880 to 1890, and becoming a member of the Republican state committee in 1884 was elected secretary of that body in 1890. His capacity has been tried in several hard-fought campaigns, and he served as chairman and manager of the Republican canvass in 1892 and 1894, winning signal victories in both instances.

In the New Hampshire house of representatives he has served as clerk, assistant clerk, and engrossing clerk. In 1894 he was elected as a representative

Col. Stephen S. Jewett.

from Ward 2, and served as speaker of the house, in which capacity his long public service in political matters and extensive acquaintance peculiarly fitted him.

Colonel Jewett was a member of the staff of Governor Goodell in 1889, and he was a member and chairman of the New Hampshire delegation to the Republican national convention which nominated President McKinley at St. Louis in 1896. He is still a member of the executive committee, of the state committee, and the executive committee of the Republican national league.

At the last state election Colonel Jewett was elected to the New Hampshire senate from the sixth district, and was the leading member of that body during the session, directing, to a large extent, the action upon most of the important measures.

Colonel Jewett was married June 30, 1880, to Annie L. Bray of Bradford, England, and he insists that most of his success in life is due to his wife. They have one son, Theo S.

William A. Plummer.

Colonel Jewett is a thirty-second degree Mason, has been an officer in all of the local Masonic bodies and grand master of the Grand council of New Hampshire.

He served as a member of old Company K, New Hampshire National Guard, and is connected with several other social and fraternal organizations.

William A. Plummer.

William A. Plummer of the well-known law firm of Jewett & Plummer, and a prominent member of the Belknap County bar, is a native of Gilmanton and can trace his family back to the very first settlers of New England. The Plummers were among the early settlers in Newburyport, Mass., in 1635, and Governor Plummer of New Hampshire was of the same stock. On the maternal side, William Moody came from England to Ipswich, Mass., in 1633, and settled in Newbury, Massachusetts, in 1635. John Moody of Kingston is a collateral line from William, and was the father of Capt. John Moody who lived in Gilmanton. He moved to Gilmanton from Kingston, November 15, 1764. He settled on No. 5 of the upper one hundred acres in the first parish. At that time he had no neighbors within four miles on the south and none nearer than the Canada line on the north.

In 1776, Capt. John Moody enlisted twenty men, joined the army, and marched under Washington as a captain to New York. They were out three months and eight days. He had seven children; one son, Elisha Moody, was born Sept. 28, 1773, and died Sept. 21, 1833. He had twelve children: one son, Stephen S. Moody, was born in Gilmanton, June 25, 1806, and died April 27, 1893; he had six children. Mary H. Moody, a daughter, was born in Gilmanton, Dec. 5, 1830, and now lives in Gilmanton. She married Chas. E. Plummer. They had three children, one of whom is the subject of this sketch.

William Alberto Plummer was born in Gilmanton, Dec. 2, 1865. His father, Charles E. Plummer, was born in Gilmanton and still resides there, a large landowner, his property covering over a thousand acres, and he is extensively engaged in farming, stock-raising, and lumbering. William A. Plummer was educated at Gilmanton academy, Dartmouth college, and Boston University School of Law. He was admitted to the bar, July 26, 1889, and previous to this date he read law with J. C. Story at Plymouth, G. W. Murray at Canaan, and was also in the office of C. T. & T. H. Russell of Boston. Sept. 2, 1889, he became the partner of Col. S. S. Jewett, and the law firm of Jewett & Plummer is one of the best known in the state, and it has gained much

Residence of William A. Plummer.

legal prestige from the ability of both members of the firm.

In politics, Mr. Plummer is a Democrat, but not what is known as a Silver Democrat. He was a representative in the legislature in 1893, has been a member of the Laconia board of education since 1893, and president of the board for the past three years. He was a delegate to the Democratic national convention at Chicago in 1896.

He is a director of the Laconia board of trade, a director of the Laconia National bank, a trustee of the City Savings bank, and a director of the Laconia Building and Loan Association.

Mr. Plummer is a Mason, a Knight of Pythias, and a member of the Ancient Order of United Workmen. He was master of Mt. Lebanon lodge, 1895-'96, and is an officer in Union chapter, Royal Arch Masons, and in Pilgrim commandery, Knights Templar.

Mr. Plummer married Ellen F. Murray, daughter of George W. Murray, Esq., of Canaan, N. H., a well-known and able lawyer, who has achieved great success in his chosen profession, and during the active years of his professional life enjoyed as extensive a law practice as any lawyer in the state. Mr. and Mrs. Plummer have one son, Wayne Murray Plummer, and their residence on Pleasant street is one of the most beautiful and elegant homes in the city of Laconia.

Dr. William A. King.

Although a resident of Laconia for comparatively a few years, Dr. William A. King has practised his profession here long enough to be recognized as a skilful and proficient dentist, and to acquire a wide reputation for scientific work in his line, which has resulted in building up a large and prosperous practice.

Dr. King was born in Leeds, P. Q.,

Aug. 6, 1863, son of Henry and Mary Ann (Kirtland) King. He went to Littleton, N. H., in 1881, and thence came to Laconia in 1888, where he studied dentistry in a local office, then took a course at the Boston Dental college, and afterwards attended the Baltimore Dental college, graduating from the latter institution in 1890.

Upon completing his professional studies, Doctor King returned to Laconia, and has been in successful practice here since that time. He is located at No. 79 Main street, where he has handsomely fitted apartments for his office, while his residence on Lincoln street is generally admitted to be one of the most beautiful and comfortable homes in the city.

He was married in 1893 to Miss Helen Abbott Martin, daughter of the late Henry Martin and Mrs. Lucy J. Martin of Canaan, N. H. They have one son, Martin Ronald King, who is four years old.

Dr. William A. King.

Residence of Dr. William A. King.

The Laconia Grist-mill.

One of the very first industries in Laconia was a grist-mill, which was established very soon after the Province road was built, about 1770. The grist-mill was first erected on the Meredith side of the river, but was swept away by a freshet in 1779, and then rebuilt on the Gilford side. In 1775, the grist-mill was conducted by Stephen Gale, and afterwards by Col. Samuel Ladd, and from him handed down to one person and another until the present day.

The mill building has been several times destroyed by fire, but always immediately rebuilt, and the location of the Laconia Grist-mill to-day, conducted by Miller J. S. Morrill is not very far from the first location on that side of the river, the grist-mill which was erected in 1780 being built a trifle nearer the Mill street bridge.

A century and a quarter of time has made considerable change in the grist-mill industry, but the Laconia Grist-mill has always managed to be classed as an up-to-date establishment, and is, to-day, equipped with modern machinery and conducted on modern principles. In the olden times, the principal branch of this business was the grinding of corn and grain for the farmers, and this feature has not yet entirely passed away, and Miller Morrill still makes a special feature of custom grinding, although this is now a small part of the grist-mill business. The Laconia Grist-mill carries a large stock of all kinds of grain, feed, hay, straw, etc., and handles a larger quantity of flour than any other concern in this section of New Hampshire. Mr. Morrill is agent for the well-known Pillsbury mills, which are the largest flour mills in the world, and produce the standard bread flour. During the past few years, the Laconia Grist-mill has

The Laconia Grist-Mill.

built up a good trade in entire wheat flour, graham, bolted meal for cooking purposes, etc.

Joseph S. Morrill, the present proprietor of this long-established industry, is a native of Canterbury, N. H., born April 22, 1869. He completed his education at New Hampshire Conference Seminary, from which institution he graduated in 1889, and soon after commenced learning the grain business and miller's trade. Mr. Morrill came to Laconia in April, 1890, and formed a partnership with Mr. W. L. Melcher and G. G. Brown, and engaged in business at the Laconia Grist-mill. Mr. Melcher retired from the concern in 1892, and three years later, in 1895, Mr. Brown sold out his interest in the busi-

Joseph S. Morrill.

ness to Mr. Morrill, who has since conducted the mill alone. Mr. Morrill married Ina M. Stone of Webster, N. H., September 7, 1892. He has been quite successful in the management of the grist-mill business, and has built up a large trade in all departments of the business. Grist-mills in many parts of New Hampshire have been abandoned and rendered almost useless by the march of progress, but the Laconia mill has always kept up with the procession, and under the enterprising management of Mr. Morrill bids fair to be a necessary and profitable industry for a century or two longer at least.

The Late John O'Loughlin.

The late John O'Loughlin, who died in Boston, October 26, 1896, was a young Laconian who rose by his own enterprise and ability, from a poor boy, starting in life without a penny, to be postmaster of Laconia, and recognized as one of the active business men of the city. He was the son of Martin and Nora O'Loughlin, who were industrious and excellent people, but very poor. At an early age, John O'Loughlin found employment in the Pitman mills, and later on was a clerk in the Pitman grocery and hardware store. He then entered the store of Lougee Brothers, and after several years was with the O'Shea Brothers for some time, until he attracted the attention of the late Hon. John C. Moulton, who made him manager of the Moulton opera house, and finally employed him nearly all the time in looking after the Moulton real estate and other interests. It was largely through Mr. O'Loughlin's efforts that the old gas company was merged into the present Winnipesaukee Gas company, and the new modern gas plant constructed. In March, 1895, Mr. O'Loughlin was appointed postmaster of Laconia, after one of the hardest

The late John O'Loughlin.

contests in the history of Laconia. He went into the fight with almost no prospects of success, and but very little influential backing, and that he was successful was due almost entirely to his own energy and persistency. He took much pride in moving the post-office from its old quarters to the handsome quarters in Masonic temple, and in having the establishment fitted in metropolitan style. Mr. O'Loughlin worked hard with the department at Washington for the free delivery system, and was finally successful in securing this service for Laconia.

Light-hearted, jovial, loyal to his friends and generous to a fault, tenderly caring for his widowed mother and trying to keep the family together after the death of his parents, Johnny O'Loughlin was a young man with many commendable traits of character. He was but twenty-eight years old at the time of his death, but had accomplished more in his brief business career than most men similarly situated would have achieved in a whole lifetime.

Dr. Alfred W. Abbott.

Dr. Alfred Wells Abbott has practised his profession in Laconia for nearly twenty years, and has won a wide reputation as an able physician.

He was born in Concord, N. H., May 7, 1842, son of Alfred C. and Judith (Farnham) Abbott. He studied medicine with Dr. S. S. Emery at Fisherville (now Penacook), and graduated with honor at Dartmouth Medical college in 1868. He commenced the practice of his profession at Lawrence, Kansas, but soon returned to New Hampshire, locating at Suncook, where he remained until July, 1870, and then removed to Sanbornton, where he remained ten years, acquiring a large and lucrative practice, and gaining a host of friends. Runnells's history of Sanbornton, published while Dr. Abbott was a resident of that town, says of him: "He has won much esteem for his social qualities, and as a well-read, scientific physician, enjoying an extensive practice in this and adjoining towns."

In 1880 he came to Laconia, and here, preceded by his reputation for skill and knowledge, he made rapid strides in his profession, and to-day he occupies an assured position among the leading practitioners of New Hampshire. His practice is large and lucrative, he has acquired a competency, and is considered one of Laconia's best financiers. He has long been a trustee of the Laconia Savings bank, and has been president of the Citizens' Telephone company since its organization in 1896.

Dr. Alfred W. Abbott.

He was the first vice-president of Winnipesaukee Academy of Medicine, and its second president. In his political affiliations Dr. Abbott is a staunch Republican, but has never sought political preferment, and has steadfastly refused official positions, although often urged by his political friends to accept positions of honor and trust. He is distinctively a professional man, and devotes his whole time and attention to the calling which he loves so well and in which he has been so successful.

He was married December 30, 1869,

to Julia Ann Clay of Manchester, N. H., by whom he has had three children: Clifton Smith, born Jan. 16, 1871, a graduate of the Dartmouth Medical college in the class of 1893. Dr. Clifton Abbott is now in partnership with his father and has a well-deserved reputation as a learned and skilful physician. Blanche Newall Abbott was born April 10, 1872, is a young lady of many accomplishments, and a teacher in our Laconia public schools. Carl Benning Abbott was born August 29, 1877, and died March, 1888.

Dr. Clifton S. Abbott.

Dr. Clifton S. Abbott is one of the youngest, but by no means the least, of Laconia's physicians. He was born in Sanbornton, Jan. 16, 1871, the son of Dr. A. W. and Julia Abbott, and is one of a family of physicians. He was educated in the public schools of Laconia, and studied the medical profession at Dartmouth Medical college, where he graduated in 1894, afterwards taking a post-graduate course at Harvard Medical school. Dr. Clifton Abbott commenced practice in this city in the office of his father, with whom he is still associated.

He was elected a member of the board of education in March, 1899, and is county physician for Laconia and Sanbornton, also surgeon at the Laconia Cottage hospital. He is a member of the Winnipesaukee Academy of Medicine, Winnipesaukee lodge, I. O. O. F., and is also a member of the Order of Golden Cross. He is unmarried, and an attendant at the Congregational church.

The Laconia Democrat.

Laconia has had numerous newspapers during the last sixty years, but with the exception of the *Laconia Democrat* at this end of the city, and the *Belknap Republican* at Lakeport, none of them has survived the journalistic storms for more than a dozen or fifteen years. The *Democrat* was founded in 1849, and is consequently half a century old, and it has always been a thriving and progressive newspaper. The paper was started by Keach & Seaver, and among its editors and proprietors have been the late S. C. Baldwin, the late Joseph Batchelder, the late O. A. J. Vaughan, William M. Kendall, and Col. Edwin C. Lewis, with his partners. Col. Lewis was connected with the *Laconia Democrat* for about eighteen years, and under his editorship the paper was exceedingly prosperous.

In the year 1897 Colonel Lewis sold his interest in the concern, and the Laconia Press Association was organized, with Ex-Gov. Charles A. Busiel as president and a frequent contributor to the editorial columns, and Charles W.

Dr. Clifton S. Abbott.

Vaughan as general manager. As an advocate of state reform and the development of New Hampshire, during the past two years, the circulation and influence of the *Laconia Democrat* have largely increased, and from a merely local paper covering only Belknap county the paper now enjoys an extensive circulation in all parts of the Granite State.

E. P. Jewell.

Erastus P. Jewell was born in the town of Sandwich, N. H., March 16, 1837. He came to Laconia in 1859 and studied law with the late Col. Thos. J. Whipple. The law firms of Whipple & Jewell, Jewell & Smith, Jewell & Stone,

Erastus P. Jewell.

The foregoing is the full extent of the information which Lawyer Jewell was willing to furnish to the Illustrated Laconian, for a sketch of himself, but the publishers take the liberty to add that Mr. Jewell has a wide reputation as a safe and careful counselor and has won especial fame in argument and pleading before the jurymen of Belknap county and in fact in all the courts of New Hampshire. He has always been intensely interested in matters of history, especially pertaining to the early settlement of this section of New Hampshire, and probably but few men in New England can talk so intelligently and interestingly of the Indians of the Granite

Residence of Erastus P. Jewell.

Jewell, Stone, Owen & Martin, have been well and widely known. Mr. Jewell's law firm is now Jewell, Owen & Veasey.

state as "Perry" Jewell. In this connection, he has made a large and valuable collection of Indian relics, stone implements, arrow-heads, hatchets, knives, etc., which he treasures highly, but which will probably some day be turned over to the custody of the city for preservation for future generations.

The Late Nathaniel Edgerly.

Nathaniel Edgerly was born in the Iron Works village in Gilmanton, Sept. 22, 1802, and died in Laconia, Sept. 26, 1874. He was one of a family of ten children of David and Anna (Lougee) Edgerly. After receiving such education as could be obtained at the common schools and at Gilmanton academy, and serving for a time as a bookkeeper in Boston, he learned the clothier's trade, at which he worked in his father's mill in Gilmanton, and later carried on the same business on his own account. He also, for a time, kept a general store in Gilmanton. Subsequently, he was employed in the Strafford county registry of deeds at Dover, N. H.

He served two terms as one of the selectmen of Gilmanton, and in 1840 was elected to the legislature from that town.

In 1841, the county of Belknap having been recently organized, he was appointed register of deeds, to which office he was annually re-elected until 1859. For a short time after his retirement from the register's office, he was engaged in the boot and shoe trade.

The late Nathaniel Edgerly.

Mr. Edgerly was married, Nov. 9, 1830, to Lucy Thurston of Gilmanton, who died in 1858. Eight children were born to them, of whom four survive.

In religion, Mr. Edgerly was a Universalist; in politics, a Democrat.

Laconia Water Company.

No city or town in the United States can boast of a better, purer, or more inexhaustible water supply than the city on the lakes. New Hampshire is noted for its clear lakes, ponds, and the largest lake in the state, and one of the purest and clearest, is Lake Winnipesaukee, from whence the city of Laconia draws its entire water supply. The matter of a city water supply had been agitated for several years, and a survey was made as far back as 1869, but largely through the efforts of Hon. W. L. Melcher and Col. B. F. Drake, a charter was obtained in 1883, and a company organized in August, 1884, as the Laconia and Lake Village Water-Works, with a capital of $60,000.

The plant was constructed in 1885, and water was first let on in December of that year. The pumping-station is located on Union avenue, at Lakeport, and the reservoir is upon the high hill overlooking Lake Paugus, on the easterly side of Union avenue. The system has, of course, been extended from year to year, and the capital stock has been increased to $100,000. The total cost of the plant, up to date, is about $175,000. The name of the corporation was changed to Laconia Water Company, by the legislature, in 1897.

The original officers of the corporation were: President, Hon. John C. Moulton; treasurer, Hon. W. L. Melcher; clerk, John W. Ashman; superintendent, Benj. F. Drake; directors, John C. Moulton, Woodbury L. Melcher, Benj. J. Cole, Ellery A. Hibbard, Benj. F. Drake, Gardner Cook, Henry B. Quinby.

The total amount of pipe laid at the present time is twenty-three and one fourth miles, and there are now 1,489 consumers taking water from this system. The corporation can supply 3,000,000 gallons of water per day if necessary. There are about ninety-two hydrants for fire purposes attached to the system. The capacity of the reservoir is 2,750,000 gallons.

The present officers of the corporation are: President, Hon. Woodbury L. Melcher; clerk and treasurer, Edmund Little; superintendent, Frank P. Webster; directors, Woodbury L. Melcher, Ellery A. Hibbard, Benjamin F. Drake, Gardner Cook, John S. Crane, William B. Fellows, Geo. H. Roby, Frank E. Busiel, Wm. H. Pepper.

The Late Samuel H. Martin.

The untimely death of the late Samuel H. Martin, on April 26, 1898, re-

Laconia Pumping Station.

moved from the Belknap Bar association one of the brightest and most promising young lawyers of Laconia. Mr. Martin was a native of Bangor, P. Q., and the son of Mr. and Mrs. George A. Martin. His age at the time of his death was thirty-one years and nine months. He came to Laconia with his parents when a mere boy, and obtained his education in our public schools. He studied law with Jewell & Stone, and was admitted to the bar in July, 1892, entering the office of Stanton Owen, the firm being known as Owen & Martin. About a year later, the partnership of Jewell, Stone, Owen & Martin was formed, and continued until broken by Mr. Martin's decease.

Mr. Martin never enjoyed robust health, and on several occasions during the few years previous to his death his life was despaired of, but he was ambitious and possessed of great will power, which enabled him to fight against disease, and he persisted in attending to his professional duties long after most men would have given up the fight and merely waited for death.

Mr. Martin was admitted to be one of the most studious, logical, and eloquent young lawyers which the city on the lakes ever produced. He was popular with his associate members of the bar and highly respected by the entire community. Strictly honorable and upright in all his dealings with clients and opponents, his conduct of legal affairs was a model of professional etiquette. He was easy and convincing in his address, and at times rose to genuine eloquence. He was a self-made man, for he carried himself along to success by his own unaided efforts, by pluck and ambition, in spite of the disease which fastened itself upon him in his early manhood and hampered him from pursuing his studies and in his professional life.

With a full knowledge that he was to be an early victim of consumption, he was always cheerful and hopeful regarding his physical condition, and persisted in going to his office and devoting himself to his professional work just as long as he had the physical strength to get out of doors.

In 1892 he married Miss Nellie A. Schoffe, who survives him.

Charles W. McDaniel.

Charles William McDaniel was born in South Berwick, Maine, May 5, 1852. His father was Charles S. McDaniel, who was a descendant from the Scotch McDaniel brothers, who were among the first settlers of Maine. His mother, Sarah Minerva Frost, was closely related to the Indian fighter Charles Frost, and Prophet Frost, whose names were household words in Elliott and other parts of Maine, in their day. He was educated in the schools of his native town. At the age of eighteen years he began to learn the machinist trade in North Andover, Mass., where he worked about one year, completing the trade of tool making two years later at the shop of Frank Perkins in Lowell. In 1877, he went with a large prospecting party from Franklin, N. H., to the Black Hills. This was before the railroad went into the hills, and Mr. McDaniel covered the entire distance from Cheyenne to Deadwood City, about 350 miles, on foot, and was the only one of the party that

The late Samuel H. Martin.

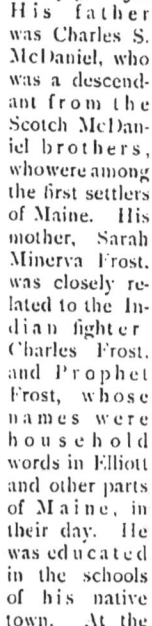

held out to walk the entire distance. He remained in this section about a year and then he and three others went down the Missouri river from Fort Pierre to Sioux City in a flat-bottomed boat of their own manufacture. Returning east he resumed his trade as a machinist in Franklin Falls.

June 26, 1879, he married Ida Frances Sanders of Bristol, N. H., daughter of Benjamin and Priscilla (Blake) Sanders. Her father, Benjamin Sanders, was a member of the Twelfth New Hampshire regiment, and was in the battle of Fredericksburg, December, 1862; battle of Chancellorsville, May 2, 1863. He was wounded in the right arm at this battle and was captured by the Confederates, and held eleven days and then exchanged. After being confined in the hospital several weeks he was discharged in October, 1863, for disability. He enlisted again on March 16, 1864, in Company A, First New Hampshire Cavalry, was taken prisoner, and died at Andersonville. Her mother, Priscilla Rundlett Blake, was great-granddaughter of Maj. Joseph Prescott of Bunker Hill fame.

This union has been blessed with three children: Harry Sewal, who is a clerk in Plummer & Thompson's drug store in Laconia; Jessa Saunders, who is a student at the Laconia High school, and Charles Stanley, a bright little fellow of nine years.

Mr. McDaniel resided in Bristol from 1879 to 1887, where he was engaged in the paper mills of Mason, Perkins & Co., and as assistant superintendent of the Train, Smith & Co. paper mills. In 1887, after the death of Mrs. McDaniel's mother, they removed to Lakeport, where they now reside. Mr. McDaniel was made a Master Mason at Franklin, and is now a member of Mt. Lebanon lodge, Union chapter, and Pilgrim commandery of Laconia, and also a member of Chocorua lodge, I. O. O. F.

He was appointed by Gov. C. A. Busiel, in 1896, as inspector of steamboats for the state of New Hampshire, which position he still holds.

Although not an aspirant for political honors he is in principles a staunch Republican. In religious faith, Mr. McDaniel is a Baptist, and the family attend the Union Avenue Baptist church at Lakeport.

Charles W. McDaniel.

Gordon & Booth, Jewelers.

Gordon & Booth, jewelers, are proprietors of the oldest jewelry establishment in the city of Laconia, the business having been started by the late Richard Gove, who came here from Boston in 1833, and opened a store in this line in a little one-story wooden building, which stood just below the Main street bridge, on a portion of the site now occupied by the Smith brick block.

Mr. Gove built up a very prosperous trade and erected several large business blocks on Main street, one on the present site of Folsom block, and another fine fire-proof building near the location of the present Gordon & Booth store

The building did not prove to be fireproof, however, and was destroyed in the great conflagration of 1860. Mr. Gove was one of the most public-spirited and enterprising citizens of his day, and he fitted up Gove Point, which projects into Lake Winnesquam, at his own expense and at great cost, for the benefit of the public, as a common pleasure resort free to all.

Under Mr. Gove's management and under its present management by Messrs. Gordon & Booth, the jewelry establishment has always been one of the leading stores in this line in this

River and Bradford, Vt. He came to Laconia in 1874 and was with Mr. Gove (his uncle) in the store from that time until Mr. Gove's death in April, 1883. Since that date he has continued the business himself, Mr. Booth entering the partnership in the summer of 1898. Mr. Gordon is a Democrat in politics and served as selectman three years under the old town government. He is a director of the Laconia Building and Loan Association, a trustee of the Laconia Savings bank, and president of the Laconia Land and Improvement company. In fraternal orders

Gordon & Booth's Jewelry Store.

section of New Hampshire. It carries a large stock of gold and silver jewelry, watches, clocks, optical goods, silver and plated ware, china, and, in fact, everything which can be found in an up-to-date metropolitan jewelry establishment.

Mr. Alburtis S. Gordon, the senior member of the firm, is a native of Hebron, N. H., the son of Levi S. and Mary (Gove) Gordon, born May 17, 1848. He was educated in the public schools, and then learned the tinsmith's trade when eighteen years of age, and worked at this trade five years in Wells

Mr. Gordon is a member of the Knights of Pythias, Knights of Honor, and a thirty-second degree Mason, being a member of the local branches of Masonry, including Pilgrim Commandery Knights Templar, and Raymond Consistory of Nashua.

John Booth, the junior member of the firm, was born Sept. 19, 1871, in Aberdeenshire, Scotland, his parents being George and Annia (Mellis) Booth. He has been employed at Danville, P. Q., and St. Johnsbury, Vt., and was in business at Windsor Mills, P. Q. He came to Laconia in June, 1898.

Pease's City Band.

Pease's City Band of Laconia was reorganized in the spring of 1893, with Charles R. Pease as leader and director. This organization was composed of some of the best musicians in the city, and at once sprang into popular favor. It has progressed rapidly, and to-day ranks with the best bands in the state. It is in a very prosperous condition, having two sets of uniforms, and has had a new band-room built for its especial convenience, and furnished in modern style throughout. It also has a large library of music. Its present membership is twenty-five musicians, with the following instrumentation: Director and leader, Charles R. Pease; cornets, Ernest Ringer, William F. Sanborn, Harry W. Smith, Henry Turcotte, Albert B. Ladd; flute and piccolo, Robert S. Foss; clarinets, Clarence R. Davis, William H. Hawkins, Geo. Ringer, John Webber, Leon Ladd; altos, Sidney H. Smith, Geo. R. Bowman, Austin Folsom; baritone, Archie L. Bean; trombones, Chas. H. Hoyt, John H. Swain, James Harder; bassos, Jas. Ringer, F. A. Clement, J. B. Morrill; drums, Leon Hale, H. P. Dimond, F. A. Carleton; drum-major, I. M. Cottrell.

Albert S. Glidden.

Albert S. Glidden, manager and proprietor of the concern known as A. S. Glidden & Co., brass founders, is a native of Lynn, Mass., born Sept. 26, 1859, the son of Levi and Emily (Coleman) Glidden, both of whom are now deceased. He removed to New Hampshire with his parents when only two years old, and was educated in the public schools of Laconia. Mr. Glidden learned the foundry business at the shops of the late George Rollins, which were located on Gove Point in this city. After learning his trade, Mr. Glidden removed to Manchester and remained there about three years, then returned to Laconia, and has been connected with the various foundries in this city. He went into business for himself in Boston, in partnership with W. H. Wilkinson, under the firm name of W. H. Wilkinson & Co., but retired from this business to return to Laconia, where he started a brass foundry of his own, located on Somes court, in a new building which was erected especially for this purpose.

The concern does business under the firm name of A. S. Glidden & Co., and manufactures all kinds of brass and composition castings. It is the only concern in this line in this city and the work turned out is considered of high quality. The business has been very prosperous and is constantly increasing.

Mr. Glidden is an Odd Fellow, and a Knight of Pythias. He was married in 1882 to Miss Ida J. Davis of Laconia. They have no children.

Albert S. Glidden.

Laconia National Bank.

The Laconia National bank, with a capital of $150,000, is the largest and easily the most important banking institution in this section of New Hampshire. The bank was organized December 28, 1865, and commenced business May 1, 1866, with the following board of officers: President, John C. Moulton; cashier, Daniel S. Dinsmoor; directors, John C. Moulton, Ellery A. Hibbard, Samuel T. Thomas, William N. Blair, Benjamin J. Cole, Samuel C. Clarke, Hanson Beede. The bank hired vault room of the old Belknap County bank, and occupied rooms in the same building. This bank has always transacted a large and profitable business, and has always been regarded as one of the most reliable and soundest financial establishments in this vicinity.

April 25, 1879, the bank was burglarized, the safe blown open, and $3,500 in cash, and $2,600 in bonds, besides securities to the amount of nearly $145,000, were taken. The burglars forced the front door, drilled into the safe, and opened the steel chest with an explosion which almost wrecked the entire building. The explosion alarmed the citizens in the vicinity, but the robbers boldly reëntered the bank, hastily gathered up the booty and escaped. The windows in the entire block were shivered, the plastering torn off, and one side of the entire building started from its fastenings. The securities were afterwards recovered, being found where the burglars discarded them as of no value, and the loss of the cash and bonds did not of course cripple the bank.

In 1889 the bank was moved to its present location at Bank square, where

Interior of Laconia National Bank.

it owns and occupies a handsome, three-story, brick block, handsomely and elegantly equipped, and furnished in modern style, with tile flooring, mahogany finish, steel ceilings, fire and burglar-proof vault, etc.

The present officers of the establishment are: President, Charles A. Busiel; vice-president, Henry B. Quinby; cashier, Orran W. Tibbetts; assistant cashier, Charles W. Tyler; directors, George H. Clark, Meredith; Ellery A. Hibbard, Charles A. Busiel, Charles F. Pitman, Henry B. Quinby, Dennis O'Shea, William F. Knight, Stephen S. Jewett, all of Laconia; J. Alonzo Greene, Moultonborough; Orran W. Tibbetts, William A. Plummer, Laconia.

City Savings Bank.

The City Savings bank, which occupies rooms with the Laconia National bank, is the youngest banking establishment in the city, being chartered in 1895. An organization was effected, and the bank commenced business April 1, 1897, and from the date of opening the increase of deposits has been rapid and steady. The bank has been enabled to invest its deposits in first-class, gilt-edged securities, nearly all its money being loaned upon valuable real estate in Laconia and vicinity. The aim of this bank is to invest the money of its depositors carefully and conservatively, paying as high a rate of interest as can be earned from strictly safe investments. Local real estate is given the preference in all cases over Western or Southern securities.

Judging from the increase of business during its two years of existence, the City Savings bank bids fair to soon become one of the strongest and most popular savings banks in the state.

Laconia National Bank.

The present officers of the City Savings bank are: President, Charles A. Busiel; vice-president, Henry B. Quinby; treasurer, Orran W. Tibbetts; secretary, Charles W. Tyler; investment committee, Charles A. Busiel, William A. Plummer, John F. Merrill, Julius E. Wilson; trustees, Charles A. Busiel, Thomas Cogswell, Henry B. Quinby, Stephen S. Jewett, William A. Plummer, John F. Merrill, Dennis O'Shea, Julius E. Wilson, Chas. F. Stone, Addison G. Cook, Edw. P. Thompson, Charles W. Vaughan; members of the corporation and associate trustees: William F. Knight, Laconia; Joseph W. Pitman, Laconia; Horace H. Wood, Lakeport; Henry F. Dorr, Centre Sandwich; Oliver J. M. Gilman, Alton; William B. Fellows, Tilton; Herbert J. Jones, Alton; Edwin C. Bean, Belmont; Chas W. Tyler, Laconia; Orran W. Tibbetts, Laconia.

City Clerk Simeon C. Frye.

Simeon Cheney Frye was born in Sanbornton, N. H., April 26, 1865, son of Jonathan J. Frye of Grantham, and Ruth H. Leavitt (Frye) of Sanbornton. He is a descendant of some of the oldest families in New England, and is a lineal descendant of Thomas Dudley, second governor of the Massachusetts bay colony. His great-grandfather was a soldier in the Revolutionary War and was engaged in the battle of Bennington.

Simeon C. Frye.

Another great-grandfather, George Avery, also served in the same war.

Mr. Frye was educated at the New Hampton Institution, and came to Laconia in January, 1887, as bookkeeper for O'Shea Bros.' store and hosiery mill. He left this firm in March, 1890, to engage in the "ice harvest," caused by a famine of frozen water down country, which resulted in a boom in this industry in Laconia and vicinity. From Jan. 1, 1891, he was with Coburn & Leavitt as bookkeeper until the firm went out of business, and then entered the office of the Crane Manufacturing Co., September, 1893, as bookkeeper, and remained with them until elected city clerk March 29, 1894. Mr. Frye has been re-elected city clerk at each subsequent election annually and still holds the position, for which it is but justice to say he is admirably equipped and thoroughly efficient. His books and records are models of neatness and correctness, and in the discharge of his official duties he has no superior in this line in New Hampshire. He was auditor of the state treasurer's accounts in 1897, appointed by Governor Busiel.

Mr. Frye is connected with several of the secret and fraternal orders. He is a member of Mt. Lebanon lodge, No. 32, A. F. & A. M., of which at the present time he is junior warden. He is also a member of Chocorua lodge, No. 51, I. O. O. F., and of Granite lodge, No. 3, Ancient Order of United Workmen, of which latter organization he has been recorder since 1892.

Street Commissioner William Nelson.

William Nelson, street commissioner of the city of Laconia, and also superintendent of the sewer department and city engineer, is a native Laconian, born

William Nelson.

April 20, 1871, his parents being Dr. David B. and Susan E. Nelson. He was educated in our public schools and graduated from the Laconia High school in the "Class of '87." The following year, Mr. Nelson commenced the study of civil engineering, and he is generally admitted to have acquired a very proficient education in this profession. He was appointed superintendent of the Laconia sewer department in 1892, city engineer in 1894, and street commissioner in 1897, and still holds all three positions, managing these three important departments of municipal work very acceptably. In addition to these official positions, Mr. Nelson has served several times as moderator of Ward 4, is sealer of weights and measures for the county of Belknap and city of Laconia, and a justice of the peace.

He is an attendant at the Congregational church, and member of Golden Rule lodge, I. O. G. T., Granite lodge, A. O. U. W., Senior Warden of Mt. Lebanon lodge, A. F. & A. M., and a member of the Boston Society of Civil Engineers.

Mr. Nelson was married to Mina L. Flint of Danville, P. Q., May 17, 1892. They have three children: Thomas L., Arthur R., and Marion Ruth.

City Treasurer Arthur W. Dinsmoor.

Arthur W. Dinsmoor, city treasurer of Laconia, is a native Laconian, the son of the late Hon. Daniel Stark Dinsmoor and Amelia M. (Whittemore)

Arthur W. Dinsmoor.

Dinsmoor, born Jan. 11, 1870. Mr. Dinsmoor is a descendant of the famous Gen. John Stark, the Revolutionary hero, while the Dinsmoors are descendants of John Dinsmoor, one of the early settlers of New Hampshire, who was noted for his honesty and uprightness both by white men and Indians in the old colonial days.

Mr. Dinsmoor was educated in our public schools and at New Hampshire Conference seminary at Tilton. For ten years he has been a faithful and trusted attaché of the Laconia National bank, and he also holds several other positions of trust and honor. He was elected city treasurer in March, 1894, and has held the office ever since that time, being re-elected at each subsequent annual election. He was one of the New Hampshire state auditors in 1895, is treasurer of the Belknap County Fish and Game League and also treasurer of the Laconia Press Association.

He is an attendant at the Congregational church, and is a member of the Masonic fraternity, holding the office of junior deacon in Mt. Lebanon lodge at the present time. He is also a member of the Ancient Order of United Workmen.

Mr. Dinsmoor married Amy W. Hatch, June 21, 1893, and they have two sons, Daniel S. and Theodore Weston.

Frank S. Peaslee.

Frank S. Peaslee, dealer in fruit, confectionery, tobacco, cigars, and periodi

Frank S. Peaslee.

cals, is a native of this city, born at Lake Village, April 19, 1871. Mr. Peaslee received a common school education, and is a knitter by trade, being employed in our local hosiery mills in his boyhood. He started in business in March, 1888, with a small stock of goods, in the room occupied by the Lakeport post-office. He met with fair success, but sold out the business in December, 1892, and then worked in the hosiery mills three years, as a knitter. In July, 1895, he again embarked in trade, at No. 47 Elm street, where he is

Mr. Peaslee is married, and resides at No. 60 School street. He has two little daughters, aged three and five years.

The Late Hon. John W. Busiel.

The late Hon. John W. Busiel was the founder of the hosiery establishment in Laconia, which still bears his name, and one of the pioneers in this industry

The late Hon. John W. Busiel.

still located, and has built up a successful and prosperous business.

He carries a large stock of all the popular cigars and tobacco, supplemented by a choice line of pipes and other smokers' goods. Fresh fruits in all seasons of the year are a specialty with Mr. Peaslee, and he handles large shipments in this line. In periodicals, Mr. Peaslee sells the daily and weekly newspapers, all the popular magazines, and literature usually found at a first-class newsstand.

in the United States. He was born in Moultonboro', N. H., March 28, 1815. His parents were Moses F. and Relief Busiel, and he was the eldest of a family of seven sons and one daughter. Only three of his brothers are now living, Albert H., of Laconia; Harrison M., of East Andover, N. H., and George H., of Providence, R. I.

Mr. Busiel's education was obtained in the country district schools, at a time when schooling was limited to a few weeks per year, but he was quick to learn and made the most of his limited opportunities. In his early youth he determined to be a woolen manufacturer, and started out at the age of only twelve years, with his scanty wardrobe tied up in a handkerchief, to walk to Loudon, N. H., where he entered the mill of his great-uncle, Lewis Flanders, who carded rolls and made flannels and cloths used at that period. A boy of unusual energy and determination, he remained with his uncle until he was nineteen years old, improving every opportunity to learn the business, and at the same time proceeding methodically with his studies while his companions were at play. At nineteen years of age, with a new suit of clothes, and one hundred dollars in his pocket, young Busiel left his uncle's roof and went to Amesbury, Mass., where he was employed in a woolen mill and completed his trade. Many times during his stay in Amesbury, he walked home, and out of his scanty earnings assisted in maintaining the family.

From Amesbury, Mr. Busiel returned to New Hampshire and located at Meredith where he remained ten years in business for himself, as a manufacturer of satinet cloth, knitting yarns, etc. In 1846 he came to Laconia and founded the J. W. Busiel mills, which he continued very successfully until his death which occurred July 26, 1872.

On December 23, 1841, he married Julia M., daughter of Stephen and Julia Tilton, of Meredith. Of this union were born three sons and one daughter. The daughter died in infancy, but the sons have lived to be an honor to their father's name. The eldest is Hon. Charles A. Busiel, ex-governor of New Hampshire. The other sons, John T. and Frank E., now carry on the hosiery business founded by their father.

Mr. Busiel was a strong Democrat in politics, and represented Laconia in the legislature in 1870-'71. He was a man of public spirit, enterprise, and progress. He manufactured the first gas burned in Laconia, and laid the first slate used here for roofing purposes. He also put in the first boiler and steam heat in the town. He took great interest in the welfare of Laconia, and gave generously to public buildings and all plans for the advancement of Laconia's prosperity. He was a liberal supporter of the Congregational church, of which Mrs. Busiel is a member, and assisted materially in remodeling the church edifice. He was kind-hearted, generous, and devoted to the interests of town.

Residence of Mrs. J. W. Busiel.

Ex-Governor Charles A. Busiel.

Probably no man has been more prominently and actively identified with the manufacturing, business, financial, and social life of Laconia, during the past thirty years, than Ex-Governor Charles A. Busiel. In the construction of the Lake Shore railroad, the erection of the new passenger station, the establishment of a city hospital, the inauguration of the city government, and in a thousand and one other enterprises, all in the direction of progress and advancement, Mr. Busiel has made his mark and built for himself a monument as a public-spirited, broad-minded, progressive Laconian, which will do honor to him for centuries to come.

Charles Albert Busiel was born in Meredith, N. H., Nov. 24, 1842. He was the eldest son of the late John W. and Julia (Tilton) Busiel. He received his education in the public schools of Laconia and at old Gilford academy, and after graduating he entered his father's hosiery mill and acquired a practical knowledge of the entire business by actual labor in each department. In 1863 he engaged in business on his own account, but within a few years sold his interest in the establishment which he had put into operation, and with a brother, in 1869, he entered into partnership and engaged in the manufacture of hosiery. Another brother joined the firm in 1872, and the name became J. W. Busiel & Co. This business is still continued and ranks as one of the most important industries in Laconia.

Ex-Governor Busiel is president of the Laconia National bank and also president of the City Savings bank. He has attained much prominence in railroad circles by his investments in this kind of property, by his success in organizing and constructing the Lake Shore railroad, and as one of the managing directors of the old Concord & Montreal railroad. In later years his attention has been given to electric roads which he believes are destined to supersede less advanced means of transportation, and to greatly assist in the progress and development of New Hampshire.

In politics Ex-Governor Busiel is an Independent, but has always supported the party which he believed represented the best interests of the people upon local, state, and national issues. He represented Laconia in the legislatures of 1878 and 1879; he was a delegate to the Democratic national convention in Cincinnati in 1880; as a Republican candidate he became the first mayor of the new city of Laconia, although at that time the city was strongly Democratic. He was reëlected mayor for a second term by a largely increased majority. In 1895 he was the Republican candidate for governor of New Hampshire, and was elected by one of the largest majorities ever received by any candidate in this state,— about 10,000 majority and 13,000 plurality. For the first time in history, every county in New Hampshire returned a Republican majority at this election. As governor of the state he advocated and even compelled retrenchments and reforms, which saved the treasury hundreds of thousands of dollars, and it was universally admitted by opponents

Ex-Governor Charles A. Busiel.

as well as friends, that Governor Busiel was one of the best governors who ever held the position of chief executive in this state. He was prominent as a candidate for United States senator in 1896, and was undoubtedly the choice of his state for a secretary's portfolio in President McKinley's cabinet.

Ex-Governor Busiel attends the Congregational church. He is very prominent in Masonic circles, as well as in the Knights of Pythias and other beneficial, social, and charitable organizations.

During his administration as governor he paid $200,000 of the state debt, and $75,000 to defray expenses left due by previous administrations. By his vetoes of the unnecessary measures passed by the legislature, Governor Busiel practically saved the state a million dollars, and when he retired from office he left in the state treasury, $590,706.07 according to the report of the state auditing committee.

In 1864 he married Eunice Elizabeth Preston, daughter of Worcester Preston. They have one daughter, Frances E. Busiel, who is the wife of Wilson Longstreth Smith of Germantown, Pa., and they have one son, Charles Albert Busiel Smith, born March 1, 1895.

John T. Busiel.

John T. Busiel, of the firm of J. W. Busiel & Co., woolen hosiery manufacturers, was the second son of John W. and Julia M. (Tilton) Busiel, born Oct.

Residence of Hon. Charles A. Busiel.

12, 1847, in that part of the old town of Gilford which was afterwards annexed to the town of Laconia, and now forms a part of the city. He was educated in the public schools, graduated at Phillips Exeter academy, class of '64, and at Harvard university, class of '68. Since completing his education, Mr. Busiel has been engaged in the hosiery industry in Laconia, as a member of the firm of J. W. Busiel & Co.

Mr. Busiel was a member of the New Hampshire legislature in 1883. He is president of the board of trustees of the Laconia public library; vice-president

John T. Busiel.

of the People's National bank; trustee of the Belknap Savings bank; and a director in the Winnipesaukee Gas & Electric Co.

He is active and aggressive in public matters pertaining to the welfare of Laconia, and he is one of the trustees and building committee under the will of the late N. B. Gale, to lay out public grounds for a park, and erect the Gale Memorial building for a public library and historical museum.

He married Nellie M., daughter of James E. and Sarah (Brock) Pinkham, July 6, 1870, and has one daughter, Helen J. Busiel.

Frank E. Busiel.

Frank E. Busiel, of the well-known concern of J. W. Busiel & Co., woolen hosiery manufacturers, is a native Laconian, born Oct. 31, 1852, the youngest son of the late John W. and Julia (Tilton) Busiel.

Frank E. Busiel was educated in the public schools of Laconia and at Gilford academy. His father was one of the pioneer hosiery manufacturers of this country, and after completing his education, Frank E. entered his father's factory to thoroughly learn the details of the industry. He worked several years as a second hand, and was then given charge of the knitting department of the factory, a position which he filled at the time of his father's death, in 1872. He was then admitted to partnership in the concern, which still continues in business under the firm name of J. W. Busiel & Co. Mr. Busiel is a natural mechanic, and assumes the oversight of the entire mechanical department of the business. In politics Mr. Busiel is a Republican, and while he has no ambi-

Residence of John T. Busiel.

tion for political honors, he consented to serve as a member of the Laconia police commission, and has been chairman since its organization, in April, 1895. Under his direction the police department of Laconia has been thoroughly reorgan-

Frank E. Busiel.

ized and put upon a model metropolitan basis, and it is generally admitted that the police department of the city is to-day one of the best, most efficient, and most economically sustained of any in New Hampshire. On Nov. 19, 1874, Mr. Busiel married Hattie A. Sanborn, and he has two children, Grace and Edith, both residing at home.

The Busiel & Co. Hosiery Mill.

The J. W. Busiel & Co. hosiery mill is the largest industry in this line in the city of Laconia, and was founded by the late John W. Busiel in 1846. Previous to coming to Laconia, then Meredith Bridge, Mr. Busiel was engaged in business as a woolen manufacturer at Meredith Village, carding woolen rolls for hand-spinning, and finishing the cloths which it was then the custom for farmers' wives to weave. He also began there the manufacture of satinet cloth and knitting yarn. When he first came to Laconia, he continued this business in the old Bean mill, which then stood upon the site of the present dye-house of the J. W. Busiel Co. During the great fire of the Strafford mill this old one-story wooden structure was partially burned, and in 1853 Mr. Busiel purchased the land and water-power formerly used by the Strafford company. On this site he erected the first of the buildings now used by J. W. Busiel & Co. He here added to his list of manufactures, Saxony and Germantown yarns. At the Crystal Palace exhibition in London, Mr. Busiel received a gold medal for the best mixture of cotton and woolen yarns.

The invention of the circular ribbed knitting machine by Jonas and Walter Aiken in 1856 led Mr. Busiel to introduce the manufacture of Shaker socks and underwear. At the beginning of the Civil War, the mill started upon the production of army socks, and after the close of the war, the manufacture of the different varieties of hosiery became the sole product of the mill, and in this line the J. W. Busiel hosiery mills have achieved a national reputation in knit goods circles. Since the death of John W. Busiel in 1872 the business has

Residence of Frank E. Busiel.

been continued and enlarged by the three sons, Charles A., John T., and Frank E. The Busiel mills are the most substantial and modern structures of the kind in this vicinity, are equipped with all the modern improvements and labor-saving devices, and employ the largest number of operatives when running at their full capacity. The firm has a long-established reputation with the trade throughout the country for manufacturing a superior quality of hosiery, and some of the specialties of this concern have been very popular with the public and profitable to the manufacturers.

Mass., to wind up the financial affairs of a dry goods house, and after remaining there one year came to Laconia in 1862, and became associated with Albert G. Folsom in the clothing and dry goods and millinery trade, carrying on two stores, under the firm name of Folsom & Smith. When the Folsom brick block was completed in February, 1863, the firm moved into the store now occupied by Patsey O'Shea and continued until 1869, when Mr. Folsom sold out

The Busiel Hosiery Mill.

Ex-Mayor Samuel B. Smith.

Although now retired from mercantile pursuits, in which he was active for many years, ex-Mayor Samuel B. Smith is still prominent in financial, political, and real estate circles in Laconia, and is one of the largest owners of rental property in the city.

He was born in West Newbury, Mass., May 11, 1837, and was educated in the public schools of that town and at Phillips Academy at Andover, Mass. After completing his education in 1855 he started to learn shoe manufacturing and worked five years as a cutter in this industry. He then went to Lawrence,

his interest to Mr. Smith, who continued the business alone. In 1875 he took Messrs. Frank and Oscar Lougee into partnership, and soon afterwards the firm occupied the entire first floor of the whole block, carrying clothing, dry goods, carpets, boots and shoes, millinery and custom tailoring. In 1884 Mr. Smith commenced to withdraw from mercantile business, selling a part of the establishment to Lougee Bros., and later other departments to W. D. Middleton, retaining the boot and shoe business for several years, but finally selling this branch to Messrs. Donovan & Stoughton.

Mr. Smith is a large real estate owner. Besides his handsome residence on Harvard street, he together with Mr. Folsom erected the substantial Smith block on Main street, built the five tenement block on Beacon street, remodeled the seven-tenement building on Hanover street, erected another large block for stores and tenements on Mill street, besides other work in the same line on a smaller scale.

Mr. Smith is a director in the People's National bank and a trustee in the Laconia Savings bank, being quite prominent in the management of both these institutions. He has been a large stockholder and a leader in the management of the Laconia Street railway most of the time since the road was constructed. It was largely through Mr. Smith's efforts that Laconia's admirable system of sewerage was constructed, and he served as chairman of the construction committee in this great public improvement. He is a director of the Winnipesaukee Gas and Electric Co., has been president of the Board of Trade, which was organized largely through his efforts, and he is also interested and active in numerous other local enterprises of a public nature.

One of the recent public improvements which ex-Mayor Smith has taken a leading part in promoting, is the laying-out and construction of the new boulevard from Lakeport to The Weirs.

Ex-Mayor Samuel B. Smith.

Largely through his efforts the city of Laconia was induced to build the highway and he also arranged the deal by which the electric road was extended over this boulevard, which will be the pride of the city for many years to come.

Mr. Smith has always been an active Republican, and represented Laconia in the legislature of 1888-'89. He was elected the second mayor of the city of Laconia, in 1895, and was re-elected in 1896, devoting his valuable knowledge of financial matters to public affairs during his two years of service, with good results. Mr. Smith married Ada, daughter of Hon. A. G. Folsom, and they have three children: Katherine Olive, wife of Harry S. Chase, James S., connected with the People's National bank, and Louise C., who resides with her parents on Harvard street.

The Late Stephen Perley.

The city of Laconia owes to the Perley family many of its important enterprises, and the late Stephen Perley was the father of the industrial life in this place. He was born in Ipswich, Mass., Oct. 7, 1770, a son of Allen Perley. The Perley family is said to have had its origin in Wales, and Allen Perley (first) came to Massachusetts from England in 1630, and settled in Ipswich.

Stephen Perley obtained his education in the public schools of Ipswich, and then worked for a time in a store in Salem, Mass. He came to Laconia when still a young man, and was one of the first settlers, and for many years was, perhaps, the most important citizen in town. At one time he owned most of the land on which the city stands to-day. He was a large farmer, raising some years six hundred bushels of corn. He managed a general store, which was the centre of trade, not only for the village, but for those in the shops, and which furnishes power, to-day, for a portion of the car industry. He was a man of great enterprise and foresight, and many of his plans have been adopted and carried out by the wise men of to-day.

Mr. Perley was a Jeffersonian Democrat, and quite active in politics. He was one of the electors for Van Buren, a representative in the state legislature, and was postmaster here for thirty years.

The late Stephen Perley.

entire farming country around. He had a number of sawmills, where he converted the lumber into marketable shape from the lands which he cleared. As the town increased, he established a nail factory, a starch factory, a cotton factory, and a linseed oil mill. The cotton mill was subsequently sold to Daniel Avery. Mr. Perley dug the present Perley canal, which connects the Winnipesaukee river, near Church street, with the same river near the car

He was a strong Universalist, and his house was always a home for ministers of his faith. He invited such men as Rev. Father Ballou of Boston, Rev. Messrs. Sebastian and Russel Streeter, to come to this place and preach, and in this way he was instrumental in forming what was for many years a strong and zealous Universalist society, which erected the church building on Union avenue now occupied by the Methodists.

Mr. Perley married twice. His first wife, Abigail, died young, leaving one daughter, Sarah, who married Dr. John Durkee of this place, a prominent physician at that time. His second marriage was with Mehitable, daughter of Colonel Samuel Ladd, who was one of the first settlers, and a prominent citizen of Gilmanton, now Belmont. He was a large landowner, and Ladd Hill was named for his family. Mrs. Mehitable Perley was a most worthy, charitable woman, and an exemplary wife and mother. She died October 25, 1834, aged fifty-one years and six months. Mr. Perley died April 13, 1855, at the ripe old age of eighty-four years and six months, leaving four children: John Langdon, Louisa, Abigail, and Martha Maria. A resident of the town for sixty years, he was a most essential factor in its growth and prosperity.

The late John L. Perley.

The Late John L. Perley.

One of the most prominent and best known men of Meredith Bridge and Laconia in its early days was Dr. John Langdon Perley, who was, in fact, one of the leading men in this part of New Hampshire in financial and political matters, in the early years of the present century.

He was born in Laconia, then Meredith Bridge, June 10, 1805, the son of Stephen and Mehitable (Ladd) Perley. His father was a very prominent man in the early history of this community, and the Ladd family, of which his mother was a member, figured extensively in the settlement and development of Laconia.

unsettled country, returned to Laconia with renewed interest in its welfare.

He was for many years extensively engaged in farming and the manufacture of lumber, owning a large extent of woodland in this section. At East Tilton he owned a sawmill, grist-mill, and valuable water privilege, but this property he finally sold.

Dr. Perley was much interested in banking, and was one of the incorpo-

The late Lieut. John L. Perley, Jr.

John L. Perley studied medicine with Dr. Durkee, one of the first practitioners at Meredith Bridge, and graduated M. D. from Bowdoin college, Brunswick, Me., in 1829. He engaged in the practice of his profession until about forty years of age, and then retired to give more attention to other matters in which he became interested. He went West in 1837, but after spending some time in that then lawless and rators of the Meredith Bridge Savings bank, a member of its board of trustees, and its president for some time. He was also one of the incorporators of the Belknap Savings bank, and its president until about ten years previous to his death, when he resigned.

He was a member of the old Whig party, and was appointed postmaster of Meredith Bridge during President John Quincy Adams's administration in 1829.

He was appointed by Gov. Benjamin Pierce, surgeon of the Twenty-ninth regiment of New Hampshire militia, in 1829. In 1834 he was elected to the state legislature, and distinguished himself as a champion of the people's rights. He introduced and secured the passage of the bill reducing the salary of the governor of New Hampshire from two thousand to one thousand dollars, on the ground that the honor of being governor of the state should satisfy the chief executive, and that the salary should be merely nominal.

He was twice married, first to Mary A. Eastman, of Franklin, N. H. His second wife was Dora P. Randlett, of Gilmanton, N. H., and this union was blessed with five children: John L. Perley, Jr., who died from the exposure of his military service in 1862; D. Augusta Perley, wife of Jacob Sanborn; Mary A. Perley, who married Josiah T. Sturtevant; Lewis S. Perley, who resides upon the ancestral farm to-day; and Clara E. Perley, who married Dr. A. L. Norris, and resides at Cambridgeport, Mass.

Dr. Perley was one of the strong men of early Laconia, a man of excellent judgment, strict integrity, and much financial sagacity.

Lewis S. Perley.

The Late Lieut. John L. Perley, Jr.

The late Lieutenant John L. Perley, Jr., in whose honor the Laconia Post of the Grand Army of the Republic is named, was a native of Laconia, born at Meredith Bridge, Dec. 10, 1839, the eldest son of John L. and Dora (Randlett) Perley. He was educated in the public schools of this town, and completed his education at Gilford academy, New Hampton Institution and the Lawrence Scientific school, Cambridge, Mass.

After completing his education, he commenced to study law, with the intention of adopting this profession in life, but on the breaking out of the Civil War, he laid aside his books and enlisted, August, 1861, in Troop M, New England cavalry, and the following November was promoted to the rank of second lieutenant. He was taken ill in May, 1862, and returned home, and died shortly after from the effects of exposure during his military service, at the age of twenty-two years.

Lewis S. Perley.

Lewis S. Perley, son of the late John L. Perley and Dora (Randlett) Perley, was born in Laconia, August 22, 1845. He was educated in the public schools in this town, and then attended Gilford academy, afterwards taking a course of special study in Boston, and completed his educational training at Professor Hyatt's academy in Pennsylvania. Mr. Perley is a civil engineer by profession, but has devoted much of his time to managing the large Perley farm, and also engages quite extensively in lumbering and clearing wood lots. He is a Republican in politics, and a liberal in religion. He is a member of Winnipiseogee lodge, No. 7, I. O. O. F. At the present time, Mr. Perley is a member of the Laconia board of city assessors, elected by the city council in March of the present year.

In 1888 he was united in marriage with Clara L. Knowlton of Meredith. They have two children, Lew K., and Marion Louise.

Charles F. Richards.

Charles Francis Richards, member of the Laconia city council from Ward 2, was born in Lebanon, Me., Nov. 11, 1850. He was educated in his native town, and in Rochester, N. H. In 1879, he started in the planing mill and box business with his brother, Geo. O. Richards, at East Rochester. Mr. Richards came to Laconia in April, 1883, and has been employed in the several wood-working establishments, and also as a contractor and builder.

He held the office of trial justice in York county, Maine, from 1879 to 1883. He served as selectman in Ward 2 of Laconia, and was elected to the city council in 1896, and

Charles F. Richards.

Residence of Charles F. Richards.

reëelected in 1898, being a member of the present city government.

Mr. Richards is a member of Cocheco lodge, Independent Order of Odd Fellows, and also of Laconia encampment, I. O. O. F. He is also a member of the Ancient Order of United Workmen, and a director of the Laconia Building and Loan Association.

Mr. Richards married Etta Maria Morton, of South Norridgewock, Me., June 1, 1881, and they reside in their comfortable and handsome home on Gilford avenue. Mr. Richards is an attendant at the Congregational church, and one of the reliable citizens of his adopted city.

published poems have been widely copied and circulated. He is a good French scholar, and speaks, reads, and writes that language with ease and fluency. He is a Democrat in politics, was county solicitor from 1891 to 1893, and was chairman of the Democratic city committee, this city, in 1896-'97. He is a charter member of Winnesquam colony, No. 14, U. O. P. F., and a member of Pontahum tribe, No. 18, Red Men, of Laconia. Besides a father and brother already mentioned, Mr. Peaslee has one sister, Mrs. Jennie C. Johnson, formerly of Lakeport, who now resides in Lowell, Mass.

W. S. Peaslee.

Walter S. Peaslee was born in Wilmot, N. H., Nov. 14, 1854. His parents were Geo. W. and Caroline T. (Burbank) Peaslee. He received his education in the public schools of this state and at Colby academy, New London, and at the Symonds High school, Wolfeborough, where his father and one brother, Eugene L. Peaslee, now reside. He taught in the public schools of this county for five years, and was for two years teacher of the old South Grammar school, in this city. He studied law with Col. Thomas J. Whipple, was admitted to the bar at the July law term, 1885, and has since practised his profession in Laconia. He has found time to cultivate the literary side of his profession to some extent, and many of his

Walter S. Peaslee.

The Late Joseph S. Tilton.

The late Joseph Sullivan Tilton, one of the pioneers of the hosiery industry in this city, was a native of London, N. H., born on June 13, 1818, the son of Stephen and Julia (Bachelder) Tilton. His parents removed to Meredith, where the early years of his life were passed, mostly on the farm. His education was acquired in the public schools, and was very thorough. Mr. Tilton was one of the early pioneers of California, moving there with his family soon after the discovery of gold. He located in San Francisco, and followed the business of a dairyman, also taking an active part in the politics of the rapidly-growing city. During the troubles with the turbulent and law-breaking element, Mr. Tilton was an officer of the famous Vigilants, and saw much service in those days of riot and trouble. In 1857 he returned to New Hampshire, and, locating in Laconia, commenced the manufacture of hosiery in 1859, in a mill which stood where now stands the dye-house of J. W. Busiel & Co. In 1862 Mr. Tilton suspended business at his mill to assist in raising the Twelfth regiment of New Hampshire Volunteers for the Civil War, and he went into the service as first lieutenant risen to high command, for he had, in an eminent degree, the dash and courage which go far to make the successful soldier. His record in the army was above reproach, courageous, and unflinching to a fault. In camp, or on the battlefield, he was ever the same bright, active, intelligent soldier,—one to whom his men could always look with strong confidence, and from whom they always received kind and just treatment. Lieutenant Tilton was one

The late Joseph S. Tilton.

of the Laconia company. At the battle of Chancellorsville, while in command of his company, he was badly wounded. For some time after receiving his wound he remained with his command, but loss of blood finally obliged him to leave the field. After a season in the hospital, he was returned to New Hampshire, and finally was obliged to resign on account of disability. But for the unfortunate wound at Chancellorsville, Lieutenant Tilton must have of the original members of John L. Perley, Jr., post, G. A. R., of this city.

When his health was sufficiently recovered, Mr. Tilton again resumed the hosiery business, retiring in 1877, and he died, Nov. 6, 1879, at the age of sixty-one years. He was of a warm-hearted and kind, though impulsive and impetuous, nature, and was a man of most profound and sincere convictions. He was frank and outspoken in his opinions on all subjects, and when once his mind was made up was never slow to act.

Mr. Tilton married Betsey Ham, Feb. 5, 1842, and they had four children: George Henry, Frank S., Emma Susan, who married Horace W. Gorrell, and died, April 20, 1890, and Nancy A., who married C. W. Gilman, of Emporia, Kan.

George Henry Tilton.

George Henry Tilton, the well-known hosiery manufacturer of Laconia, was born in Dorchester, N. H., May 13, 1845, son of Joseph Sullivan and Betsey (Ham) Tilton. His early life was passed in California, returning with his parents to New Hampshire in 1857. Mr. Tilton was educated in the public schools and at Gilford academy.

When the Civil War broke out, in 1861, young Tilton enlisted Sept. 14, in the Laconia company (Company D), of the Fourth New Hampshire Regiment of Volunteers, and served for three years.

In the employ of his father, he learned the details of the hosiery manufacturing industry, which business he, for many years, carried on in Laconia. In 1891 he purchased the mills known as the Jeremiah Tilton mills at Tilton, which he with his son, Elmer S. Tilton, are running at the present time very successfully, producing hosiery in large quantities, and employing several hundred hands. Mr. Tilton also has large manufacturing interests in the South.

Within a few weeks Mr. Tilton has leased the large brick mill on Mill street in Laconia, owned by the Belknap Mills corporation, and has purchased most of the hosiery machinery formerly owned and operated by the Hodgson & Holt Manufacturing Co. This industry was originally equipped at an expense of about $75,000, and the mill has a capacity of six hundred dozen hosiery per

George Henry Tilton.

day, employing nearly two hundred operatives. When purchased by Mr. Tilton this industry had been suspended for several months, but under his management operations were at once resumed, and the mill is now run in connection with the mills at Tilton and in the South. As this hosiery industry is one of the largest in the city, the resumption of business under Mr. Tilton's management is a matter of no little importance to the welfare of Laconia.

Although of late years, until recently, devoting most of his time to the hosiery business at Tilton and in the South, Mr. Tilton has retained his residence in Laconia.

He is still a resident of Laconia, never having lost his interest in this town, which has been his home for more than forty years, and which he represented in the legislature in 1891 and 1892.

Mr. Tilton is a member of the New Hampshire Society of Colonial Wars, of John L. Perley, Jr., post, No. 37, G. A. R., of the New England Society of California Pioneers, and of the Masonic fraternities, as follows: Mt. Lebanon lodge, A. F. & A. M., Union chapter, Pythagorean council, and Pilgrim Commandery, K. T., also a thirty-second degree Mason, being a member of Edward A. Raymond Consistory of Nashua, N. H.

He was married at Laconia, June 19, 1866, to Marietta, daughter of Osgood and Mary (Lamprey) Randlett of Upper Gilmanton, now Belmont, who died August 15, 1874, leaving one son, Elmer S. Tilton. He married the second time, April 11, 1883, in Columbia, S. C., Calista E. Brown, daughter of David and Hannah (Fox) Brown of Sanbornton.

Elmer S. Tilton.

Elmer Stephen Tilton, who is associated with his father in the manufacture of hosiery in Tilton, is a native Laconian, born Oct. 11, 1869, the son of George Henry and Marietta (Randlett)Tilton. He was educated in the public schools of this city, and graduated from the Laconia High school in the class of '87. Although engaged in the management of the hosiery industry in Tilton, he resides in Laconia. In politics Mr. Tilton affiliates with the Republicans, and he represented Ward 3 in the New Hampshire legislature during 1897-'98.

Elmer S. Tilton.

In 1892 he was united in marriage with Lillian G., daughter of E. B. Harrington of Laconia. Mr. and Mrs. Tilton have two sons: Charles Henry and Elmer Harrington.

Fraternally, Mr. Tilton is a member of the various Masonic fraternities, and of Mt. Belknap lodge, No. 20, Knights of Pythias. He is a past master of Mt. Lebanon lodge, No. 32, A. F. and A. M., and eminent commander of Pilgrim commandery, Knights Templar. Mr. Tilton is a thirty-second degree Mason, being a member of Edward A.

Raymond Consistory of Nashua, N. H., and also a member of Aleppo Temple, Mystic Shrine, of Boston, Mass.

Harry S. Chase.

Harry Sumner Chase was born in New Hampton, N. H., July 17, 1859, son of John B. and Sarah A. (Marston) Chase. He received his education in the public schools and at New Hampton Literary Institution, where he graduated in the commercial course in the class of '82.

Mr. Chase came to Laconia when about twenty-four years old, and entered the employ of O'Shea Brothers, as clerk, remaining with this firm about three years. He then

Harry S. Chase.

then entered his present position as traveling salesman for Wise & Cooper, of Auburn, Me., shoe manufacturers, covering the principal cities in New England for this concern.

Mr. Chase was married in 1895 to Miss Katherine Olive Smith, daughter of Samuel B. and Ada (Folsom) Smith. They have a little daughter, Olive Louise, born April 22, 1899. Mr. Chase located here for a permanent residence in 1895, and resides in an elegant home on Harvard street.

Mr. Chase is an attendant at the Congregational church. He is a Democrat, and in secret orders he is a member of Mt. Lebanon lodge,

Residence of Harry S. Chase.

went to Boston, where he had charge of a shoe store for about three years, and

A. F. & A. M., Union chapter, and of Pilgrim Commandery, Knights Templar,

Lougee Brothers.

Almost from the date of the building of the old Province road from Portsmouth to Canada over a century ago, first Meredith Bridge and then Laconia has been recognized as a trading centre for nearly all the necessities of life. That the city on the lakes is an important trade centre to-day is amply demonstrated by the fact that it boasts of several mercantile establishments which are among the largest in their line in New Hampshire. During the past twenty years no retail establishment in the Granite state has had a wider reputation than the dry goods, clothing, carpet, and furniture store of Lougee Bros., of Laconia. Although a comparatively young concern, the firm of Lougee Bros. has always done an immense amount of business, and has handled many thousands of dollars worth of goods every year.

The firm started in the store in Folsom block, now occupied by Baker Shannon, in 1877. This store was perhaps one-tenth the size of their present establishment in Smith block. Frank H. and Oscar A. Lougee were at that time the junior members of the firm of Smith, Lougee Bros. & Co. This firm was dissolved in 1885.

Taking in Orman T. Lougee as a partner at this time, the firm of Lougee Bros. was formed, and they at first confined their business to their original quarters, where the bakery now is. Their business increased very rapidly, and the necessity of larger and more convenient quarters was soon apparent. In 1886 the Smith brick block was built, and Lougee Bros. moved into what is now their dry goods department. The rapid increase of their business and enlarging of their stock in trade is shown by the fact that they now occupy the entire first floor and basement of the Smith block, besides a large two-story wooden addition in the rear of the Smith block and connected therewith, giving them nearly thirty thousand square feet of floor space, or about ten times the space required in 1886.

At first the firm carried only dry goods and carpets, but from time to time other departments have been added to meet the public demands, and to-day the concern handles dry and fancy goods, garments, ready-made clothing, carpets, furniture, stoves, bicycles, curtains and window shades, boots and shoes, men's furnishings, underwear of all kinds, and, in fact, everything which can be found in a large department store in any of the large cities of the United States.

The firm of Lougee Bros. is a progressive one, as their success indicates. They were the first to put in a pneumatic cash carrier, and they have always been liberal advertisers, not only in this city but throughout the entire northern portion of New Hampshire, in their efforts to draw trade to Laconia.

The Lougee Bros. personally are influential and public-spirited citizens. They are not only promptly interested, but always ready to assist by contributing their time and money to any attempt to locate new industries, or to inaugurate any movement to help build up Laconia. They are shrewd buyers, upright and honorable merchants, and they hold the strict confidence of the entire community. Their establishment furnishes employment to a large number of clerks, and by purchasing their goods in large quantities they are enabled to retail their stock at lower prices than can be obtained in many of the larger cities of New England, — a fact which is generally admitted by those in a position to know, and a fact which frequently causes surprise to summer visitors who come here from Boston and New York, and are astonished to find that they can purchase dry goods and other wares in this line fully as cheaply here "in the country" as they can at home.

Frank H. Lougee, the senior member of Lougee Bros., was educated in the public schools, supplemented by a few terms at Gilford academy and one term at Tilton seminary. He was employed for a year with White Mountain Ice Cream Freezer Co., but in 1870 he entered the employ of S. B. Smith to learn the dry goods, clothing, and carpet business, and has continued successfully in this line from that date, with the exception of about two years, when he took a commercial course at Comer's Commercial college, at Boston, and was salesman at Jordan, Marsh & Co.'s for about a year and a half.

Since 1890 Mr. Lougee has given much attention not only to the Laconia store but to the Lougee Bros. & Smythe store, which was opened at St. Johnsbury, Vt., and has also proved very successful.

In public life Mr. Lougee has served as president of the Laconia board of trade for one or two years, and was also a member of the board of education for two years. He is a director in the People's National bank and a trustee in the Laconia Savings bank. He has always been especially prominent in the board of trade, and has taken an active part in every effort of this organization to promote the welfare of the city.

Oscar A. Lougee has devoted himself more closely to the business of the establishment,

but found time to serve a term as a member of the Laconia city council, where he proved himself a valuable member, and just the kind of citizen who is needed in such a body.

Hotel Picard.

Hotel Picard is the new name of the well known hostelry on Pleasant street, for many years known as the Kirtland House, and more recently as the Victoria Hotel. The entire establishment has been thoroughly repaired, remodeled, and newly furnished by the new proprietor, Mr. George Picard, and is now as neat, clean, handsome, and comfortable as could be desired. The location of Hotel Picard, at 28 Pleasant street, makes this hotel very desirable, as it is convenient to the business portion of the city, and close by the railroad station, the telegraph and the telephone offices, electric cars, etc. Under the management of Landlord Picard the guests will be sure of excellent food, comfortable beds, and all the conveniences of a first-class hotel.

George Picard, the landlord and proprietor of Hotel Picard, was born at

Frank H. Lougee.

Residence of Frank H. Lougee.

St. Charles, P. Q., Aug. 20, 1860. He was educated in the common schools, and was in Quebec for five years. He came to Laconia in 1880, and was employed in some of our hosiery mills for three years, and then engaged in the confectionery and cigar business on Mill street. Later he added diningrooms to the business, and has been very successful as caterer. In 1897 Mr. Picard removed his business to 159 Main street.

He was married in 1883 to Miss Emma Morin, and they have three children. In secret fraternities Mr. Picard is a member of the Catholic Order of Foresters, and also of the Foresters of America and the Improved Order of Red Men. He is an attendant at Church of the Sacred Heart, and a member of the Society St. Jean the Baptiste.

place in his early manhood in 1830, entering into the employ of the Gilford Manufacturing and Mechanic Company, at their store, then known as the " Company Store," but now called the " Old Corner Store," situated on the corner of Main and Court streets.

The Gilford Manufacturing and Mechanic Co., chartered in 1828, owned all of the water power on the south, or Gilford, side of the river, and were then operating a sawmill and a grist-mill, located near the dam, about where the

Hotel Picard.

Hodgson machine shop now stands. They afterwards built a new grist-mill and a machine shop further down the river. They contemplated the erection of a mill for the manufacture of cloth, and recognizing in Mr. Melcher business qualifications which they believed would be of advantage to them in their future operations, the proprietors proposed to him to take an interest with them, and become their managing agent. He accepted the proposition, and thus became associated with some of the leading men of the growing village. Amos Smith,

The Late Woodbury Melcher.

The history of "Meredith Bridge" would be incomplete without mention of Woodbury Melcher. He came to the

Charles Morgan, Alvah Tucker, Thomas Babb, James Mollineaux, Stephen K. Baldwin, and John T. Coffin, his associates, are names which are still familiar to the older citizens of Laconia. The mill was built, and is the same now owned and operated by the Pitman Manufacturing Co. The company engaged in the manufacture of tickings, making a superior grade of goods, which became almost world-renowned, a considerable part of the production being exported. This company had a long, honorable, and successful career. As one and another of the owners, for various reasons, disposed of their stock, Mr. Melcher was always ready to buy, until at last he became owner of the entire property. He built the brick building now known as the Gilford Hosiery Co. mill. It being completed about the time the Civil War broke out, with characteristic foresight he determined to go into the manufacture of army goods. The mill was speedily equipped with hosiery machinery, and during the whole war it was run almost constantly, day and night, in the manufacture of hosiery for the soldiers. This was the beginning of the hosiery industry in Laconia.

He was for many years a trustee of the Meredith Bridge Savings bank, now the Laconia Savings bank, and at the time of his death was its president. He was an earnest advocate and worker in connection with the building of the Boston, Concord & Montreal railroad, and for a while connected with its management. He was always adverse to holding public office, and save the representing of his town in the legislature for two years and the accepting of an appointment as a trustee of the asylum for the insane, he declined to contest for political honors. He died Nov. 10, 1870, lamented by the entire community.

Woodbury L. Melcher.

The late Woodbury Melcher.

Woodbury L. Melcher was born Oct. 7, 1832, in the house on Main street next below the "old corner store," and has always resided within almost a stone's throw of the place of his birth. He was fitted for college at Gilford academy, which was then in a very flourishing condition under the instruction of Prof. Benj. F. Stanton, and was graduated from Bowdoin college in 1856. After teaching elsewhere a short time, he was elected the principal of Gilford academy, where he taught for two years. But not intending to make teaching a profession, he entered as a student the law-office of Hon. E. A. Hibbard, and was admitted to the bar in 1862. Mr. Melcher still retains his connection with the Belknap County bar, although not now in active practice. In 1861 he was appointed register of probate and held the office for ten years, when he felt compelled to resign on account of the pressure of other business. In 1864 he was elected treasurer of the Laconia Savings bank, which position he held for twenty-one years, when, feeling the necessity for a more active, outdoor life, he resigned. He then engaged extensively in the insurance business and was the founder of the Melcher & Prescott Agency, now one of the largest insurance agencies in the state. He did not, however, give up his interest in the savings bank. Being elected one of its trustees, he has been intimately connected with its management ever since. For a few years he was a director and vice-president of the Laconia National bank. He was a member of the constitutional convention of 1889.

Mr. Melcher has always been interested in promoting the material interests of Laconia. He drew the original charter for the street railway and assisted in procuring its passage through the legislature. He aided materially in procuring subscriptions for stock, and was the first treasurer of the corporation. In these days of electrics it is interesting to note some of the rebuffs he met with, being laughed at for being so sanguine, and told that "the income would not pay for the oats which the horses would eat," "the rails would rust out before they would wear out," and many other similar remarks. He was also largely interested in establishing the Laconia water-works, another enterprise which was looked upon by many as a doubtful investment. He, however, showed his faith in it by a larger subscription to its stock than that of any other individual. He became one of the first board of directors, and since the death of the Hon. John C. Moulton has been its president. He was interested in organizing the Laconia Hospital Association, and was elected its first president, which position he still holds. For a long series of years Mr. Melcher was connected in an official capacity with the public schools, being a member of the school committee when his district was annexed to Laconia, and a member of its board of education afterwards, until, feeling that he had done his whole duty in this respect, he declined further service. For eleven years he was president of the board of education.

Although recently circumstances have compelled him to be away from home during a considerable portion of each year, he is still proud of his birthplace and deeply interested in everything tending to its progress.

Woodbury L. Melcher.

The Late Rev. A. D. Smith.

The late Rev. Alpheus D. Smith, who died at Canterbury, N. H., Feb. 9, 1886, was pastor of the Free Baptist church in Laconia from July, 1857, to the spring of 1873, and was one of the most forcible preachers and strongest Christian characters who ever officiated in this city.

He was born in Lebanon, N. H.,

Aug. 25, 1813, but was brought up in Vermont, where he was "bound out" until he was twenty-one. He became converted at the age of seventeen, and felt called to hold meetings and preach.

The late Rev. A. D. Smith.

As soon as he was of legal age to act for himself he became an itinerant preacher, and traveled nearly all over the state of Vermont, visited various towns in Maine and New Hampshire, holding revival services and meeting with great success. On the second Sunday in July, 1857, he commenced his labors in Laconia at the Free Baptist church, and remained here four years, gathered a large congregation, and saw a glorious work of grace. He then went to East Tilton and did excellent work there, and came back to Laconia at the end of three years, remaining here until 1873. He died at Canterbury, Feb. 9, 1886, in the seventy-third year of his life.

Rev. Mr. Smith's preaching was largely emotional, intensely interesting and convicting, thoroughly evangelical. Few men saw so great immediate results of labor as he did, and many will rise up and call him blessed.

He was twice married, his first wife who died Oct. 10, 1872, being Emily B. True of Corinth, Vt. Jan. 14, 1874, he married Mary E. Clough of Canterbury. He is survived by one daughter, Mrs. Josie Sanders of Laconia.

The Late Samuel W. Sanders.

The late Samuel W. Sanders was one of the marked characters of Laconia, so few of whom now remain, one of the sturdy, wide-awake, pushing citizens of the old times, who believed in Laconia and worked for the advancement and prosperity of the town in every way.

He was a native of Mason, N. H., and learned the tinsmith trade. He came here in 1841 and embarked in business with no capital, but built up a successful business, and at the time of his retirement from trade, about six years before his death, was one of the oldest merchants on the street. His establishment was burned in 1846, and again in the big fire of 1860, and the present Sanders brick block on Main street was erected by the subject of this sketch after the last conflagration.

The late Samuel W. Sanders.

He was an ardent Republican, took an active part in the setting off of Laconia from Meredith, and was one of the first selectmen of the new town. He was twice married. His first wife was Serena Ranlet, who died in 1871. His second wife, Mrs. Josephine E.

Prescott, daughter of the late Rev. A. D. Smith, survives, together with two sons, J. Warren, of St. Louis, and Charles F., of San Francisco. Another son, the late Col. George A. Sanders, died in 1898.

Mr. Sanders died Jan. 16, 1892, and his death removed a good and valuable citizen, one of the solid, substantial men of the town.

Hampshire. Mr. Tilton was a leader in financial circles in Laconia, was vice-president of the People's National bank, and a trustee of the Belknap Savings bank, besides holding numerous other positions of trust and taking an active interest in nearly all the public enterprises which tended to improve and build up Laconia. In secret orders he was a Mason, and he was also a mem-

The late James H. Tilton.

The Late James H. Tilton.

The late James H. Tilton was for half a century engaged in mercantile life in Laconia, first as a clerk, and then for many years as proprietor of the Old Corner Store on Main street. Mr. Tilton entered this store as clerk for H. J. French, and from a boy he worked up to clerk and assumed control of the business in 1859. He largely increased the business and was for many years one of the most successful merchants in this section of New

ber of the board of trade. Mr. Tilton did considerable to beautify Laconia by improving his real estate and erecting one of the finest residences in the city. Mr. Tilton was a native of Sanbornton Bridge, N. H., born April 1, 1828, and died in Laconia, March 15, 1894.

Rebecca Weeks Wiley, M. D.

It was in the dreamy old town of Gilford, in a large two-story house, a typical New Hampshire home of the better sort, that she of whom we write first opened her eyes upon the light of this world. The ancestral lines through which she is able to trace her kindred stretch back through families distinguished for education, patriotism, and statesmanship. These include Horace Greeley and Daniel Webster. She was named for her great-grandmother, Rebecca Webster, who was a cousin of Daniel Webster. For the sake of brevity and euphony, at marriage, she dropped the Webster, and has since been known as Rebecca Weeks Wiley.

Her immediate relations were characterized for quick discernment, executive ability, and sterling integrity. Her father, John Gale Weeks, was a successful manufacturer of hats and caps at the time of her birth. She was educated at Laconia academy, New Hampshire Female college, and Boston University School of Medicine, graduating from the latter with the class of '82.

Dr. Wiley at once began the practice of her profession at Laconia, being the first woman physician in the state north of Concord. Her reception by the people of Laconia was most cordial, and the circle of her friends and patrons has steadily widened. She has a large office and correspondence practice, in addition to regular outside work; all of which perfect health enables her to heartily enjoy.

Several of Dr. Wiley's ancestors and an older sister were successful physicians, and she has marked hereditary tendencies towards the profession. The dream of her youth was a prophecy of which the practice of medicine is a fulfilment, and she is an enthusiast in her profession. She has from the first been a close student, and is up to date in all that pertains to both medical science and practice.

Dr. Wiley is a member of the New Hampshire Homeopathic Medical society and the American Institute of Homeopathy. In church relations she is a Free Baptist. She is sympathetic and coöperative with her husband, the Rev. Frederick L. Wiley, in his literary and philanthropic pursuits. Their only son, Maurice G. Wiley, after a four years' course, was graduated from a medical college in '94, and is practising his profession in Boston.

Dr. Rebecca Weeks Wiley.

H. D. Cilley.

Harry D. Cilley, carbonater and wholesale dealer in malt liquors, is a native of that part of Gilmanton which is now Belmont, and was born on Oct. 7, 1857, the son of Joseph Plummer Cilley, a prominent citizen of that town. He was educated in the public schools of Concord, N. H., and came to Laconia about twenty years ago. He is a carbonater and manufacturer of light summer drinks, such as bottled soda, ginger ale, pear cider, and other liquid refreshments in this line, and is also a wholesale dealer in malt liquors. Mr. Cilley manufactures his beverages at No. 489 Main street, and has a well-established reputation for using the purest syrups and flavors, and manufacturing wholesome, healthful, and delicious summer drinks. He has built up an excellent business in this line, and there is a constant demand for his goods at all seasons of the year, and especially in the summer, during the hot weather, his establishment is driven to its full capacity.

In politics, Mr. Cilley affiliates with the Republicans, but should perhaps be classed as an independent, as he always acts and votes with that party which he considers to be advocating the best interests of the people.

He served as a deputy sheriff of Belknap county in 1891 and 1892, under Sheriff William P. Lang of Tilton.

In fraternal societies Mr. Cilley is a member of the Order of Elks at Manchester, N. H., and he is also a member of New Hampshire's historic military organization, the Amoskeag Veterans, the headquarters of which are at Manchester.

Mr. Cilley is an active member of the Belknap County Fish and Game league, and takes great interest in all matters pertaining to fishing and hunting. He has a comfortable and convenient summer home on the shores near the headwaters of Lake Winnesquam, and devotes most of his spare time to enjoyment out of doors with gun and rod.

Harry D. Cilley.

Residence of Harry D. Cilley.

Laconia Board of Trade.

During the past ten years the Laconia Board of Trade has been an important factor in dealing with many questions of town and municipal government, railroad matters, and the location of new industries. The board was first permanently organized May 27, 1889, as the Laconia and Lake Village Board of Trade. The first officers were: President, John C. Moulton; vice-presidents, Henry J. Odell and James H. Tilton; secretary and treasurer, Samuel B. Smith; directors, John T. Busiel, E. C. Lewis, Dennis O'Shea, H. B. Quimby, B. F. Drake, Dr. Henry Tucker, and H. H. Wood.

The present officers of the board are: President, D. O'Shea; vice-president, W. F. Knight; secretary, S. C. Frye; treasurer, Edmund Little; directors, Oscar A. Lougee, Frank P. Holt, S. B. Smith, James McGloughlin, and W. A. Plummer.

Edwin F. Burleigh.

Edwin F. Burleigh, chairman of the board of assessors of the city of Laconia, has been a prominent figure in mercantile and financial circles here for the past thirty years. He is a native of Sanbornton, N. H., born Jan. 24, 1841, son of James M. and Harriet G. (Kentfield) Burleigh. He was educated in the common schools, and at the old Woodman and Sanborn academy at Sanbornton square, and also attended the New Hampshire Conference Seminary at Sanbornton Bridge, now Tilton, N. H.

After completing his education, he remained on the home farm in Sanbornton for a few years, and came to Laconia in March, 1864. In 1865, he engaged in the boot and shoe business in the store in Burleigh's block, now occupied by McCarthy Bros.

He continued in business very successfully for about thirty years, always remaining at the same stand, where he retailed boots, shoes, hats, caps, and men's furnishing goods. He was a shrewd buyer, and handled reliable goods, which, perhaps, accounts for his success, and it is a fact, that, when he retired from the shoe business in 1892, he was the oldest merchant in the town in point of service, and had continued his trade without any change of firm or location for almost thirty years.

In 1894 Mr. Burleigh was elected a member of the board of city tax assessors, a position for which his excellent judgment and knowledge of business affairs and real estate admirably fitted him. He has served as chairman of the assessors since that time, and still holds the position. Since the retirement of the late Major N. B. Gale, Mr. Burleigh has served as president and trustee of the Belknap Savings bank, and he is a director in the People's National bank. He is also one of the executors of the will of the late Maj. Gale, and a trustee of the estate under the will; also a trustee and a member of the building committee for the city of Laconia to manage the Gale bequest, and erect the forthcoming Gale memorial building. He was one of the committee that erected the High school building in 1887.

Edwin F. Burleigh.

Mr. Burleigh married Clara Richardson of Reading, Mass., Dec. 23, 1867, and they have one son, Harry T. Burleigh, a law student in this city.

Vue De l'Eau Hotel.

The Vue De l'Eau Hotel, under the efficient management of H. H. Caldon, proprietor, is one of the ideal summer resorts in New Hampshire. The hotel is located on an eminence on the shores of Lake Winnesquam, is only three hours' ride from Boston, and is but a short distance from the end of the electric railroad system of Laconia, connecting with The Weirs and Lake Winnipesaukee. The Vue De l'Eau is most beautifully situated, commanding a magnificent view of Lake Winnesquam and the city of Laconia, with the Sandwich, Ossipee, and White Mountain ranges in the distance, and the Belknap mountains only a few miles away on the east. The hotel is connected with the outside world by long-distance telephone, and offers all the charm of country life, together with the facilities and conveniences of the city close at hand. Lake Winnesquam is a widely-known sportsmen's resort, these waters abounding with lake trout, salmon, bass, pickerel, and smaller fish. The lake is nine miles long, and from half a mile to two miles in width. A prominent writer and admirer of New England scenery says :

"The scenery of which it is a part is primitive and wonderfully attractive. Its shores rise abruptly in many parts to hills often of considerable height, these being usually well wooded, the forest growth coming down often to the water's edge. The shore winds inward and outward among these hills in graceful lines and curves, and all the scenes are of natural loveliness not to be described. This tortuous coastline multiplies little bays and inlets throughout the basin occupied by these waters, and affords a succession of scenes not often surpassed in beauty in any section in New England."

Central House.

The Central House, at No. 603 Main street, Laconia, is a first-class hotel, open all the year, and under the management of H. H. Caldon, proprietor. It is centrally located, near the railroad station, electric cars, and business portion of the city, and the hotel is

Vue De l'Eau Hotel.

equipped with every convenience, such as steam heat, electric lights, baths, etc. Rates are from $1 to $2 per day, and this hotel is very popular with commercial travelers, on account of its good service and excellent location.

Judge John G. Jewett.

For nearly half a century, Judge John G. Jewett has served the public in various positions of trust and honor, and he has been for many years one of the best known citizens in this section of Belknap county. He was a son of Smith and Statira (Glines) Jewett, born Sept.

4, 1829, in Laconia, then, of course, known as Meredith Bridge.

His grandfather, Samuel Jewett, was the first permanent settler in Laconia on the east side of the Winnipesaukee river, coming here in 1782, when the land was covered with heavy timber. He owned more than half of the land which now comprises Ward 5, and sold the water privilege and seven acres of land on the east side of the river for seven dollars. His first dwelling was near the present site of Judge Jewett's residence, and a part of the estate is still owned by the Jewett family. He was in the Battle of Bunker Hill, and served through the war.

John G. Jewett was the sixth child of his parents. He attended the public schools of Meredith Bridge and the Gilford academy, and after completing his education he taught school in this vicinity for ten years. In 1855 he went to South America as a goldhunter, returning in March, 1857.

He was employed for eight years in the Laconia car shops, and in 1876 was appointed judge of the Laconia police court, a position which he filled with dignity and justice for sixteen years. In 1891 he resigned, and was appointed postmaster by President Harrison. He resigned the postmastership in May, 1895, and since that time has been retired from public life. Besides these two positions mentioned, Judge Jewett has held numerous other offices, both town and county. He was register of probate for two years, was collector of taxes in 1859, was a selectman of Gilford for three years, and in 1863 was recruiting officer for that town. He was in the New Hampshire legislature in 1867 and 1868, was a member of the Laconia board of education for twelve years, and was superintendent of the school committee in Gilford back in 1858.

In December, 1855, he married Caroline E. Shannon, a native of Barnstead. They have three children: Stephen S., the well-known lawyer, John B., and Katie B.—all married.

Judge Jewett has been a Free Mason for over thirty years, having joined Mt. Lebanon lodge in 1864, and he is past master of the lodge. He is also a member and past officer of Union chapter, and belongs to Pilgrim Commandery, Knights Templar. In religious affairs he affiliates with the Congregationalists, and in politics he is a staunch Republican.

Judge John G. Jewett.

Col. Edwin C. Lewis.

As editor of the Laconia *Democrat* from June, 1878, to January, 1897, Col. Edwin C. Lewis has been an important factor in all phases of Laconia life. He came here from New Hampton, with no journalistic training and no knowledge of the newspaper business, but with an abundance of "horse sense," a good education, and the ability to write tersely and interestingly of current events and to indite editorials which compared favorably with those in newspapers of much greater pretensions. In fact, it has been frequently and truthfully said that for good English, good common sense, and good judgment, the editorials of Colonel Lewis were not excelled by any newspaper published in New Hampshire.

Edwin C. Lewis was born in New Hampton, N. H., Nov. 28, 1836, the son of Col. Rufus G. and Sally (Smith) Lewis. His father was for many years the prominent man of New Hampton, a large property owner and influential citizen, and was a leader in obtaining the charter for and establishing New Hampton Literary Institution. Edwin C. Lewis fitted for college at New Hampton Institution, and graduated at Harvard in the class of '59. He read law for a time in Lowell, Mass., but the sickness of his father called him home and caused him to abandon this profession. In 1878 he came to Laconia with Fred W. Sanborn and purchased the Laconia Democrat. The firm of Lewis & Sanborn was changed at the end of two years by the retirement of Mr. Sanborn, and the concern continued as Lewis, Vaughan & Co., with Charles W. Vaughan and Albert P. Brown as the junior partners, until Colonel Lewis disposed of his interest to Gov. C. A. Busiel in January, 1897. Politically Colonel Lewis is a Democrat. He served two terms as treasurer of Belknap county, was in Governor Tuttle's executive council in 1890 and 1891, was a member of the Laconia school board for some time, and was for many years a trustee and member of the executive committee of New Hampton Institution. Colonel Lewis is a member of the several Masonic fraternities in this city, including Pilgrim Commandery, Knights Templar. In 1890 Colonel Lewis married Eliza B., daughter of David and Sally (Wallace) Hilton of Sandwich, who died April 15, 1899.

Col. Edwin C. Lewis.

Postmaster F. L. Gilman.

Postmaster Frank L. Gilman is a Laconia boy, though born on the Gilford side of the river, and he has perhaps served the public in one capacity or another more than any other man of his years in the city. He was born Sept. 29, 1858, his parents being Lyman W. and Dorothy E. Gilman. His education was obtained in the public schools of Laconia, and he then entered the Laconia passenger depot as telegraph operator and ticket seller, holding these positions from 1876 to 1880. He went to Old Orchard beach in the summer of 1881, where he held a position as telegraph operator, and in October of the same year went to Boston, where he was employed in the

Western Union Telegraph company's office on State street, until July, 1882, when he resigned his position to return to Laconia and accept the assistant

Frank L. Gilman.

postmastership under Postmaster Perley Putnam. Mr. Gilman held the assistant postmastership during Mr. Putnam's term, and when Postmaster Nath'l Edgerly took the office in March, 1887, he continued as assistant until October of the same year. During the next year or two Mr. Gilman was collector for the *Laconia Democrat*, clerk for Geo. R. Leavitt in the wood and coal business, and agent for the Singer Manufacturing Co.

In the fall of 1888, Mr. Gilman was elected register of probate for Belknap county, which office he filled for two years, from July, 1889. In 1891, he was appointed assistant postmaster by Postmaster John G. Jewett, and held the place until Postmaster John O'Loughlin came into office in May, 1895, remaining with the latter until October, 1895.

He was elected tax collector of the city of Laconia in 1895 and again in 1896, acting as agent for the New York Life Insurance company at the same time. Mr. Gilman was appointed postmaster of Laconia by President McKinley, July 2, 1897, a position which he still holds to the general satisfaction of the patrons of the office, for in his long service of the public in the various positions he has held, Mr. Gilman has always been a popular official, courteous to all, and in short, an ideal public servant.

Mr. Gilman married Miss Ruth Barber of Lewiston, Maine, Dec. 31, 1881. She died April, 1883, leaving one son, R. Frank Gilman, a member of the Laconia High school, class of 1900. Mr. Gilman married Miss Emma Jones, of this city, June 16, 1896.

He is a member of Winnipiseogee lodge, a past chief patriarch of Laconia encampment, is at the present time lieutenant of Canton Osgood, No. 5, Patriarchs Militant, I. O. O. F. Mr. Gilman is also connected with the Laconia Lodge and Chapter of Masons. He has served as president and member of the board of managers of the First Free Baptist church of this city.

Residence of Frank L. Gilman.

Laconia Post-office.

The Laconia post-office is in every respect a model institution, and is the largest and best-equipped office in New Hampshire north of Concord. For many years the post-office was kept in drug stores, bookstores, etc., and then for about twenty years in old Post-office block, so called, near the river, in quarters which answered well enough for the times, but which finally proved inadequate. When the handsome Masonic temple was erected, in 1895, the most desirable quarters in the building were leased and fitted up in elegant and convenient shape for the handling of the United States mails, and for the accommodation of patrons of the office. It is equipped with all modern improvements, including a Bundy time recorder, fire and burglar proof safe, and stamping

1889; a native of Laconia, born March 31, 1867. Mrs. E. Gertrude Sanborn, appointed May, 1894; a native of Laconia, born July 16, 1870. Charles F. Shastany, appointed September, 1895; a native of Laconia, born Nov. 15, 1877.

The regular letter-carriers are: John M. Guay, appointed April 1, 1896; a native of Canada, born Sept. 20, 1861. Eben P. Merrill, appointed April 1, 1896; a native of Laconia, born July 10, 1863. Oliver F. Griffin, appointed Aug. 9, 1898; a native of Attleboro, Mass., born Dec. 12, 1858. Arthur F. Turner,

Laconia Post-Office.

machine. Frank L. Gilman, the present postmaster, was appointed by President McKinley, July 2, 1897, and was already admirably fitted by several years of subordinate service in this office for the more responsible position of postmaster.

The office was removed to the Masonic temple in September, 1895. The free delivery service was established April 1, 1896.

The present force of clerks in the post-office are as follows: Edward S. Cook, chief, appointed July, 1897; a native of Laconia, born May 6, 1864. Miss Belle V. Dixon, appointed March,

appointed April 1, 1896; a native of Chelsea, Mass., born Sept. 28, 1869.

The employés of the post-office are in the classified service, and the members of the Civil Service Examining Board (local) are: Edward S. Cook, chairman; Belle V. Dixon, secretary; and Arthur F. Turner.

The Late Col. Thomas J. Whipple.

The late Col. Thomas J. Whipple, who died Dec. 21, 1889, was perhaps the most noted citizen who has ever resided in Laconia, having a national reputation as a brave soldier—the hero of two wars—a brilliant lawyer, and a strong character, whose like we shall not look upon again.

Colonel Whipple was born in Wentworth, N. H., Jan. 30, 1816. His father was one of the noted men of his time. Young Whipple was educated at the academies in New Hampton, Bradford, Vt., and at the Norwich university, where he developed his early taste for military affairs. At the age of seventeen he had been aide-de-camp on the staff of General Cook of the New Hampshire militia, and he organized a company known as the Wentworth Phalanx, which had quite a brilliant reputation. He read law with Hon. Josiah Quincy of Rumney and Salmon Wires of Johnson, Vt., and commenced practice in his native town. He was one of the first to enlist in the Mexican War, was taken prisoner at Vera Cruz, afterwards exchanged, and made adjutant-general on the staff of General Lewis. Returning from Mexico he opened an office in Laconia in 1849, and was until his death one of the most prominent figures among the lawyers of New Hampshire. At the breaking out of the War of the Rebellion he served as lieutenant-colonel of the First New Hampshire regiment and as colonel of the Fourth regiment, resigning the latter March 18, 1862. Later he was prominent in raising the

The Late Col. Thomas J. Whipple.

famous Twelfth regiment, and was elected its colonel, but did not serve.

Although for years recognized as one of the trusted and foremost leaders of the Democratic party in New Hampshire, he filled but comparatively few offices. Almost any place in the gift of the party could have been his, but he steadily refused them all. He was assistant clerk and clerk of the house of representatives, secretary of the constitutional convention of 1850, and a member of the convention of 1876. He was once moderator of the old town of Laconia.

Colonel Whipple married Belinda Hadley of Wentworth, and he is survived by one granddaughter, Mrs. C. O. Downing of Laconia.

Colonel Whipple was a man of remarkable ability, a profound and original thinker, and a most effective orator. His manner and bearing, the erect form, the flashing eye, the resolute tones of his voice, and his personal magnetism, seemed like special gifts of his own. The place of this brilliant man is likely to remain forever unfilled.

Dr. John G. Quimby.

John Grant Quimby, physician at Lakeport, was born at Sandwich, N. H., April 8, 1862, son of Joseph H. and Nancy J. (Fogg) Quimby. He was educated at New Hampton Literary Institution, and Nichols Latin school, Lewiston, Me., from which he was graduated at the head of his class in June, 1885. He then became a student of Bowdoin university, medical department, and obtained the degree of M. D. on June 27, 1888.

He began the practice of his profession in July, 1888, at Lakeport, and has since been a resident of Ward 6, except the years 1892-'93 when he was at New Hampton, N. H. For several years he has been city physician, and holds that position at present. He is a member of the U. S. board of examining surgeons at Laconia, and a member of Laconia board of education.

He is a member of the New Hampshire Medical society, and Winnipesaukee Academy of Medicine; a Knight of Pythias, past chancellor of Endicott Rock lodge, and member of grand lodge of New Hampshire; a member of J. A. Greene company, U. R. K. of P.; a member of Mount Lebanon lodge, A. F. A. M; of Pilgrim commandery, and a thirty-second degree Mason.

In politics he is a Republican. He married May I. Davis on June 28, 1888. They have one child, Havene May Quimby.

Dr. John G. Quimby.

Laconia Street Railway.

The Laconia Street Railway, which now sends its handsome and comfortable electric street cars from the lower end of Laconia, almost at the Belmont line, through the heart of Laconia and Lakeport's business and residential streets, and thence along the shores of Lake Paugus over the magnificent boulevard just completed from Lakeport to The Weirs, was chartered in 1881 by the New Hampshire legislature as the Laconia and Lake Village Horse Railroad.

The grantees were Albert G. Folsom, J. P. Hutchinson, James H. Tilton, and Richard Gove. The capital stock was only $15,000, and the first car was run over the road August 18, 1882. Bela S. Keniston was the first superintendent, and the tracks extended only from the Willard hotel in Laconia to the steamboat wharves in Lakeport.

The road was always a successful institution, but for the past ten years there has been a public demand for

President H. L. Pierce.

electricity to replace the old-fashioned method of horses for motive power. Dr. Joseph C. Moore obtained control of the road in 1889, and planned to introduce electricity, but in 1896 the control came back into the hands of A. G. Folsom and his associates, who built and operated the road at first.

In the summer of 1898, a controlling interest in the corporation was purchased by Messrs. Harry L. Pierce and Charles T. Foster, of Leominster, and George H. Cook of Athol. These gentlemen at once proceeded to equip the system with electricity, and in September, 1898, the electric cars were running over the road, and the system was kept open for traffic during the winter, while in previous years, with the horse-motors, the track was usually abandoned at the first heavy fall of snow, and transportation furnished during the winter in cumbersome and inconvenient sleigh-barges.

In the spring of 1899. Messrs. Pierce, Foster, and Cook extended their tracks from Lakeport to The Weirs, a distance of about five miles, over one of the most beautiful routes for an electric ride to be found in New England. The tracks follow the shore of Lake Paugus very closely, and command a most beautiful view of water and mountain scenery over the entire route, while at The Weirs, the summer resort of central and northern New Hampshire, the system crosses the outlet of the famous Lake Winnipesaukee, and has its terminus near the camp-grounds of the New Hampshire Veterans' Association, and the Winnipesaukee Campmeeting Association (Methodists), where musical festivals, religious and social gatherings and reunions are held every week during the summer season.

Treasurer C. T. Foster.

Thus the little horse railroad has grown from a small system, merely connecting the business centres of two ends of the city, to an electric system which runs practically from Belmont on the south to Meredith on the north, through one of the most enterprising cities of New Hampshire, while the new extension affords an opportunity for a ride through the world-famous lake region of New Hampshire.

The motive power is supplied by an equipment of the latest pattern of gasolene engines, located at the car stables on Union avenue, and the road is supplied with modern and elegant cars, and everything to make the service first-class, and just what an electric road should be. Messrs. Pierce, Foster, and Cook are entitled to much credit for their enterprise in giving Laconia such a desirable service, and they certainly deserve the success with which their efforts seem likely to be rewarded.

The present officers of the road are: President, Harry L. Pierce; treasurer, Charles T. Foster; superintendent, Lewis S. Pierce; directors, H. L. Pierce, Charles T. Foster, Geo. H. Cook, S. B. Smith, A. G. Folsom, Edmund Little, Chas. F. Stone.

President H. L. Pierce, of the Laconia Street Railway, was born in Somerville, Mass., June 9, 1865, and entered the electric business in 1889, when he started in the manufacture of electric supplies at Leominster, Mass. In 1890 he formed the Pierce Construction Co., and has since built about two hundred miles of electric roads, from Bath, Me., to Austin, Tex. In 1887 he gave up the construction business to devote his entire attention to his several railways and his real estate interests, among

Superintendent L. S. Pierce.

which is the Fitchburg & Suburban of Leominster, Mass., and the Laconia Street Railway, in both of which concerns Mr. Pierce is president.

Charles T. Foster of Leominster,

Mass., was born in Canterbury, N. H., July 22, 1869. His father, Moses A. Foster, was a farmer and breeder of fine blooded horses. Mr. Foster's early education was acquired in the district schools at home. At sixteen years of age he entered Tilton seminary, from which he was graduated in 1889.

The following fall he was admitted to the Bryant & Stratton Business college in Boston, and at the completion of his course he was offered a position in the Leominster National bank at Leominster, which position he accepted, and held for four years, resigning to connect himself with the Whitney Reed Chair Company of that place. During the past few years he has been an active real estate dealer, and has been fortunate in purchasing unimproved land in advance of the rapid development of the city where he lives, and has built a great many new streets and houses in connection with his land improvement. He was one of the promoters of the Fitchburg & Suburban Street Railway, and at the present time is one of the managing directors and treasurer of that road. He is also one of the managing directors and treasurer of the Laconia Street Railway of Laconia, and has other railway interests where he is not an active officer.

At the present time he is a member of the Leominster board of selectmen, and previously one of the town auditors.

Superintendent L. S. Pierce was born August 4, 1863, and became connected with the electric railway business in 1887, at which time there were but two roads in operation. He was at that time electrician on the Belt line, in Lynn, Mass. The next year he become superintendent of overhead construction and electrician for the Pierce Construction Co. In the past ten years he has superintended the setting of poles, stringing of wires, etc., for twenty-two different lines of electric roads, on most of which he has been the first to start a car. Superintendent Pierce became connected with the Laconia Street Railway on August 1, 1898.

Bayshore, Residence of William C. Marshall.

Hon. E. A. Hibbard.

Hon. Ellery A. Hibbard.

Hon. Ellery A. Hibbard, senior member and president of the Belknap County Bar Association, is one of the most widely known of Laconia's legal fraternity. He was born in St. Johnsbury, Vt., July 31, 1826, and was admitted to the bar in Plymouth, N. H., in July, 1849. In January, 1853, he came to Laconia, and in course of time won a place as one of the ablest and most successful lawyers in New Hampshire. He was appointed judge of the supreme court in March, 1873, but retired after being on the bench a little over one year. In politics Judge Hibbard has always been a firm and consistent Democrat. He served Laconia as moderator from 1862 to 1873 inclusive, has been assistant clerk and clerk of the legislature, represented the town twice in the general court, and was a member of the forty-second United States house of representatives. Judge Hibbard was a member of the original board of directors of the Laconia National bank, and still retains his connection with that institution; he is a trustee of the Laconia Savings bank, and has been prominent in numerous local enterprises, besides holding many other positions of trust and honor.

December 5, 1853, he married Mary, daughter of Jacob Bell of Haverhill, N. H., and they have had four children: Charles B., his father's law partner; Jennie Olive, wife of Orman T. Lougee; Walter, who died at the age of seven; and Laura B., who resides with her parents.

The Late Hon. Warren Lovell.

Quarter of a century ago the late Hon. Warren Lovell was one of the leading citizens of Laconia, and a man who was largely in public life. He was a native of Rockingham, Vt., born Dec. 3, 1802, and died Aug. 18, 1875. He read law at Bellows Falls, Vt., with Judge Kellogg, and was a student in the same office with the late Chief Jus-

The Late Hon. Warren Lovell.

tice Bellows. Admitted to the bar, he came to Meredith, N. H., in 1825, where he remained in practice until 1843, at which time he changed his residence to Laconia. He was several times elected representative from Meredith, was state senator from this district two years, and was solicitor and afterwards judge of probate for Strafford county. When Belknap county was set off from Strafford county, Judge Lovell was appointed judge of probate and held the office until he attained the age of seventy, and thereby became disqualified. He was quite prominent in local financial circles and was president of the Belknap County bank from its organization until it closed up its business.

Dr. John Alson Wrisley.

Among the skilful physicians for which Laconia has always been, and still is, noted, is Dr. John Alson Wrisley, who at the present time is the only homeopathic physician at the Lakeport end of the city.

Dr. Wrisley was born in Stafford Springs, Conn., son of John J. and Melissa S. (Franklin) Wrisley. He was educated in the common schools, supplemented by courses at Tilton seminary, and Fort Edward institute, of New York. His professional studies were commenced with Dr. W. E. Keith, of Franklin Falls, N. H., after which he took his first course of lectures at Boston University Medical school, and then a two years' course of lectures at Hahnemann college, of Philadelphia, where he graduated M. D. in 1881. Dr. Wrisley remained in hospital practice in Philadelphia for one year, and came to Laconia in August, 1894, purchasing the practice of Dr. Geo. F. Roby.

Dr. Wrisley is a member of the American Institute of Homeopathy, the New Hampshire Homeopathic Medical society, Winnipesaukee Academy of Medicine, and an honorary member of the Homeopathic Medical society of Philadelphia.

Dr. Wrisley has been very successful in his practice in Laconia and vicinity, and has been favored with the liberal clientage which his success has merited.

Dr. John A. Wrisley.

The Late Jonathan L. Moore.

Although a native of Sanbornton, the late Jonathan Lovejoy Moore was for almost half a century a most prominent, most reliable, and esteemed citizen and business man of Laconia. He was born at Sanbornton Square, Dec. 13, 1828, and was educated at the Sanbornton academy. Mr. Moore was a blacksmith and machinist by trade in his early days, and first settled in Wolfeborough, where he engaged in business and remained there three years. He moved to Laconia in 1852, and for many years conducted a blacksmith shop on the Gilford side of the river. He sold out this business in 1876, and went into the machinist business, being one of the firm of Moore, Diamond & Co., at what is now the Huse machine shops.

In 1887, he became the senior member of the firm of J. L. Moore & Son, undertakers and dealers in wall papers, etc., continuing in this business successfully until his decease.

Mr. Moore was a Republican in politics, and was selectman of the town of Gilford from 1871 to 1876, and was chairman of the Laconia board of city assessors for five years, from the time the city was incorporated until his death, May 27, 1898.

In his leisure hours, the business laws of New Hampshire were his continual study and he was an unusually well-informed man upon matters in this line, and many estates were placed in his hands for settlement.

He was a charter member of the I.O.O.F., and was treasurer of that society for over thirty consecutive years.

The late Jonathan L. Moore.

The Late Joseph P. Pitman.

The late Joseph P. Pitman was for more than half a century an honored, prominent, and influential citizen of Laconia. He was not only a leading figure in financial and manufacturing circles, but as one of the managing directors of the old Boston, Concord & Montreal railroad, he saved the corporation from financial ruin and secured its prosperity.

The Pitman family has been favorably known in Belknap county from the first settlement of this region. At the first town-meeting held in Meredith, the name of Ebenezer Pitman appears among the officers elected, and he afterwards served the town as representative and town clerk. His son, Ebenezer Pitman, Jr., was also a prominent man in colonial days, serving the town as clerk for many years, and also as representative to the legislature several terms. He was the legal authority in his section of the town and for many years made out most of the legal documents for his fellow-townsmen.

Joseph P. Pitman was the second son of Ebenezer Pitman, Jr., born on the old homestead in Meredith, Jan. 12, 1809. He passed his early years upon the farm, attended the common schools, and then entered the academy at New Hampton. Before he was twenty years of age he had taught several terms of school and served two years as a clerk in Concord. At the age of twenty-one he began business for himself in Laconia, in connection with the late Daniel M. Gale, and afterwards with his brother, John M. Pitman, and still later for more than thirty years, with his intimate friend, the late Daniel A. Tilton. This business has not yet passed from the Pitman family and is now conducted by his sons, Messrs. Joseph W. and Walter H. Pitman.

From 1836 to 1841 he was agent and treasurer of the Winnipesaukee Lake

Cotton and Woolen Manufacturing Co., and during a part of this time was also engaged in business at Lake Village in company with the late John V. Barron.

Mr. Pitman at this time was only about twenty-five years old, and as agent for the Lake Co. (a position afterwards held by the Hon. James Bell), he was superintendent and manager of all the mills at Lake Village, and sold all of the goods manufactured. These mills were owned by Mr. David Pingree, and Mr. Pitman was agent for him.

He was a director in the old Winnipesaukee bank, and during the twenty years of its existence a director of the Belknap County bank, and subsequently in 1876 he was chosen a trustee of the Belknap Savings bank, an office which he continued to hold during the remainder of his life.

Mr. Pitman was the founder of the Pitman Manufacturing Co., commencing the manufacture of knit goods in 1868. At this time he held the controlling interest in the firm of Pitman, Tilton & Co., which was in 1874 incorporated as the Pitman Manufacturing Co., and in this corporation Mr. Pitman was president and principal owner.

In railroad affairs in New Hampshire, Mr. Pitman was especially prominent. He was a director of the Winnipesaukee Steamboat Co., of the Concord railroad, and president of the Pemigewasset railroad, and at the time of his death was senior director of the Boston, Concord & Montreal railroad, having been elected in 1858. It was largely through Mr. Pitman's financial tact, energy and foresight that this corporation was restored to prosperity when failure of the enterprise seemed almost unavoidable.

Mr. Pitman was a life-long Democrat, but never cared for political honors, although he represented Meredith in the legislature in 1851 and 1852. He was

The late Joseph P. Pitman.

for forty-three years an active member of the Congregational church, and prominently identified with all its affairs. He was the principal member of the building committee under whose direction the church was rebuilt in 1874, making it at that time one of the finest church edifices in New Hampshire.

Perhaps no better estimate of Mr. Pitman's character and of his importance to the growth of Laconia can be given than to quote the following resolutions which were adopted by his townsmen who were called together for that purpose immediately after his death, which occurred Feb. 16, 1883:

"We deeply lament the loss which we, in common with others, have sustained by the death of one so intimately connected with the substantial history and prosperity of our town. Mr. Pitman was widely and most favorably known as a strong business man, of undoubted integrity and great sagacity, always punctual in meeting every engagement, and faithful in performing every duty, and combining energy with prudence to a rare degree. No one has contributed more largely to give Laconia its enviable rank as a business center than Mr. Pitman, and his loss will be long and severely felt far beyond the immediate circle in which he moved."

Mr. Pitman was married May 9, 1841, to Charlotte Abby, daughter of Charles and Abigail Parker. The Parkers were also prominent people in old Laconia, and Mrs. Pitman as a young lady was noted for her great beauty, and

Charles F. Pitman.

she was a woman of great strength of character and many estimable qualities. Their children were Elizabeth W. (now the wife of Hon. Charles U. Bell of Lawrence, Mass., associate justice of the superior court of Massachusetts); Helen M., deceased (the first wife of Mr. Bell); Charles F., the present manager of the Pitman Manufacturing Co.; Joseph W., and Walter H., who continue the mercantile business of their father under the established partnership name of J. P. Pitman & Co.

The Pitman Manufacturing Co.

The Pitman Manufacturing Co. was incorporated in 1874, but was established in 1868 by the late Joseph P. Pitman, and has always been one of the most important industries of Laconia, furnishing employment to a large number of operatives, and having a widespread reputation among the trade for the manufacture of fine hosiery. Both woolen and cotton hosiery are produced at the Pitman mills, and their output at the present time is larger than that of any similar concern in the city. The present officers of the corporation are: President and manager, Charles F. Pitman; clerk, Joseph W. Pitman.

Charles F. Pitman, the present head of the Pitman Manufacturing Co., is a native of this city, the son of Joseph P. and Charlotte Abby (Parker) Pitman, born Oct. 6, 1847. He was educated at New Hampton academy and Phillips academy at Andover.

Upon leaving school he entered the store of Pitman & Tilton, with which he was connected from 1865 to 1870. He then turned his attention to the hosiery manufacturing business, and was in company with his father and Daniel A. Tilton from 1870 to 1874, thoroughly mastering the details of the management of the concern. In 1874 the Pitman Manufacturing Co. was incorporated, and he has been general manager from the start, and president of the corporation since his father's death in 1883. Mr. Pitman applies himself very closely to the management of the concern, is thoroughly familiar with every detail of the industry, and is considered one of the best and most successful hosiery manufacturers in this section of the country.

He is a director in the Laconia National bank, trustee of the Belknap Savings bank, trustee of the Gale fund for a city library and park, one of the managing trustees of the Laconia hospital, president of the Congregational society, and a deacon of this church. He is a member of the New Hampshire Society of Colonial Wars, his ancestors in Essex county, Massachusetts, having served with distinction in the Colonial and Revolutionary Wars.

In politics Mr. Pitman is a Republican, and although never an aspirant for any political honors he takes great interest in public affairs, and is recognized as one of the public-spirited citizens of Laconia, always ready to assist in any enterprise or charity for the benefit of the community.

He married, Oct. 15, 1890, Grace Anna, daughter of the late O. A. J. Vaughan. They have had two children: Ruth Marion, who died in infancy, and Charles Joseph, born Jan. 22, 1895.

Station Agent C. E. Leavitt.

Charles E. Frye.

Charles E. Frye, general foreman at the Laconia car shops, is a master car builder who has grown up with the car industry in this city, and has been for many years an important man in this concern. He was born in Sandwich, N. H., Oct. 6, 1846, and was educated in the public schools. He came to Laconia in 1870, and worked at his trade as carpenter for two years and then entered the car shops under the old Ranlet Manufacturing Company. He has been connected with the car shops ever since that time, and was superintendent of the works under the old Laconia Car Co. He is now general foreman under the present management, the Laconia Car Company Works.

He is not only a skilful workman and thoroughly efficient car builder, but he is a man of much executive ability, and understands the business of constructing cars in all its branches and various departments. In politics Mr. Frye is a Democrat and represented Laconia in the legislature in 1892, and

Charles E. Frye.

also served one term in the council as a member of the first city government of Laconia in 1893.

In secret orders Mr. Frye is a thirty second degree Mason, a Knight Templar, a member of the Mystic Shrine, and Ancient Order of United Workmen. He is an attendant at the Congregational church.

Mr. Frye married Olive M. Vittum, on June 5, 1870, and they have three sons.

Adelbert Clark.

Adelbert Clark, New Hampshire's young poet, whose verses have attracted much attention, both in the Granite state and throughout New England, and who is also a short story writer of no mean ability, is a native of Laconia, born Feb. 27, 1870, and has spent nearly all his life in this city. He acquired his early education in the public schools at Lakeport, and even at an early age his thirst for books was apparent, caring more for his studies and reading than for sports, games, and out-of-door amusements. He left school at the age of fourteen years, but continued to devote all his spare time to the reading of standard works, both poetry and prose.

He commenced writing both stories and poems at an early age merely for his own amusement and gratification, but some four years ago he submitted one of his poems to the *Waverley Magazine* of Boston. The poem was accepted, and since then he has written many verses for that publication. All of his poems are of a serious nature, and are noted not only for the beautiful thoughts expressed in them, but for the way they are handled. He has contributed for *Godey's Magazine*, the *Midland Monthly*, the *Army and Navy Journal*, the Philadelphia *Times*, the *Saturday Globe*, the Manchester *Union*, and nearly all of the local newspapers. His short stories have also been very favorably received, possessing good plots, interesting characters, and fine descriptions.

Mr. Clark is an enthusiastic collector of the autographs of famous men, and has one of the largest and finest collections in this line to be found in New England, comprising the signatures of celebrated poets, authors, statesmen, musicians, actors, army and navy officers, presidents of the United States, etc.

When the Laconia company went to Chickamauga Park with the First New Hampshire Regiment during the summer of 1898, Mr. Clark took great interest in their welfare, and when many of the company were sick with fever and lacking home comforts and luxuries, Mr. Clark worked steadily night and day in their behalf, arranging a booklet

Adelbert Clark.

of appropriate verses which was placed on sale for the benefit of the boys of Company K, and which netted a snug little sum for their relief.

Mr. Clark is a great lover of nature, very sympathetic, and his pleasant disposition and pleasing manners win him a host of friends wherever he is known. He is acquiring much more than a local reputation as a poet, and his work thus far gives promise of a brilliant future.

George F. Mallard.

Although comparatively a young man, George F. Mallard can claim to be the oldest merchant, in point of service, at the Laconia end of the city, having established his drug business in its present location, No. 537 Main street, in 1861, and he has continued in the same store and with no change of firm until the present date.

Mr. Mallard is a native Laconian, the son of the late Ephraim and Mercy (Barker) Mallard of this place. He was educated in our public schools and has always resided here.

Mr. Mallard's drug business is not only the oldest, but the largest, establishment in this line in the city. He carries everything in the way of drugs, herbs, and barks, and all the standard patent remedies; besides cigars, toilet articles, sponges, and, in fact, everything usually found in a first-class drug

George F. Mallard.

store. Mr. Mallard also carries a large line of trusses of all the different makes.

Dr. Helen L. Story.

Dr. Helen Louise Story was born in Campton, N. H., April 16, 1860, the daughter of Hazen D. and Lydia (Walker) Smith. Her parents moved to Plymouth when she was five years of age, where she was educated in the common schools and finally graduated in the Belles Lettres course at Tilton Female college. Fitting for a teacher at the State Normal school at Plymouth, she continued the work until the fall of

1881, when she married Jos. Clement Story, a young lawyer practising at Wentworth, who with his family afterwards removed to Plymouth, where he became known as one of the brilliant men of the Grafton county bar, and continued in active practice until overcome by disease, and died Jan. 27, 1894, after a lingering illness, leaving the wife and two children, Charlotte Louise and Marion Walker.

It was during her husband's illness that Mrs. Story conceived the idea of following the medical profession, and she thus began the study of medicine at that time with Dr. Haven Palmer of Plymouth. In the fall of 1894 she entered the Woman's Medical college of Pennsylvania at Philadelphia, remaining two years, when she went to Boston to accept a position as assistant surgeon in the Boston Dispensary, and continued her studies at Tufts Medical college, from which she took her degree of Doctor of Medicine in June, 1897. She passed the Massachusetts State Board the following July, and commenced practice at 23 Dartmouth St., Boston,

Marion Walker Story.

with a position of assistant physician at Trinity Dispensary. She also opened an office in Lowell for a few days in each week, in company with Dr. Sophia R. Peabody. Dr. Story continued in these several capacities until May, 1898, when on account of failing health she was forced to seek rest and change, joining her family at Laconia, and

Dr. Helen L. Story.

opened an office for practice in Masonic Temple on July 1, 1898, having passed our own State Board of Examiners the previous year with the highest record of any candidate during 1897.

Dr. Story's present place of business and residence is at 395 Main St., where she resides with her two daughters. Dr. Story makes no specialty in her profession, but is of the regular school of practice and has had large experience and opportunities in the diseases of women and children, while she has done some creditable work in general surgery.

Miss Marion Walker Story, youngest daughter of Dr. Story, has won a wide reputation as the smallest lady cornetist before the public, having made her first appearance in Montreal three years ago at the age of seven. She has appeared in Boston and many of the large cities of New England, and her ability, execution, tone, and expression have received the warmest praise from the press and musical critics wherever she has been heard.

T. H. Worrall's summer residence, Lake Shore Park, Lake Winnipesaukee, N. H. This property includes sixty acres of land and five buildings.

T. H. Worrall's steam yacht: *Goa.ie.* Fifty feet long, ten feet wide.

T. H. Worrall's winter residence, Laconia, N. H.

Shannon's Bakery.

During the past half a century, Laconia has had bakers and bake shops galore, some good, some bad, and some indifferent, but none of the bakers ever appeared to make a financial success of their industry, until the advent of the subject of this sketch, Mr. William P. Shannon.

Mr. Shannon was born in Hampstead, N. H., Jan. 1, 1862, and he was educated in the public schools of Haverhill, Mass. He came to Laconia in 1886, and in 1891 started a bakery in a small way on North Main street. The fame of Shannon's bakery spread and the bake shop prospered and outgrew its original quarters in a very short time. He then removed to Mill street, where he continued very successfully, constantly increasing his production and capacity for goods in his line, until in 1897 he secured still more convenient quarters at 501 Main street, where his establishment is now located.

Mr. Shannon has always devoted his personal attention to the supervision of the business and his baked goods are recognized as first-class and always reliable. He has the patronage of the best people of the city and manufactures everything in the line of breads, cakes, pies, and fancy cooking known to the trade.

He married Miss Emma M. Griffin of Gilmanton in 1882, and they have one child, a son of three years. Mr. Shannon is a Republican in politics and is connected with the Knights of Pythias and Ancient Order of United Workmen.

Lake City Laundry.

The Lake City Laundry, on Canal court, is one of Laconia's metropolitan establishments, conducted by Frank R. Folsom, and equipped with all new and up-to-date machinery. This laundry was established by Mr. Folsom about four years ago. Previous to this time numerous attempts had been made to establish and maintain a first-class laundry in Laconia, under various managements, but until Mr. Folsom's advent in the business none of the ventures was very successful. Mr. Folsom, however, with modern methods, hard work, and close attention to the details of the laundry business has built up a large trade and created a successful business in this line.

Branch offices have been established in the principal surrounding towns in this vicinity, and laundry work from all sections of Belknap county, from the Pemigewasset valley and even as far north as Vermont, is now sent to this establishment. Mr. Folsom has won a reputation for turning out first-class work, and the fame of the Lake City Laundry has spread throughout northern and central New Hampshire and in many adjoining towns in Vermont.

The establishment employs only skilled help, and with the improved machinery of the present day is enabled to turn out the very finest work. Goods are collected and delivered in all parts of this city by the laundry teams, and out-of-town work is collected by the local agents in each town and forwarded and returned by express.

Will P. Shannon and son, Dana P.

Mr. Folsom, the proprietor and manager of this industry, is a native of Belmont, born Oct. 21, 1857. He was ness, which was then conducted here by Mr. J. H. Toof, a Concord laundryman. Since that time Mr. Folsom has

The Lake City Laundry.

educated in the public schools of Belmont and Laconia, and started in the piano and organ retail business about devoted his entire time and attention to building up a successful business in this line, and his efforts have been re-

McCarthy Bros.' Stores.

twenty years ago, following this line of business until about four years ago, when he purchased the laundry business warded with a liberal patronage and the establishment of a prosperous business.

Mr. Folsom is connected with several secret societies, being a Mason, Odd Fellow, and a member of the Ancient Order of United Workmen.

McCarthy Bros.

Although one of the latest established of Laconia's large retail dry goods and clothing firms, McCarthy Bros. are recognized as the proprietors and managers of one of our most successful and reliable concerns. The firm of McCarthy Bros. started in the dry goods business in April, 1891, with a store eighteen feet wide by sixty feet deep. In June, 1896, owing to the constant and rapid increase of their trade, they were obliged to add a second floor, twenty feet wide by sixty feet deep. Their business still continued to grow, and it again became necessary to add more space to afford facilities for their increasing trade and larger stock of goods, and in December, 1896, they bought out the Laconia One-Price Clothing Co., and added to their business a clothing department, with a floor space thirty feet wide by ninety feet deep. But the increase in trade still kept pace with the increase in accommodations, and in November, 1898, they leased the Burleigh shoe store, which is twenty-two feet wide and sixty feet deep. This store they annexed to their dry goods department, and the establishment is now as modern, convenient, and well-lighted a store as will be found in New Hampshire.

The members of the firm are Stephen J. McCarthy, John E. McCarthy, and Dennis W. McCarthy, all of whom are Laconia boys, who were educated in our public schools, and who have grown up to manhood in the dry goods and clothing trade in this city, thoroughly understanding every detail.

By close and constant attendance to their business, and by merchandizing only strictly first-class goods, they have gained the confidence of the public, and built up a splendid business in their dry goods and clothing departments.

The Esty Sprinkling Company.

The protection of property, especially that consisting of mill, factory, and business buildings, against fire, has been and is still receiving the closest attention by the most skilful engineers of the present day. Efforts are being made constantly to render such buildings more fireproof, and endless contrivances have been made and improvements have been effected whereby the disastrous effects of fire may be lessened.

One of the best known and most successful of these devices ever placed up-

The Esty Sprinkler, full size.

on the market is the "Esty" automatic sprinkler, a full sized cut of which appears above. This sprinkler is universally approved and accepted by insurance companies, and where installed, lowest rates are secured.

The "Esty" sprinkler was invented and patented by Mr. William Esty of Laconia, N. H., and in 1893 a stock company known as the Esty Sprinkler company was formed, with Mr. Esty as president and general manager. This company is located in the Esty mill, 59 Mill St., Laconia, N. H., and its works have been in constant operation since the date of its incorporation, and is one of the few concerns in this city not forced to shut down at any period during the recent "hard times." Through this trying period, the company continued doing a good business, and during the few years they have been in business, have manufactured and sold over 300,000 sprinklers, an average of over 50,000 each year, furnishing steady employment to its employés.

The "Esty" sprinkler is well known not only in this country, but is in use in many of the most progressive foreign countries, including England, Australia, Japan, Sweden, France, Belgium, and Austria.

The officers of the Esty Sprinkler company are: President and general manager, William Esty; secretary and treasurer, Fred A. Phelps; directors, William Esty, Fred A. Phelps, and Henry Richardson.

The company is ever ready to furnish any information at its command relative to sprinkler protection, and respectfully solicits correspondence from all parties contemplating the installation of a first-class sprinkler equipment.

Fred R. Adams.

Fred Russell Adams, proprietor of the West End Grocery and Provision

Fred R. Adams.

Store at Lakeport, is a native of Gilmanton Iron Works, born March 24, 1859, son of Albert A. and Mary A. (McNeal) Adams. He was educated in the public schools of Concord and Loudon, and then attended the Tilton seminary. At the age of sixteen he commenced to serve an apprenticeship at the carpenter's trade.

Mr. Adams came to Lake Village May 1, 1882, and until the spring of 1887 was employed in the Boston & Maine railroad shops. He next engaged in the contracting and building business and erected several fine residences in Lakeport.

Mr. Adams was employed at his trade for about two years at different times by Boulia, Gorrell & Co., of

West End Grocery and Provision Store, Lakeport.

Laconia, and afterwards by J. Boulia & Co., at Lakeport. In the fall of 1889 he engaged in the grocery business with George P. Colby, and the following year formed a partnership with E. L. Hadley in the grocery and provision trade in the "Brawn store." In 1893, Mr. Adams erected his present home and store, known as the West End Grocery and Provision Store, F. R. Adams, proprietor.

He joined Harmony lodge, I. O. O. F., at Tilton, in 1882, and is now a member of Chocorua lodge of Lakeport, and has served as secretary since June, 1898. Mr. Adams was elected secretary of the Odd Fellows' Mutual Relief association in March, 1898, and he is also a member of Hannah Frances Rebekah lodge, No. 41. Mr. Adams is a special officer on the Laconia police force.

Mr. Adams married, November 13, 1878, Emma E. Abbott, daughter of G. W. and Annie (Lorimer) Abbott. They have had two children: Bertha Blanche, born August 20, 1879, who resides at home, and Eva May, born August 21, 1881, who died April 13, 1892.

Capt. Stephen B. Cole.

On March 24, 1633, there landed on these shores, one Thomas Cole who came in the *Mary and John*. He was

Capt. Stephen B. Cole.

an original proprietor of Hampton, and is mentioned as there in 1638. He was at Salem in 1649-'50, and is recorded as a husbandman.

The subject of this sketch, Stephen B. Cole, is the eighth generation from the above-named Thomas Cole. Stephen B. Cole was born in Gilford, or that portion of this city now known as Ward 6, April 30, 1840. His father was the late John A. Cole of Gilford, and his mother, Abigail Davis of Canterbury, N. H. His early education was obtained in the public schools of Gilford, later, he attended the seminaries at Tilton and New Hampton. Captain Cole has been interested in numerous business enterprises from time to time in all of which it is understood he was quite successful.

He was wedded November 8, 1876, to Miss Caroline A. Sanborn, daughter of the late John Jervis Sanborn, well known in railroad circles. He has one daughter, Miss Virginia L. Cole, fifteen years of age, now taking the classical course in the Laconia High school.

Captain Cole was commander of the steamer *Lady of the Lake*, on Lake Winnipesaukee, for a number of years, was representative from the town of Gilford in 1869 and 1870, one of the board of selectmen in 1889 and 1890, and also county treasurer for two years. He has been cashier of the Lakeport National bank until recently, and is treasurer of the Citizens' Telephone company.

Captain Cole is a member of Chocorua lodge, No. 51, I. O. O. F., and in politics is a Republican.

W. D. Heath's Jewelry Store.

The jewelry store of W. D. Heath at Lakeport was established in 1890, at

that time occupying one side of the clothing store of Waldo H. Jones, in the Osgood block on Union avenue, then Main street. The jewelry store was at first something in the nature of an experiment, but finding that a successful business could be carried on in this place, Mr. Heath added musical instruments to his stock, and then put in a line of bicycles. He finally found his space in the store too small for his increasing trade and larger stock, and to remedy this lack of room he purchased the clothing stock of Mr. Jones, and remodeled the entire premises.

Mr. Heath now occupies the entire store, which is twenty by fifty-five feet, and equipped with fine modern fixtures. He carries a large stock of watches, diamonds, clocks, silverware, jewelry, musi-

W. D. Heath's Jewelry Store.

cal goods, bicycles, etc. The Heath jewelry store has won a reputation for reliable goods and square dealing, and this well-deserved reputation has secured for the proprietor a profitable and constantly-increasing patronage.

Mr. W. D. Heath was born in Groton, Vt., and learned the jewelry and watch business with A. J. Stone of Montpelier, Vt., after which he worked as a journeyman in Waltham, Mass., with an English watchmaker, and there attended the Waltham Horological school.

After attending this school, he secured a position as watchmaker with J. R. Murdock of Woodstock, Vt., where he was employed four years, then he was with E. E. Cheney at Nashua, N. H., until he came to this city and engaged in business for himself.

Mr. Heath is a member of Chocorua lodge, No. 51, I. O. O. F., of Endicott Rock lodge, Knights of Pythias, and Hannah Frances lodge, Degree of Rebekah.

He married Maud Fuller, daughter of A. E. Fuller of Woodstock, Vt., in 1888. They have one son, Lewis Heath.

Charles J. Pike.

Charles J. Pike.

Charles J. Pike, foreman of the Crane Manufacturing Co. shops at Lakeport, is a native of Franklin, N. H., born Jan. 18, 1842, the son of Major Samuel and Hannah (Wells) Pike. He was educated in the common schools and remained at home on the farm until Aug. 13, 1862, when he enlisted in Co. E, Tenth regiment, New Hampshire Volunteers. This regiment was assigned to the Army of the Potomac, and remained in this department of the army until discharged, June 12, 1865.

On returning to New Hampshire, Mr. Pike obtained a situation in the machine shop of the late Walter Aiken at Franklin, and remained there two years. In 1867 he came to Lake Village and was employed by the late B. J. Cole in the machine shops until the spring of 1872, when Mr. Pike formed a partnership with the late E. F. Woodman and removed to Newark, N. J., where they engaged in the manufacture of light machinery. Having sold out his interest in this business, Mr. Pike returned to Lake Village in the spring of 1882. He entered the machine shop of J. S. Crane, assembling and testing machines. He remained in this position until Jan. 1, 1898, when he was appointed foreman of the shops, which position he still holds.

Dec. 30, 1865, Mr. Pike was united in marriage with Mary, a daughter of Horace Carlisle of Hartford, Vt., and has one daughter, E. Eva Pike, residing at home. In politics Mr. Pike is a Republican. Fraternally, he is a charter member of Chocorua lodge, No. 51, I. O. O. F., and its first presiding officer and representative to the state grand lodge. He is also a member and P. C. P. of Laconia encampment, No. 9, I. O. O. F.

The Late O. A. J. Vaughan.

From 1857 until his death on April 30, 1876, the late Orsino A. J. Vaughan was an active citizen, in many ways prominent in Laconia life. He was born in Hanover, N.H., on March 11, 1819, son of Silas T. and Polly (Ingalls) Vaughan. He studied law with Judge Kittredge of Canaan. He was admitted to practice and became a member of the Belknap county bar in 1846.

He located in Gilmanton, and practised there until 1857, when he came to Laconia and was for a time associated with the late Col. George W. Stevens, and in 1868 he became editor and proprietor of the Laconia *Democrat*, continuing in this capacity until his death. He was register of probate from 1849 to 1856; he was clerk of the supreme court for Belknap county at his decease, and also the first justice of the Laconia police court. He became identified with the militia system of New Hampshire; in August, 1841, was appointed adjutant of the Thirty-seventh regiment; and in 1844 was promoted to lieutenant-colonel. He represented the town in the legislature, and the sixth district in the state senate in 1866–'67. He was for many years a member of the Democratic state committee. In 1866 he received the degree of A. M. from Dartmouth college.

He was twice married, his first wife being Julia Cogswell of Gilmanton, who lived but a few years after her marriage. June 11, 1855, he married Mary Elizabeth Parker of Laconia, who died on December 18, 1898. The survivors of the family are,— Charles W. Vaughan, manager of the Laconia Press association; Grace Anna, wife of Charles F. Pitman, and Mary Alice Vaughan, all of whom yet reside in Laconia.

The late O. A. J. Vaughan.

Leon J. Merchand.

Leon Joseph Merchand, for quite a number of years an active young business man of Laconia, but now located in Boston, where he conducts a prosperous business in the handling of patented machinery, is still a resident of Laconia. He is the son of the late Lewis Merchand, born in Champlain

P. Q., April 8, 1868. He came to Laconia with his parents when a boy of eight years, and was educated in our public schools.

Mr. Merchand started in life as a cash-boy for O'Shea Bros., and later was employed in a similar capacity for Smith & Lougee Bros. He then worked as clerk in S. B. Smith's shoe store for seven years, and in 1891 went into business for himself as a boot and shoe merchant, and conducted one of the finest equipped shoe stores north of Boston until November, 1898, when he sold out to E. L. Hearn.

Mr. Merchand then purchased the Model Menu Maker, a newly-patented printing device, and also several other patents, and took up headquarters in Boston at 220 Devonshire street, where he has finely-appointed office rooms and is conducting a large business in the sale of menu makers. This machine was the invention of a Laconia boy, and enables hotels, restaurants, summer boarding-houses, etc., to make their own menu cards in first-class style, handsomely printed, at comparatively no expense, except for the blank cards or paper on which the menu is printed.

Mr. Merchand was married in the year 1894 to Miss Abbie S. Heywood, daughter of the late Harrison O. Heywood of Lakeport, and they have one child, a bright little girl of four years of age.

Maher's News Stand.

Maher's News Stand is the popular periodical establishment in Laconia and is located at No. 497 Main street, "On the Bridge." This store handles the New York, Boston, Manchester, and Concord, daily and weekly newspapers, as well as the local weekly papers, all of the popular magazines, latest novels, sheet music, etc. In the line of reading matter Maher's stand carries a larger and more complete stock than any other establishment in this section of the state.

In addition to the periodical business, the Maher store has the sole agency for the celebrated Baker chocolates and bonbons, and also carries a choice line of confectionery, cigars, soda-water, and summer drinks. Charles Maher, the proprietor, is a native of Boscawen, N. H., born July 17, 1850. He was educated in the common schools, and learned the machinist's trade, being employed in Brown's machine shop at Penacook for about nineteen years.

Mr. Maher came to Laconia in the year 1886, and opened a billiard and pool room which he conducted successfully for twelve years. In 1895 he purchased the news stand of Hutchinson & Lord, and last year disposed of the pool and billiard room business to devote his entire attention to the news stand and confectionery store, this business having been very successful and largely increased within the past year or two.

Leon J. Merchand.

Mr. Maher was married in 1874 to Miss Mary A. Thornton of Penacook, and they have two children: Mamie E. Maher and Fred Maher. In secret orders, Mr. Maher is a member of the local lodge of Knights of Pythias.

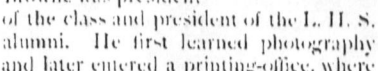

Maher's News Stand.

Lewis Allen Browne.

Lewis Allen Browne was born in North Sandwich, Jan. 18, 1875, but came to Laconia when five years old, in 1880, where he has since resided with the exception of three years spent in Virginia and the South. He was educated in the public schools of Laconia and a private school for boys in Wytheville, Va. He graduated from the Laconia High school in 1893, with a class of fifteen, the first class to graduate after Laconia was made a city. Mr. Browne was president of the class and president of the L. H. S. alumni. He first learned photography and later entered a printing-office, where

from printer's devil he became local reporter. Mr. Browne has been employed upon the *Laconia Press* and *Laconia Democrat*; was at Dover, N. H., as correspondent of the *Manchester Mirror* and Concord papers, and at the present time is Laconia correspondent of the *Manchester Union*, and covers the lake region for the *New York World*. He entered the law office of Judge F. M. Beckford as a law student, a short time ago, but will continue in the newspaper work also for a while. Mr. Browne married Miss Minnie Mae Breck, Oct. 8, 1898, and they reside at 123 Church street.

Eagle Hotel.

The Eagle Hotel, located at the junction of Main and Pleasant streets, on Bank square, is Laconia's most popular hotel for commercial travelers and others who desire strictly first-class accommodations. The Eagle Hotel is under the successful management of "the two

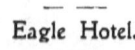

Lewis Allen Browne.

Eagle Hotel.

Franks," Messrs. Farwell & Gilman, and accommodates one hundred guests. The table is superb, the rooms and beds are clean and comfortable, the house is illuminated with electricity, supplied with a pool room and barber shop, while the location, directly in the business centre of the city, makes the Eagle a very convenient and desirable home for "the stranger within our gates."

Frank E. Farwell, the senior landlord, is a native of New London, N. H., but resided in Farmington nearly twenty-five years, coming to Laconia about three years ago. He is a Red Man, a member of the Knights of Pythias, and the Elks He is married and has one child.

Frank A. Gilman is a native of Gilford. He has been connected with various hotels in this vicinity, having been connected with the late Levi B. Brown, a veteran hotel landlord, for about six years.

Messrs. Farwell & Gilman took possession of the Eagle Hotel in 1897, and as both of them are men of experience in the business and have an extensive acquaintance with the traveling public, they have always enjoyed a very liberal patronage, the Eagle being often filled with guests to its full capacity.

Residence of Eugen O'Shea.

LACONIA CHURCHES

Congregational Church.

The Laconia Congregational church was organized June 28, 1824, with a membership of nine persons, and on the

Congregational Church.

same day Mr. Francis Norwood of Andover seminary preached his first sermon. A parish society was organized May 2, 1825, and united with the church in inviting Mr. Norwood to the pastorate. Having accepted the call, he was ordained July 5, 1825, and continued in service until June 8, 1830.

On the 29th of November, 1831, Rev. John K. Young, D. D., was installed as pastor of the church, and after serving for thirty-five consecutive years was dismissed Feb. 12, 1867. In the earlier part of his ministry the church edifice (the only one in the village) was burned to the ground. But on the 6th of June of the same year (1836), a new house of worship was erected on what is now the corner of Main and Church streets, and with various modifications has been preserved until the present time. Rev. Harvey M. Stone was pastor from Feb. 11, 1868, until Dec. 20, 1870, and was succeeded by Rev. Wm. F. Bacon, who began his labor as acting pastor Nov. 1, 1871, and resigned Dec. 31, 1876. During his ministration the church edifice was rededicated after it had been greatly beautified by essential changes in its structure. At the public service the building committee received a vote

Rev. Chas. A. G. Thurston.

of thanks from the church for keeping within the limits of the appropriation.

Rev. J. E. Fullerton, the next pastor, was installed Oct. 17, 1877, and dismissed Feb. 15, 1881. Among other good works he established a Young People's meeting, which held its session every Sunday evening a half hour before the regular service began. Some of the valued results of that organization are seen at the present day. On the 1st of December, 1881, Rev. Chas. A. G. Thurston began his labor as acting pastor. In 1889 the edifice was again repaired and rededicated, the people in the meantime worshiping for the most part with the congregation of the South church. On the 28th of June occurred the seventy-fifth anniversary of the formation of the church. Its present membership is one hundred and eighty-two.

REV. CHAS. A. G. THURSTON.

Rev. Chas. A. G. Thurston was born in Fall River, Mass., July 23, 1841, and received his earlier education in the public schools of that city. He was fitted for college by the late Chas. B. Goff, principal of the English and Classical High school of Providence, R. I. Entering Brown university in September, 1862, and taking the full classical course he graduated in 1866 with the philosophical oration and the degree of A. B. and in 1869 received from the same institution the degree of A. M. The next week after his graduation from college he entered the Theological seminary at Andover, Mass., completing the course and receiving the full diploma in August, 1869. After eight years of mission work in several places including Bradford, N. H., Danbury, Conn., and Wakefield, Mass., he was ordained and installed Oct. 17, 1877, over a Congregational church which he had organized in North Raynham, Mass., and in a new edifice built during the same year.

In 1872 he married Miss J. Anna Moore of Barnet, Vt., a graduate of Abbott academy, Andover, Mass. He has three sons,—Frederick H., now in Brown university, and Arthur D. and Everett S., both residents of this city.

During the last eighteen years Mr. Thurston has been the acting pastor of the Laconia Congregational church.

First Baptist Church.

The First Baptist church was organized May 30, 1888. Previous to this time religious services had been held for a few months in Smith's block hall, with Rev. D. M. Cleveland, state missionary, as preacher. At the meeting called to form the church, twenty persons presented letters of dismission from their various churches. In accordance with the call of the church, an ecclesiastical council convened in the Y. M. C. A. rooms on June 11, 1888, and it was voted to recognize the organization as a regular Baptist church, under the name of First Baptist church of Laconia.

First Baptist Church.

The church thus organized worshiped for some time in the Y. M. C. A. rooms in Smith block, until their own building on Union avenue was completed. The church has been unusually fortunate in its pastors. Rev. Tillman B. Johnson was the first regular pastor, from December 16, 1888, to April 5, 1891. Rev. Woodman Bradbury was pastor from May 3, 1891, to April 8, 1897. Rev. Joel B. Slocum was installed pastor June 6, 1897, and resigned the pastorate November 27, 1898. The present pastor is Rev. Charles L. Pierce, who assumed charge of the church May 1, 1899.

Through wise and vigorous leadership, faithful and unremitting coöperation, the present commodious and beautiful house of worship was erected, and on June 25, 1895, dedicated with free seats. The celebration of the tenth anniversary on June 3, 5, and 6, 1898, was an occasion of deep gratitude. At no time had the membership exceeded 114, all of whom were working people, and only a small number of whom were male members or heads of families, yet at an expense of $12,000 a house of worship had been secured, and the last dollar of its indebtedness removed. The average growth of the church has not been rapid, but sure and hopeful. For nine years the average increase was eight members per year. During the

Rev. Charles L. Pierce.

past year, twenty-three members have been added to the church, fifteen of them by baptism.

REV. CHARLES L. PIERCE.

Rev. Charles L. Pierce, the present pastor, was born in Salem, Mass., February 28, 1865. His early education was received in the public schools, for which the old historic city is noted.

Converted at the age of seventeen, he was at once impressed to fit himself for the Christian ministry; to this call he did not at first respond, but entered business life, going west where a bright business future was before him.

While absorbed in the desire to make money he heard the call, "Woe is me if I preach not the Gospel," and returning to New England he served seven years as general secretary of the Young Men's Christian Association in the cities of Brockton, Mass., Philadelphia, Pa., and Middletown, Conn. During these years he was burning the midnight oil studying under competent teachers. Twice he resigned as secretary, to enter the seminary at Newton, Mass., but each time his plans were frustrated and the pastorate was open for him.

His experience was so peculiar and positive he finally concluded that it was God's plan for him to accept the call from the country parish of Eastor, Conn., and was ordained November 4, 1891. The church in Yalesville called him to be their pastor, and he served there for two years, when a unanimous call from the Kingston church called him to Massachusetts. After a successful pastorate of nearly four years he responded to the call extended from the church in Laconia, and entered upon his duties as its pastor May 1, 1899.

While general secretary of the Brockton, Mass., Y. M. C. A., Mr. Pierce was married June 15, 1889, to Julia Woodman, daughter of Granville Packard of Salem, Mass.

Free Baptist Church of Lakeport.

The Free Baptist church at Lakeport was organized through the influence and labors of Rev. Nahum Brooks, at that time pastor of the Free Baptist church at Laconia, on July 13, 1838, at the house of Isaac Cole, father of B. J. Cole, and consisted of the following named persons: Isaac Cole, his son, Isaac Cole, Jr., Daniel Davis, Elihu Davis, their father, John Davis, William Brown, Richard Martin, Hannah Sanborn, and Arvilla Sanborn. Rev. John Pinkham gave the right hand of fellowship. The new church invited the Rev. Nahum Brooks to take pastoral charge of it, and at once applied for admission to the New Durham quarterly meeting, which request was granted, and it became a part of that body in August, 1838. The meetings of this church were held in private houses, and in the only schoolhouse in the village, for nearly two years, when a room was fitted up in what has been known as the Griffin mill. Up to this time no regular preaching services were held. Rev. Mr. Brooks came as often as he could be spared from his work at Laconia, and a supply was occasionally obtained from other sources. Several new members had been received, and the services of Rev. John Pettingal were secured for every other Sabbath. He was followed by Rev. William Johnson. Rev. Uriah Chase became regular pastor in 1843, and the church increased in numbers. A new chapel was built on Main street by B. J. Cole and John Davis, father of Olin S. Davis, where for several years the meetings were held, or until 1852, when a meeting-house was erected on Park street.

During the time the church occupied the chapel the pulpit was occupied by Revs. W. H. Waldron, Smith Fairfield, Kinsman R. Davis, J. L. Sinclair, and Ezekiel True. It was largely through the instrumentality of Ezekiel True that the old church edifice on Park street was built in 1852. He was succeeded by Revs. J. A. Knowles, S. D. Church, Hosea Quinby, C. B. Peckham, M. C. Henderson, H. S. Kimball, J. W. Scribner, Carter E. Cate, E. W. Ricker, E. W. Porter, and the present pastor, Rev. W. H. Getchell. The first church edifice was destroyed by fire on the morning of Dec. 15, 1890, and the day following was a blue day in the annals of this church. It had been burdened by debts which had just been lifted, and was, at the time of the fire, building an extension to the edifice to enlarge the seating capacity of the auditorium. There was but very little insurance, and the people felt rather poor in purse, but they were rich in faith, and with such a leader as the Rev. William H. Getchell they were bound to succeed, for it was through his earnest efforts largely, backed up by a faithful church membership, and attended by the blessing of God, that the present beautiful and commodious edifice was erected. Mr. Gurnsey, of Montpelier, Vt., was its architect and builder, and its cost was about $20,-

Free Baptist Church, Lakeport.

Rev. William H. Getchell.

000.00, including fixtures. The beautiful memorial windows on either side were presented by Mrs. Daniel Davis, Olin S. Davis, and his mother, and the front windows were given by the Sunday-school in honor of Joseph L. Odell, who, for more than thirty years, had been the much-loved and highly-esteemed superintendent of the school. Other beautiful furnishings were donated by private individuals. The selection of colors, for the interior furnishings, was under the direction of Pastor Getchell and wife, and the money for carpets and cushions was raised by the ladies of the church. All worked together with a will, and in perfect harmony, and felt repaid for their labors when the chairman of the building committee, Hon. H. B. Quinby, presented the keys to the executive committee of the church, and declared the society to be free from debt. It was a memorable day when the present church edifice was dedicated, May 27, 1892. May it stand long to beautify and bless the city!

REV. WM. H. GETCHELL.

Rev. William H. Getchell, present pastor of the Park Street Free Baptist church, Lakeport, was born in North Berwick, Me., Sept. 6, 1854. He became a Christian at the early age of fifteen, and from that time on was actively engaged in Christian work, and a great helper in his home church. From counter to pulpit has run the line of his life. His training or education for the ministry was obtained in the schools at Saco, Pittsfield, and Lewiston, Me., he being a graduate of the Cobb Divinity school, Lewiston. He was ordained to the ministry July 15, 1886, but had been licensed to preach some years previous, and had had a pastorate at Sabattus, Me., three and one half years. After remaining in Sabattus another year after his ordination, he accepted a call from the Park Street church, where he has served as pastor more than eleven and one half years, during which time many changes have taken place. A new church edifice and a beautiful parsonage have been built. In this time Mr. Getchell has married one hundred sixty-nine couples, attended three hundred fifty-five funerals, baptized one hundred twenty-four persons, and received one hundred seventy-two to church membership. Not only his church has his willing care, but he endeavors to help build up the cause of Christ all about him. He has served as president of the New Hampshire yearly meeting of Free Baptists, also as vice-president, missionary superintendent, and president of the New Hampshire State Christian Endeavor society; and, as has been truly said of him, "With old and young alike he is a magnet that never fails to draw, in the pulpit and out of it."

First Free Baptist Church.

This church was organized March 17, 1838, by the Rev. Nahum Brooks, who was for the six ensuing years its pastor. It worshiped in the court-house till Jan. 6, 1841, when, considerably increased in numbers and material substance, it was able to dedicate a meeting-house of its own, on Court square. This was a substantial structure, with seating accommodations for about three hundred. It was remodeled and enlarged in 1873, at a cost of nearly $12,000. Four years later it was reduced to ashes, with no

Rev. John B. Jordan.

Freewill Baptist Church.

insurance. But "the people had a mind to work," and in just thirteen months — November, 1878 — the present edifice was dedicated, free of debt. It stands on the original site, with seating capacity for seven hundred, has modern furnishings, and represents $15,000.

The church has encouraged long pastorates. That of the Rev. Lewis Malvern was in two installments, which aggregated about twenty years, during which the new sanctuary was built and the working power of the church greatly increased. His immediate successor, the Rev. John B. Jordan, began his pastorate with September, 1897. He is not only sustaining the congregation, which frequently taxes the full capacity of the auditorium, but is adding families to his parish, members to his church, and efficiency to all departments of Christian work. He is also a potent factor of the religious commonwealth at large.

The church is a fair exponent of what a Congregational clergyman once asserted of the denomination which it represents: "It is on the right side of all moral questions, and on the evangelical side of all controverted doctrines."

REV. JOHN B. JORDAN.

Rev. John B. Jordan, pastor of the First Free Baptist church, spent his boyhood and school-days in Auburn, Me. In 1868 he entered the employment of the First National bank of Auburn, in which institution he was bookkeeper and teller for six years, when he was elected cashier. He held this position for more than eight years, when he resigned in order to give his whole time to the ministry. He was ordained in May, 1882, and has held pastorates in Lewiston, Me., Minneapolis, Minn., Augusta, Me., Pawtucket, R. I., and in this city. For two years before coming to Laconia he was engaged in evangelistic work.

St. James Episcopal Church.

St. James Episcopal church on Pleasant street was built in 1894 by Rev. Dr. Lucius Waterman, who came here from Littleton, erected the church building, and organized an Episcopal church. The building and lot cost between $11,-

St. James Episcopal Church.

000 and $12,000. Dr. Waterman resigned his pastorate about a year ago, in order to devote more attention to literary work, and the church at the present time is without a regular settled pastor.

First M. E. Church.

The First Methodist Episcopal church is, as an organization, thirty-eight years old. The building occupied by this society is older still, having been originally the property of a Universalist church. The Methodists bought the building.

On the 1st of April, 1861, the first quarterly conference of this church was held, with James Pike, presiding elder, in the chair. The original members of the church and quarterly conference were: Hiram Gilman, S. C. Gilman, and R. T. Martin. At the annual conference, which met a few days thereafter, Rev. G. W. H. Clark was appointed by the bishop as pastor of the new church at Laconia. Of the persons here named, only R. T. Martin is now living. At an advanced age, he maintains the keenest interest in all the affairs of the church, of which he is the only surviving charter member.

Rev. A. L. Smith.

This church has been served by twenty different pastors, whose average term of service has been about two years. The present pastor has just commenced his fourth year.

It may truthfully be said that few churches have met graver obstacles, or passed through severer reverses than has the First Methodist church of this city; yet it has maintained an uninterrupted activity from its birth to the present time, and is stronger to-day than for several years past. All its bills are paid up to date, its membership is steadily increasing, it has a large body of children and youth, its several departments of work are well organized and officered, and it feels the pulse-beat of a true Christian hope and purpose.

REV. A. L. SMITH.

Mr. Smith was born in Salisbury, Mass., a town that falls within the limits of the New Hampshire Conference of the Methodist Episcopal Church. His father was a member of that conference for fifty years, and was pastor of the Methodist church in Salisbury when the sub-

Methodist Episcopal Church.

ject of this sketch was born. A. L. Smith was educated in the public schools of Concord, N. H. (at a time when his father was the chaplain of the New Hampshire state prison), and later was graduated from the Wesleyan university of Middletown, Conn. He taught in Connecticut for three years following graduation, and then, after brief service as a "local preacher," joined the New Hampshire conference in 1887, and has been an active member—i. e., an itinerant preacher—in that conference ever since. His stations have been Rumney, Auburn and Chester, Newfields, and Laconia. Mr. Smith's ministry here commenced in April, 1896, and he has just been appointed for the year ending in April, 1900.

Church of the Sacred Heart.

Early in the history of Laconia many French Canadians came here to live, and they formed so large a part of the Catholic population, that in July, 1891, the bishop organized them into a separate parish. Rev. John Monge was appointed pastor, and services were held for a short time in Moulton opera house. Rev. Father Monge at once began to raise money for the erection of a church building, and in 1892 the present parochial residence and five acres of land on Union avenue were purchased, at a cost of $10,000. In 1893 the present church edifice, the Sacred Heart, was completed at a cost of $30,000, an imposing structure, built of brick, and handsomely decorated in the interior. This parish has a membership of about two hundred families.

Rev. Father Monge.

Rev. Father Monge was born in France, in 1838. He was educated at Nimes and Paris, and ordained to the priesthood in Paris. Before coming to Laconia he was curate at St. Augustine's, in Manchester, and also at Salmon Falls. He was for some time parish priest at Marlborough, N. H.

First Unitarian Church.

The First Unitarian church of Laconia is the outgrowth of the First Universalist church of Meredith Bridge, which was organized July 19, 1838. In 1867, after the parish had been served by several Unitarian ministers, and as Unitarians constituted the majority of its membership, the corporation name of the parish was changed to that of the First Unitarian Church of Laconia. The parish continued to worship in the old Universalist meeting-house (now the Methodist church building) until the completion of the present edifice in Bank square, which was dedicated Nov. 11, 1868. The new church

French Catholic Church.

building was completed during the brilliant ministry of Rev. Thos. B. Gorman, and among those associated with him in the work of advancing the interests of liberal religion were Woodbury Melcher, Joseph Ranlet, John C. Moulton, Jos. S. Tilton, Col. T. J. Whipple, Woodbury L. Melcher, E. P. Jewell, Geo. W. Stevens, S. T. Thomas, Benj. P. Gale, Perley Putnam, Harriet Gale, Mary T. Hull, G. V. Pickering, Horace Whitcher, D. J. Dinsmore, H. E. Brawn, Rev. J. P. Atkinson, Thomas Sands.

Mr. Gorman's successors in the pastorate were C. Y. De Normandie in 1869, Clarence Fowler in 1873, James Collins in 1874, Enoch Powell in 1878, John D. Wells in 1881, John N. Pardee in 1884, N. S. Hill in 1888, James B. Morrison in 1890, Geo. Heber Rice in 1896.

This church accepts the religion of

Rev. George Heber Rice.

Jesus, holding in accordance with His teaching that practical religion is summed up in love to God and love to man. While imposing no credal subscription, it believes in the fatherhood of God, the brotherhood of man, the leadership of Jesus, the immortality of the soul, the progress of mankind onward and upward forever.

Its object is to seek and proclaim truth along the highest lines of the spiritual consciousness; to keep in step with the advancing hosts of scholars and scientists and of all gifted, honest men and women who are striving to aid humanity in its efforts to grow in knowledge; to interpret the Bible as the supreme literature of the religious life; to emphasize the dignity of human nature as the highest manifestation in this world of the Creator's love and wisdom; to affirm the priceless worth of the soul and the impossibility of its ever becoming lost or separated from God. It welcomes to its fellowship all who are in sympathy with these high aims, all who believe in intellectual and spiritual freedom as the highest outcome of the religious life.

The present officers of this church are: Rev. G. H. Rice, minister; W. F. Knight, president; John Ashman, treasurer; Miss Carrie B. Cooke, sec-

Unitarian Church.

retary; Geo. H. Everett, Horace H. Gorrell, Chas. F. Stone, trustees.

REV. GEO. HEBER RICE.

Rev. Geo. Heber Rice was born in Elmira, N. Y., Dec. 28, 1858. On the paternal side he is of Welsh-English ancestry and on the maternal of English. His father was born at Meriden, Conn., in 1817, and his mother at Springfield, Mass., in 1822. Upon their marriage they took up their residence in Elmira, N. Y., where the subject of this sketch attended the graded schools, preparing for college at the Elmira academy. Upon being graduated from Hamilton college, N. Y., he entered the Auburn (N. Y.) Theological seminary, and upon graduation from that institution went to Texas and was ordained to the ministry in San Antonio.

In 1889 he was married to Miss Clara Ree Baldwin of Columbus, Ohio. They have one son, Heber Baldwin Rice, born May 5, 1892.

In 1890 Mr. Rice decided to enter the Unitarian ministry and was received into its fellowship at Denver, Col. He has held three Unitarian pastorates, the first being at Marietta, Ohio; the second at Stockton, Cal., and the third at Laconia, N. H., to which place he came in 1896.

To be a good teacher and leader of liberal thought means hard work. Mr. Rice has a strong and courageous mind and a keen insight into the deep things of life. He is gifted as few men are with the power of expressing his thoughts upon whatever subject he may be engaged, and is thoroughly imbued with the true spirit of Unitarianism. He has done a great work for the liberal church in Laconia, especially in reorganizing and placing the society in a stronger and healthier condition. No work is ever too great for him to undertake, and no one can fail to find in him a true Christian gentleman and a faithful follower of the master. Whether his stay may be long or short, his ministry here will live forever in this community, and it is hoped the day is far distant when he will be called to other fields of labor.

Baptist Church in Lakeport.

This was the first religious organization in this community. The organization was effected in 1811. The first meeting-house of the body, of a simple, barn-frame construction, was erected in 1833, on the site occupied by the present edifice. In 1850 a vestibule and

Baptist Church.

tower were added to the primitive structure. Between the years of 1868 and 1871 the present edifice, with its architecturally beautiful front and tower, replaced the old house of worship.

Among the members of this body well deserving of honorable mention, there is one who, on account of her timely and munificent gifts, may not be omitted from an historical sketch of the organization. We refer to Mrs. Emeline S. Taylor, recently deceased. Of the seventeen pastorates within its history, the two of K. S. Hall are most notable. The present incumbent, the Rev. Geo. F. Babbitt, is the sixteenth who has served this body, he being its acting pastor since September, 1897.

St. Joseph's Church.

Among the first Catholic residents of Laconia and Lakeport were John O'Shea who came here in 1858, and Michael Scott, also a family by the name of O'Neil. At Lakeport at that time there were several Catholic families, among whom were the Dunlaveys, Murphys, Harringtons, and the Leavitts. Ever faithful to their religion, these Catholic settlers held meetings whenever possible. At first the services were held at the home of some of these families, the first meetings being held at the residence of John O'Shea, who at that time resided on Water street. Rev. Father Daley was the first priest who visited here, and after 1858 meetings were held in Folsom hall until a church was built. In 1866 land was purchased on Messer street, and in 1867 work was commenced on the building, which was dedicated by the Right Rev. D. W. Bacon, as St. Joseph's church. This was during the pastorate of Rev. Isadore Noiseux. In the summer of 1877, during a terrific thunderstorm, the spire of the church was struck by lightning, and the

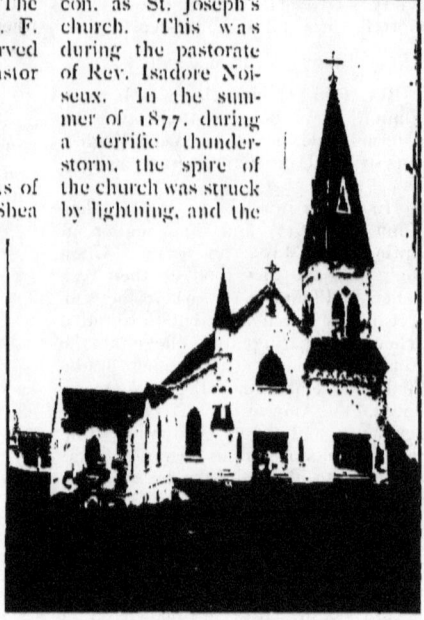

St. Joseph's Catholic Church.

entire edifice destroyed by fire. Rev. J. L. Schakers was pastor at that time, and by his energy and the loyal assistance of the members of the parish, a new building was erected upon the foundations of the old one, at an expense of $10,000. The following pastors have officiated at St. Joseph's church: Rev. Isadore Noiseux, who was the first resident priest. He was followed in 1871 by Rev. John W. Murphy. In April, 1872, Rev. M. J. Goodwin was appointed to Laconia, and he served until October, 1877. In December, 1877, Rev. J. L. Schakers, or Father Lambert as he was called, came here and served until his death, March, 1895. He was followed by Rev. John R. Power, who took charge in April, 1895, and remained here until his death, April 16, 1898. The present pastor of St. Joseph's is Rev. Charles R. Hennon, who came here January 20, 1899.

The church now has a membership of about 150 families, and besides the

Rev. Charles R. Hennon.

church edifice also owns a parochial residence and lot on Messer street, as well as the convent and school property on Beacon street.

People's Christian Church.

The People's church was formally organized July 3, 1892, with seventy-five members, and the court-house was obtained for the place of worship. After maintaining a successful existence independent of all ecclesiastical bodies until it was no longer considered an experiment, in October, 1893, it united with the Christian denomination and became the People's Christian church.
A large majority of the original members had formerly been Methodist Episcopal, but among those who soon joined by letter were representatives of eight distinct denominations, with creeds somewhat dissimilar, hence it seemed very appropriate to belong to a religious body discarding all creeds and accepting the Bible as its only standard.
In the spring of 1894, the society purchased from the county the court-house, and moved it to the present site, where it was dedicated to the service of God; thus the old temple, where justice was so long dispensed, is rounding out its years with the vibrations of the gospel within its sacred walls.
Rev. J. H. Haines was the first pastor, and remained in that capacity until his death; Rev. E. E. Colburn maintained a pastorate for a little more than a year; and Rev. J. E. Everingham, the present pastor, is the third shepherd of the flock. The church has a present membership of 156, maintains three Christian Endeavor societies, senior, intermediate, and junior—and has an

Rev. John E. Everingham.

People's Church.

average attendance in the Sabbath-school of about eighty-five.

The Christians, as a denomination, had their origin about a century ago. Three little companies of ministers, far remote and unknown to each other, separated from their respective and distinct denominations for conscience sake, and finally came together in one body, organized upon the broadest principles, having no creed save the holy Bible, no qualifications for membership save faith in the vicarious atonement and a consistent Christian life, and no name save that authorized by Scripture—Christian. Its motto is: In essential things, unity; in non-essential things, liberty; and in all things, charity.

REV. JOHN E. EVERINGHAM.

Rev. John E. Everingham, pastor of the People's Christian church since September, 1896, has been in active ministry for fourteen years, and was settled over the Christian Church of the Evangel, Brooklyn, N. Y., before coming to Laconia. He was born in Kiswick, Ontario, Oct. 7, 1861, educated in the schools of his native town, and afterwards spent nearly four years in the Christian Biblical institute, Sanfordville, N. Y., the principal theological school of his denomination. Mr. Everingham married Miss Florence M. Coleman of Portsmouth, nine years ago, and two children bless their union. Since coming to Laconia, twenty-eight have united with the church. As a preacher, he is earnest, faithful, and fearless, preferring to please God rather than man. In politics he is a Prohibitionist, and in all things Christian.

Trinity M. E. Church, Lakeport.

The M. E. church of Lake Village was organized June 15, 1872. On this date, Rev. B. W. Chase, pastor of the Laconia M. E. church, granted church letters to the following persons, in order that they might be organized into a Methodist Episcopal church at Lake Village: Henry H. Buzzell, Mary A. Buzzell, Almira P. Homan, Lizzie Ho-

Rev. Jonathan R. Dinsmore.

man, Lorenzo W. Downing, Martha Downing, Lizzie Dame, Sarah Gaskill, Jeremiah Homan, Abigail Kimball, Sarah Palmer, Albert Whitten, Elmira Whitten, Ebenezer Woodman, Harriet Woodman.

These persons were formed into a church and the quarterly conference organized on the above date at the house of Albert Whitten by Rev. S. G. Kellogg, presiding elder.

This organization continued with varying fortunes until March 7, 1877, when, for the time being, the last quarterly conference was held.

The pastors for this period were: 1872, W. C. Bartlett; 1873 '74, C. W. Tebbetts; 1875, O. T. Lovejoy.

In response to an invitation by the Methodists of Lake Village, they were reorganized into a church, March 31, 1881, by Rev. J. W. Adams, presiding elder.

The church records show a continued growth in numbers and financial strength until 1896, when the membership is reported as 112, and the Sunday-school, 110.

Since that time until the present, the membership and financial strength have decreased, resulting chiefly from the continued financial depression which has been felt with great severity in Lakeport, making it necessary for many of our people to seek employment elsewhere.

Prior to May 17, 1891, the meetings were held in what had been the Advent chapel on Gold street. In 1889 the people said, "The place is too strait for us, let us arise and build." Accordingly, in the quarterly conference held March 15 of that year, the pastor, D. W. Downs, reported that a lot of land upon which to build a church had been secured. After more than two years of heroic struggle, a church building, which is a credit to Methodism, was completed and ready for occupancy. The first service in the new house of worship was held Sunday, May 24, 1891. The dedicatory service was held on February 16, 1892.

The following have been the pastors during this period: 1881-'82, N. C. Alger; 1883, A. C. Hardy; 1884, J. H. Trow; 1885-'87, William Woods; 1888 '90, D. W. Downs; 1891 '92, L. R. Danforth; 1893 '95, W. J. Wilkins; 1896, G. W. Farmer; 1897 '98, C. E. Eaton; 1899, J. R. Dinsmore.

REV. JONATHAN ROY DINSMORE.

Rev. Jonathan Roy Dinsmore was born in New Haven, Conn., Oct. 20, 1870. His father, Charles C. Dinsmore, and his mother, Viola Hanscomb, were natives of New Hampshire. He was the youngest of four children, two of whom died in infancy. The oldest is now living in Claremont, N. H. Mr. Dinsmore took his academic training in the Claremont (N. H.) High school, at the Pittsfield (Mass.) High school, at Dow academy, Franconia, and in the N. H. Conference seminary at Tilton.

In the fall of 1890 he began preaching as a supply at West Stewartstown, N. H., and continued in ministerial work in connection with his schooling.

In 1895 he joined the N. H. conference, having served four years prior to that as a local preacher. His appointments have been: Swiftwater and Benton, 1895 '96; North Haverhill, 1897-'98; Trinity church, Laconia, 1899.

In June, 1894, he united in marriage with Mary A., youngest daughter of Rev. and Mrs. D. C. Babcock, now of Dover.

The Laconia Y. M. C. A.

The Association was organized in the parlors of the Free Will Baptist church, Feb. 26, 1886. Its first quarters were on the second floor in Smith's block. In several years it took rooms on the third floor in the First National Bank building.

Two years ago the needs of the work led the board of directors to engage the first and second floors in Edwards block on Mill St.

A gymnasium and reading-room are on the first floor. On the second floor you will find a library and social rooms with a kitchen for use at suppers.

The presidents who have served the Association in the order of their election are Dr. A. H. C. Jewett, G. H. Mitchell, C. A. Dunn, H. W. Carey, and R. C. Dickey.

The general secretaries were Thomas Johnson, H. W. Carey, J. M. Ropes, W. R. Goddard, A. C. Hunt.

The Woman's Auxiliary have performed able service in the Association.

They have purchased an excellent piano, furniture, crockery, silverware,

Methodist Church, Lakeport.

and other useful and ornamental articles.

The membership of the Association has averaged some over a hundred. Seventy boys were at one time members of the boys' branch.

Rev. Frederick L. Wiley.

By so much as pure Scotch and English ancestry are of worth, the subject

Rev. Frederick L. Wiley.

of this sketch entered at birth upon a goodly heritage. He was born in New York, spent a portion of his youth in Boston, and was educated at New Hampton Institution, Hillsdale college, and what is now Cobb Divinity school. He has held important Free Baptist pastorates in Vermont, Maine, and New Hampshire. As a pastor, Mr. Wiley has been specially successful in the organization of church forces, the payment of church debts, the improvement of church property, and the increase of church membership. He has retained his studious habits and his pulpit efforts have been well sustained.

Since failing health incapacitated him for general parish work he has been a permanent resident of Laconia. Noticing that the young men of the city had no common place where they might spend a bit of spare time except in resorts of "lewd fellows of the baser sort," he suggested, and helped organize, the Young Men's Christian Association of Laconia. He was for a term its treasurer and has always given it practical support. For the last ten years Mr. Wiley has been secretary of the Evangelical Ministers' Conference of this city. He has conducted religious services as a pulpit supply, as health would allow, and has spent most of his secular time in literary and benevolent work. For years he has held important ecclesiastical secretaryships and is now developing biographical and historical work in the interests of his denomination.

Profile Rock, The Weirs.

...THE WEIRS...

The Weirs and vicinity, which is within the city limits of Laconia, at the outlet of Lake Winnipesaukee, has been famous as a summer resort, further back, undoubtedly, than any historical or traditional records exist. Long before the Massachusetts colonists sent the first party of white men to the shores of the lake, the Winnipesaukees, a branch of the Penacook tribe of Indians, built and maintained a permanent fish-weir in the channel at the outlet of the lake, and here in the spring and fall of each year, all the red men in this section of the state would gather to partake of the shad which ran up the river from the ocean into the lake in the spring and returned to salt water in the fall. Large numbers of these fish were taken in the rude weir, and dried and smoked for winter use. The weir was maintained for many years after the white men came here, and large loads of these fish were used to enrich the land of the early farmers. The numerous dams on the Merrimack river finally stopped the annual run of shad, and then for years The Weirs was merely a stopping place for the steamer, *Lady of the Lake*, which connected at this point with the old Boston, Concord & Montreal Railroad.

Soon after 1870, the Methodists commenced holding summer camp-meetings at The Weirs, and in 1879 the New Hampshire Veterans' Association held their first annual reunion here. The first hotel, or rather boarding-house, was erected on the Methodist grounds, on the present location of the Lakeside House. It was principally for the accommodation of the Methodist people and there were but eight sleeping rooms at first.

The establishment was inadequate to meet the constantly increasing demands, and finally the Lakeside House was erected by L. R. & G. W. Weeks. Then the late Capt. W. A. Sanborn pulled down the old hotel at Diamond island, far down the lake, and used a portion of the material to construct Hotel Weirs, which hostelry has grown into the magnificent new Hotel Weirs of to-day, one of the largest and most elegant hotels in the entire lake region.

The progress of The Weirs during the past ten or fifteen years has been exceedingly steady and substantial. The state of New Hampshire and the railroad corporation have assisted the Veterans' Association in fitting up their grounds and erected suitable structures for their annual gatherings in August. Many of the regimental associations have large and handsome buildings for the use of

Soldiers' Monument,
Presented to the city by Mrs. J. F. Zebley.

N. H. Veterans' Headquarters, The Weirs, N. H.

their members. Over in the Methodist grove, on the shore of the lake, there are hundreds of handsome cottages which are occupied during the summer by their owners, while the Winnipesaukee Camp-Meeting Association has laid out streets and avenues, provided a system of water works, etc. The Methodist grove and the Veterans' grove are occupied nearly all the time in the summer season by various religious associations, while the New Hampshire Music Teachers' Association have a fine large pavilion for their annual musical festival, which is one of the summer attractions at The Weirs. An electric railroad now connects The Weirs with Lakeport and Laconia, while the place boasts of numerous other advantages and attractions such as telegraph and telephone facilities, hundreds

Steamer Mt. Washington.

and numerous boarding-houses, where good accommodations can be obtained.

A few words on beautiful Lake Winnipesaukee may not be out of place in connection with The Weirs. The lake lies in the counties of Belknap and Carroll, and is about twenty-five miles long, and varies from one to seven miles in width. Its area, exclusive of two hundred and seventy-four islands, is upwards of seventy-one square miles, and the distance around its shores is one hundred and eighty-two miles. There are ten islands which have an area of more than one hundred acres each, and Long Island has an area of one thousand acres. The lake is four hundred and seventy-two feet above the level of the Atlantic ocean. The waters of the lake are very clear and pure, abounding with

Railroad Station, The Weirs.

of row, sail, and steamboats, excursions to all parts of the lake, good train and steamboat service, etc.

Besides the two hotels mentioned, the New Hotel Weirs and the Lakeside, there are half a dozen other smaller hotels

fish of all kinds, and Winnipesaukee is becoming more noted every year as a resort for fishermen from all parts of New England.

Nearly all of the islands have one or more summer cottages, many of them substantial and in some cases elegant structures, and The Weirs is the centre for a very large proportion of the summer cottagers, fishermen, and tourists. For many years the old-fashioned horse-boats were in frequent use on the lake to transport wood, grain, and other merchandise, the first of these curious craft being constructed in 1838, but the advent of the steamboat in 1842 gradually drove the horse-boat into disuse, and to-day transportation is furnished by hundreds of beautiful steam and naphtha craft of all sizes.

From the red man's fishing ground and a mere camp-ground for a week or ten days in the summer, The Weirs has account of the beautiful grove of health-giving pines, its convenience to station, steamboat landing, etc. Its nearness to the shore of the lake suggested its name. The first hotel contained eight sleeping apartments as an addition to a rough unfinished Methodist boarding-house, and was built by Levi R Weeks, brother of the present proprietor, and run by him very successfully for three years.

In 1880 George W. Weeks united with his brother and the present house was erected, which, constantly growing in popularity, has each year been enlarged or improved, until at the present date it stands one of the most popular

The Lakeside House.

grown to be one of the most important and widely known summer resorts in New England. It is constantly increasing in valuation by the erection of new cottages and other improvements, and the place is undoubtedly permanently established as a summer home for thousands of the tired and overworked residents of our larger cities.

The Lakeside House.

In the earliest history of The Weirs as a summer resort, the site of the Lakeside House was chosen as the most desirable location for a hotel, principally on summer homes to be found in New Hampshire: noted for its cleanliness, excellent service, and homelike attractiveness, equipped with modern conveniences, electric bells, bath rooms, perfect sanitary arrangements, and refreshing spring water. One remarkable feature and a delightful wonder to all sojourners is the absence of mosquitoes and flies, which so often trouble the summer guest. One can sit on the broad verandas of the Lakeside House, day or evening, in perfect tranquility. Malaria is also unknown; air, pure and invigorating.

"In the Lakeside pines there lurks no ill,
But fragrant balsam all pain to still."

The house contains seventy-five sleeping rooms and a spacious dining hall, and with its several adjoining cottages can easily accommodate two hundred guests. The property accumulated by Mr. Weeks in these years of prosperity includes in addition to the hotel: Five cottages, casino, with pool and billiard tables, two restaurants, grocery store, barber's shop, printing office, meat market, and livery stable.

In 1882, the late L. R. Weeks gave up to the disease which had been preying upon his constitution for a number of years, leaving the business in which he had taken such a deep interest to continued in the same business five years, since which time his summer residence has been at The Weirs.

Always prominent as a worker in politics and voting in Gilford or Laconia with the exception of three years, he was postmaster three terms and represented Ward 1 in the first city council. He belongs to the order of Odd Fellows.

In 1867, he was married to Lizzie Sinclair, daughter of Jonathan M. Sinclair of Brentwood, N. H. Mrs. Weeks is by profession an artist, and the work of her brush and her artistic taste have contributed much to the charm and attractiveness of the hotel, besides the

Mrs. George W. Weeks.   George W. Weeks.

George W. Weeks, Jr., who has since been sole manager and proprietor of the Lakeside House. This pioneer of The Weirs, son of George William Weeks, was born in Gilford, removing at twelve years of age with his father to Lakeport. Here he received his early education and also attended Tilton seminary. G. W. Weeks, Sr., was an active business man and engaged in various pursuits, and here the son acquired his first knowledge of hotel keeping; also the grocery business. Later he was engaged with brothers in the dry goods business at Laconia for twelve years, removing to Concord in 1875, where he many hundred souvenirs which have been taken away into all parts of the country in the form of oil and water color pictures and decorated china. A delightful exhibition of art is constantly going on at the Lakeside House, and Mrs. Weeks finds there a ready sale for sketches of surrounding landscape and flowers, which are made in the early and later part of the season and perfected at the winter residence in the capital city. No one person has contributed so much for the building up of The Weirs as George W. Weeks. Hotel keeping is his chosen profession, and The Weirs his " Paradise on Earth."

The New Hotel Weirs.

Situated upon a commanding eminence, overlooking the world-famous Lake Winnipesaukee, at the gateway of the White Mountain region, stands Dr. J. A. Greene's "New Hotel Weirs," the most commodious and best hotel in the lake region. This hotel has been enlarged, improved, and entirely renovated and refurnished, with eighty new rooms, thirty of which are supplied with baths. Its sanitary arrangements are perfect. The proprietor, Dr. J. Alonzo is pure and bright, coming directly from the mountain springs, and a second supply, for sprinkling, bathing, and fire protection, from the lake itself. The table is supplied daily with fresh vegetables, milk, butter, and eggs from the famous Roxmont Poultry Farm and from the neighboring farmers. Spacious piazzas encircle the entire hotel, from which views of lake and mountains of unsurpassed magnificence are obtained. Electric cars leave the hotel grounds at frequent intervals for a five-mile ride to the city of Laconia.

The New Hotel Weirs.

Greene, and the manager, the ever-popular and experienced landlord, Col. Freeman C. Willis, spare no pains or expense to make the New Hotel Weirs a model of comfort to its guests. It is fully equipped with electrical appliances and connected by telephone and telegraph with the direct lines to various points. Its cuisine is excellent and up-to-date in every particular. A never-failing mineral spring is constantly flowing from a ledge of rocks on the hotel grounds. The water used in the hotel

All trains and steamboats arrive at and depart from the station and wharves directly in front of the hotel grounds. The New Hotel Weirs has a fine billiard-room and tennis court connected, and an excellent orchestra furnishes good music. The climate is conceded by all to be the best, the mountain breezes being tempered by the moisture from the waters of the lake. Lake Winnipesaukee abounds with game fish of all kinds, and has been very properly christened the fishermen's paradise, all varieties of freshwater fish being taken by anglers, including landlocked salmon, lake trout, black bass, pickerel, perch, etc. Steam yachts and row-boats can be engaged at the hotel office, and the lake affords excellent and safe bathing. Lake Winnipesaukee is unmatched in all the mountains for variety and picturesqueness, and the New Hotel Weirs is unparalleled in New England for its comfort and great variety of attractions. The view obtained here is pronounced by travelers to be superior to anything of the kind to be found in the world.

Four express trains leave the Union station on Causeway street, Boston, every day for The Weirs, with parlor and buffet cars attached, thus ensuring perfect comfort in travel. Steamboats leave The Weirs every few hours for Centre Harbor, Wolfeborough, Alton Bay, and all points on the lake, affording many delightful excursions.

Lake Winnipesaukee, on whose matchless shores Hotel Weirs is situated, is one of the most magnificent lakes in the world, surpassed by no American waters and rivaling in scenic beauty the far-famed Italian, Swiss, and Scottish lakes. Winnipesaukee is the name bestowed by the Indians, whose meaning, "The Smile of the Great Spirit," shows that even the untutored aborigines recognized that Omnipotence had placed the seal of its crowning glory upon this sparkling lake whose pelucid waters lave the foothills, an advance guard of the picturesque White Mountains.

Perhaps we can give the reader no better idea of this summer paradise than to quote from a letter written by a guest of last season:

"I had taken rooms at the famous Hotel Weirs and descended from the hot and dusty train into cool and deliciously fragrant air. It was night, and such a night! Never through life will the memory of that wondrous scene fade from my mind. Weirs was *en fête*, and the spectacle was transcendent, dazzling, beautiful. It was as if I had been suddenly translated into fairyland. At the back rose the great hotel, its hundred windows aglow with the cordial light of welcome; festoons of myriad flags and streamers waved in the soft breeze, while thousands of Chinese lanterns gleamed and twinkled among the trees and up and down the long, wide piazzas, filled with bevies of radiantly dressed women, groups of men, and promenaders. The soft strains of a Strauss waltz floated out upon the air from the hospitable, wide-open windows of the hotel parlors, and the laughter of merry dancers echoed the music of the orchestra.

"All this was pleasure in its highest personification, but a cooling zephyr from the water, upon my heated brow, caused me to turn toward that famed lake, the lake of the poet, Whittier, the lake artists rave over, the ideal lake of the sportsman—Winnipesaukee—which I then saw for the first time and which was, indeed, the Smile of the Great Spirit. Never shall I forget the shuddering ecstacy with which I drank in that wondrous scene. The hotel, the music, the life, the light, and gayety were instantly forgotten—lost in that amaze and reverent awe into which the human atom is plunged when brought face to face with the stupendous grandeur of the Creator's masterworks of nature.

"What pen can describe the sublimity of that picture, what pen portray its ineffable and transcendent beauty! For miles upon miles, in all directions, spread that marvelous sheet of water, dotted all over by the greenest isles that

Dr. J. A. Greene, Proprietor.

ever studded a blue sea; the moon at her full rode high in a heaven unflecked by cloud or shadow, dropping, as it were, the diamonds of her light in brilliant reflection down upon the distant bosom of the lake, at first in a narrow streak of shivering silver, ever widening, ever growing as in broadening band upon the shimmering waters it approached the beholder in corruscations of living, liquid light, tossed, glowing and gleaming and glittering from myriad tiny waves like untold millions of limpid, resplendent jewels; the soft air was cool and fragrant with pine and hemlock from every heavily wooded isle, bearing in every deep-drawn breath the balm of health; at my feet the gentle ripples lapped musically upon the shore. Far away, glancing athwart the moonbeams on the water, were tiny pleasure yachts, their

Tavern at The Weirs. David B. Story is one of the oldest and best known tavern-keepers in New Hampshire, and has also figured prominently in political and other circles of Laconia for many years.

David B. Story is a native of Hopkinton, N. H., born January 19, 1836. He was educated at Hopkinton academy, and was married in 1857 to Sarah J. French, and has four children living: J. Henry, Fred W., Charles F., and Benjamin F. A daughter, Ada S., died in 1877.

West End of Dining-Room, New Hotel Weirs.

lights now showing, now lost to sight. Nearer land some young people in boats were idly drifting, the faint echoes of their joyous laughter floating across the waters, while just off shore a great fish, belated by nightfall, broke water and disappeared, leaving only the rapidly widening circle where a moment before he had risen to some luckless fly. Such a scene! such a night! such a place! I felt that here at last I had found the vacationist's paradise."

Story's Tavern.

Everybody who ever stopped long in Laconia knows " Dave " Story of Story's

Mr. Story is a Unitarian, and a member of the Odd Fellows, Knights of Honor, and the Amoskeag Veterans of Manchester, New Hampshire's famous military organization.

He is a veteran Democrat, and has served as sheriff of Belknap county, deputy sheriff, justice of the peace, selectman, member of the city council, and representative in the legislature.

Mr. Story has been a hotel-keeper for thirty-six years, having been landlord of the Perkins House, Mt. Belknap House,

Laconia House, Hotel Weirs, and at the present time welcomes his patrons at Story's Tavern, on Lakeside avenue at The Weirs.

Story's Tavern is located on the shore of Lake Winnipesaukee, and situated in a grove directly facing the lake, and within two hundred feet of it, and having one of the finest views of the lake and mountains to be had at The Weirs. This hotel, although small, has all the comforts of a larger house.

The steamboat landings and depot are but one minute's walk from the hotel and in full view of the same.

Nice fishing, boating, excursions on the lake every day, and splendid drives.

The motto is: "Small but Good."

Terms from $7 to $10 per week. Transient $2 per day.

Mr. Story's long connection with the hotel business has given him an extensive acquaintance with the traveling public, and his honest welcome to the weary traveler or the sojourner from the city seeking a quiet rest in the country, is a guarantee of good lodgings, substantial food and all the comforts which can be desired.

Lake View House.

The Lake View House at The Weirs is open from June 15 to September 15, Robert C. Dickey, proprietor. The Weirs is the principal summer resort on the shores of the beautiful Winnipesaukee lake, thirty-five miles north of Concord, on the Boston & Maine railroad. There are seven trains daily each way from Boston through to Plymouth and the White Mountains. The Lake View House is pleasantly located on quite an elevation but a short distance from the railroad station and steamboat landing.

The house is neat, clean, and newly furnished, every room is pleasant, and the house accommodates twenty-five guests.

Everything is made homelike and cheerful. The location makes it cool and comfortable even in the hottest weather. There is a fine grove near by, also the G. A. R. grove, speaker's stand, etc., where band concerts and many interest-

D. B. Story.

Story's Hotel.

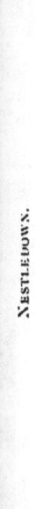

Summer residence of Mrs. John F. Zebley.   NESTLEDOWN.   W. H. Tucker, Manager.

Log Cabin at Nestled on Beach.

ing outdoor gatherings are held during the summer. The spring water with which the house is supplied has special medicinal qualities, as very many have testified after using it freely for a short time, when they could not drink ordinary city water without injury. Particular pains is taken to have a first-class table, supplied with fresh milk, fruit, vegetables, etc., from the farm daily. Boating and fishing, with the opportunity for carriage drives through delightful even by a bush or rock. On either side of this avenue many islands arranged themselves, as if to adorn with a finish that could be given only by their glowing verdure and graceful forms. That the successive beauties of the Winnipesaukee strongly resemble and equal those of Lake George, I cannot entertain a doubt, and from various elevations the scene is superior. The Winnipesaukee presents a field of twice the extent of Lake George. The islands

Lake View House.

scenery, make this one of the most desirable places to spend a quiet summer vacation at a small expense. Prices are from $7 to $10 per week.

Dr. Dwight, a noted traveler, has said of this lake: "From a delightful elevation a short distance from the highway could be seen the Winnipesaukee lake, an immense field of glass. In the centre, a noble channel spread out twenty-two miles before the eye, uninterrupted in view are more numerous, of finer form, and more happily arranged. The shores are not inferior. The expansion is far more magnificent, and the grandeur of the mountains can scarcely be rivaled." A few minutes' walk from the Lake View House the above can be at once verified, and no finer view of lake and mountain can hardly be conceived. Descriptive circular and other information sent on application to R. C. Dickey.

INTERLAKEN PARK

Interlaken Park, located on the shore of beautiful Lake Winnipesaukee, just across the channel from The Weirs, is already recognized as one of the most charming and convenient summer-resort locations in the whole lake region of New Hampshire. White Mountains in the background, while the facilities and conveniences for business and professional men who make this Mecca of tourists a place of summer resort, give it a special advantage over the majority of towns and villages catering for summer patronage.

Looking down the Channel from the Park, Endicott Rock in the Distance.

Lake Winnipesaukee is everywhere acknowledged to be the most magnificent summer resort in the Granite state. It is the largest lake in the state, containing an area of seventy square miles, and its hundreds of islands, natural bays, interesting inlets and picturesque shores, are the theme of universal praise by both press and public. The Weirs is the chief port of the lake and the most important junction of railroad and steamboat travel. The view from this point combines the lake scenery with the mountain ranges of Ossipee, Sandwich, and the Railroad and steamboat communication is prompt and frequent. The running time between Boston and The Weirs is only about three hours, and the Boston & Maine system runs several express trains each way every day between these points; the White Mountain region can be reached in a few hours; steamboats run between all the harbors and towns around the lake; while the conveniences of telegraph and telephone are the same as can be obtained in any of the large cities. Electric street cars make twenty-minute trips between The Weirs and

The Weirs, as seen from the Park.

the thriving city of Laconia, five miles distant, the electrics running directly by the entrance of Interlaken Park.

Interlaken Park is actually the coolest spot on the shores of the lake. By careful temperature tests, under like conditions, made in August by Mayor Adams of Franklin, the thermometer registered from 6 to 16 degrees cooler at his cottage at the park than at The Weirs station. Four consecutive days showed a difference of 12 degrees on each day.

Interlaken Park includes forty acres of shore property which has been surveyed and is laid out into lots for summer residences. A substantial driveway or avenue has been made at considerable expense along the whole lake frontage, and sub-avenues or broad streets intersect at regular and convenient distances. Running water is supplied from The Weirs water-works, and can be carried to any portion of the park, thus securing a bountiful supply of pure drinking water.

It is designed to make the park a summer resort for those who appreciate the beautiful attractions and the health-giving properties in which this region abounds. The scheme of allotments secures to each cottager immunity from the annoyances of arbitrary privileges which are sometimes the bane of allotment summer parks, and everything has been carefully planned and considered so that each purchaser feels that his personal purchase secures to himself comfort and security during the months of summer leisure and occupancy.

The park property is on a gradual rise (the back lots being one hundred feet higher than the lake level), and commands one of the most extensive and magnificent views to be obtained anywhere around this celebrated lake. Some of the best fishing grounds in the lake for lake trout, salmon, bass, and pickerel are within easy distance of the park, a feature which is appreciated by many summer visitors.

Combining as it does all the charm of shore and moun-

Summer Homes at the Park.

tain scenery, superbly located, free from excursion crowds and picnics, and yet within immediate communication of railroad, telegraph, and city life, Interlaken Park offers attractions which cannot be found elsewhere, and can hardly fail to rapidly become one of the most popular resorts on Lake Winnipesaukee.

For further particulars inquire of Harry W. Daniell, superintendent of the Winnipesaukee Lake Company, at Lakeport, N. H., or at the Hotel Weirs, The Weirs, during the summer season.

Plan of Interlaken Park.

Harry W. Daniell, Agent of the Winnipesaukee Lake Co.

Charles W. Vaughan.

Charles W. Vaughan, manager of the Laconia Press Association, and editor of THE ILLUSTRATED LACONIAN, is a native Laconian, born June 30, 1862, in the old Vaughan homestead, which stood on Main street, just below the railroad tracks, and which was removed to make room for the new passenger depot and railroad square. His parents were the late O. A. J. Vaughan, for many years a well-known lawyer, and also editor of the Laconia *Democrat*, and Mary Elizabeth (Parker) Vaughan. The ancestors of these families were not only among the early settlers of America, but if the family records had been properly kept the pedigree could have been traced back to the late Mr. Noah, who conducted a very successful ferryboat business at Mt. Ararat at the time of the big freshet, and whose menagerie of wild and domestic animals was at that time universally admitted to be the biggest show on earth.

Quite a number of the Vaughan family were among the early colonists of Massachusetts, and while some of them acquired fame in the French and Indian wars, and the Revolution, others had fame thrust upon them, one being tried, convicted, and hung as one of nineteen witches in Salem, while another served a term in jail for speaking very disrespectfully of one of the colonial governors of Massachusetts, which might or might not have been discreditable.

The subject of this sketch distinguished himself at the tender age of three years by burning his father's barn, thereby satisfying a vindictive antipathy towards a certain gentleman sheep with whom he had some previous misunderstanding. He was educated in the public schools of Laconia, and at the age of thirteen years entered the Pitman mills with the intention of becoming a hosiery manufacturer. A violent disinclination for work, however, induced him to abandon this enterprise for the newspaper business after one year, and since 1877 he has been connected with the Laconia *Democrat* in various capacities.

In politics he is an Independent, but always votes the Democratic ticket. He was a member of the first city council of Laconia. In religious matters he is a Congregationalist.

He married Florence N. Elliott of Bradford, Vt., October 16, 1882.

Charles W. Vaughan.

Louis B. Martin.

Louis B. Martin, publisher of THE ILLUSTRATED LACONIAN, was born in Providence, R. I., May 24, 1874, only son of the late Walter A. Martin and Hattie A. (Brown) Martin. His father died March 8, 1878, and young Martin with his mother removed to Laconia, where they have since resided. Mr. Martin attended the public schools, and learned the printer's trade and has been employed on the various papers of Laconia. He conducted the street car advertising service in Laconia for four years, has published various advertising novelties and illustrated souvenirs in different parts of the state. Mr. Martin recently invented a printing press, and was allowed a patent on the same last March, which is now being successfully placed on the market by a Boston house. He was married on October 21, 1895, to Miss Mary L. Twombly of Laconia, and they have a little daughter, Esther.

Publisher's Note.

The publisher of THE ILLUSTRATED LACONIAN takes considerable pride in presenting this publication to the public, believing the work to be the most complete and representative souvenir of the city ever issued. The publisher does not claim that the book faithfully presents every man and every industry which has helped to build up Laconia, but it is claimed that in this respect the publication is complete with but very few exceptions, and these exceptions through no fault of the publisher. The facts and dates in the various articles have been obtained so far as possible by personal interviews and are so far as known absolutely correct. The publisher is deeply indebted to quite a number of our public-spirited citizens for valuable assistance in compiling THE ILLUSTRATED LACONIAN and in making the publication a success, and would also express his appreciation for the courteous treatment and generous support received from the numerous people and concerns who appear in the book.

For the excellence of the engravings and the fine typographical appearance of this publication, credit should be given to the Rumford Printing Co., of Concord, N. H., which concern is not only by far the largest engraving and printing establishment in New Hampshire, but which also stands second to none in New England for fine work in this line. The half-tone engravings were all made by the Rumford Printing Co., and the book was printed and bound complete in their establishment.

LOUIS B. MARTIN,
Publisher.

Louis B. Martin.

INDEX.

Abbott, Dr. Alfred W................. 140
Abbott, Dr. Clifton S................. 141
Adams, Fred R....................... 206
Ashman, John W..................... 41

Baldwin, Charles W.................. 118
Babb, Rev. J. Franklin.............. 39
Beckford, Judge Frank M........... 119
Blaisdell, Joseph H.................. 83
Booth, John......................... 147
Brown, the late Levi B.............. 97
Browne, Lewis A.................... 212
Burleigh, Edwin F................... 182
Busiel, the late Hon. John W....... 154
Busiel, Ex-Gov. Charles A.......... 155
Busiel, John T...................... 157
Busiel, Frank E..................... 158
Busiel, J. W. & Co.................. 159

Carroll & Crapo..................... 35
Central House....................... 183
Chase, Harry S...................... 171
Chase, Ethan A...................... 81
Chase's Sporting Resort............. 81
Churches:
   Baptist, Lakeport................ 223
   Church of the Sacred Heart....... 221
   Congregational................... 214
   First Free Baptist............... 218
   Free Baptist, Lakeport........... 216
   First Baptist.................... 215
   First Methodist Episcopal........ 220
   First Unitarian.................. 221
   Peoples' Christian............... 225
   St. James' Episcopal............. 219
   St. Joseph's..................... 224
   Trinity M. E., Lakeport.......... 226
Cilley, Harry D..................... 180
City Savings Bank................... 151
Clark, Adelbert..................... 199
Clow, the late William.............. 66
Clow, Henry B....................... 67
Clow, William & Son................. 67
Cole Manufacturing Co............... 47
Cole, the late Hon. Benjamin J..... 47
Cole, Capt. Stephen B.............. 207
Cottrell's.......................... 105
Cottrell, Irving M.................. 106
Cox, George B....................... 101
Crane Manufacturing Co............. 128
Crane, John S....................... 129
Crane, Mazellah I................... 130

Daniell, Harry W.................... 244
Davis, the late Francis H........... 80
Dinsmoor, the late Daniel S......... 38
Dinsmoor, Arthur W................. 153
Dinsmore, Rev. Jonathan R.......... 227
Dow & Roberts....................... 57
Drake, Benjamin F................... 60

Eagle Hotel......................... 212
Edgerly, the late Nathaniel........ 143
Esty Sprinkler Co................... 205
Everingham, Rev. John E............ 226

Flanders, William H................. 58
Folsom, Albert G.................... 126

Folsom, Frank R..................... 204
Foss, Oscar......................... 123
Foster, Charles T................... 191
Frye, Charles E..................... 198
Frye, Simeon C...................... 151

Gale, the late Major N. B........... 107
Getchell, Rev. William H........... 218
Gilman, Frank L..................... 185
Gilman, Dr. Charles S............... 76
Gingras, Joseph H................... 68
Glidden, Albert S................... 149
Gordon & Booth...................... 146
Gordon, Alburtis S.................. 147
Goss, the late Dr. Oliver........... 87
Goss, the late Elizabeth H. (Flanders).... 89
Goss, Dr. Ossian W.................. 89
Greene, Dr. J. A.................... 235

Harriman, Dr. A. H.................. 56
Heath, W. D......................... 208
Hennon, Rev. Father................ 224
Hibbard, Hon. Ellery A............. 193
Hodgdon, Dr. Edwin P............... 53
Hotel Picard........................ 174
Huntress, Hamlin.................... 113
Huse Machine Shops.................. 74
Huse, Warren D...................... 75

Interlaken Park..................... 241

Jewell, Erastus P................... 142
Jewett, Judge John G............... 183
Jewett, Col. Stephen S............. 133
Jones, Hon. Frank................... 29
Jordan, Rev. John B................ 219

Kellogg, Daniel..................... 110
King, Dr. W. A...................... 137
Knight & Huntress................... 112
Knight, Gen. William F............. 112

Laconia, 1652–1899.................. 3
Laconia Board of Trade............. 181
Laconia Building and Loan Association... 32
Laconia Car Company Works.......... 29
Laconia, Census of, in 1836........ 27
Laconia Electric Lighting Co...... 125
Laconia Democrat.................... 141
Laconia Grist-mill.................. 137
Laconia Hardware Company........... 36
Laconia Lumber Works................ 92
Laconia Landmark.................... 50
Laconia National Bank.............. 150
Laconia Post-office................ 186
Laconia Street Railway............. 189
Laconia Savings Bank............... 103
Laconia To-day...................... 21
Laconia Water Company.............. 143
Lakeside House..................... 232
Lakeview House..................... 237
Lake City Laundry.................. 203
Leavitt, Charles E................. 198
Letourneau, Dr. J. N............... 109
Lewis, Col. Edwin C................ 184
Lougee Bros......................... 173
Lougee, Frank H.................... 173
Lovell, the late Judge Warren..... 193

INDEX.

Maher's Newstand	211
Maher, Charles	211
Mallard, George F	200
Marshall, Residence of William C	192
Martin, the late Samuel H	144
Martin, Louis B	245
Mayor and Council	24
McCarthy Bros	205
McGloughlin, James	33
McDaniel, Charles W	145
Melcher & Prescott Insurance Agency	130
Melcher, the late Woodbury	175
Melcher, Woodbury I	176
Meredith Bridge, Map of in 1853	10
Merrill, John F	79
Merchand, Leon J	210
Moulton, the late Hon. John C	64
Morin, Joseph P	68
Moore, Albert C	82
Moore, the late Jonathan I	194
Moore, John B	106
Morrill, Joseph S	138
Monge, Rev. Father	221
Munsey, George B	100
Mutual Building and Loan Association	45
Nelson, the late David B	52
Nelson, William	152
New Hotel Weirs	234
Oberon Ladies' Quartette	63
Old Corner Store	50
Osgood, F. George H	72
O'Loughlin, the late John	139
O'Shea Bros	42
O'Shea, Dennis	45
O'Shea, Residence of Eugene	213
Pease's City Band	149
Peaslee, Walter S	167
Peaslee, Frank S	153
Peoples' National Bank	103
Pepper Manufacturing Company	69
Pepper, William H	70
Perley, the late Stephen	161
Perley, the late John I	163
Perley, the late John I., Jr	165
Perley, Lewis S	166
Pierce, Harry I	191
Pierce, Lewis S	191
Pierce, Rev. Charles L	216
Pike, Charles J	209
Pitman, the late Joseph P	195
Pitman, Charles F	198
Pitman, Walter H	73
Pitman Manufacturing Company	198
Plummer, William A	136
Plummer, Martin B	118
Post-office	186
Prescott, True E	133
Pulsifer, Ex-Mayor Charles L	111
Quimby, Dr. John G	189
Quinby, Col. Henry B	48
Quinby, Henry Cole	49
Quinby, Albert T	37
Quinby, Edwin N	37
Richards, Charles F	166
Rice, Rev. G. Heber	223

Riley, George W	93
Roberts, John L	98
Robinson, Mark M	121
Rowe, Fred B	59
Saltmarsh, Dr. George H	78
Sanders, the late Samuel W	178
Sanders, the late George A	75
Sanders, George A	71
Sanborn, Herbert S	95
Scott, City Marshal H. K. W	96
Shannon, Edwin H	62
Shannon, Jonathan C	124
Shannon, Will P	203
Simpson, Charles L	91
Smith, Ex-Mayor Samuel B	160
Smith, John Parker	51
Smith, Joseph F	121
Smith, Rev. A. L	220
Smith, the late Rev. A. D	177
Stone, Hon. Charles F	61
Story's Drug Store	104
Story, J. Henry	105
Story's Hotel	236
Story, David B	236
Story, Dr. Helen I	200
Story, Marion W	201
Tetley, Mayor Edmund	31
The Weirs	229
Thompson, Edwin P	111
Thompson, True W	116
Thurston, Rev. Charles A. G	215
Tilton, the late Daniel A	86
Tilton, the late James H	179
Tilton, the late Joseph S	167
Tilton, George Henry	169
Tilton, Elmer S	170
Trask, Julian Francis	55
True, the late Noah I	53
True, Dr. Walter H	54
Tucker, Hoyt H	84
Twombly, the late Orison	97
Vaughn, the late O. A. J	210
Vaughan, Charles W	245
Vue de L'Eau	182
Wallace, William	105
Wardwell Needle Co	39
Ward, Edwin D	77
Waverly Shoe Company	98
Weeks, George W	233
Weeks, Mrs. George W	233
Wells, Dr. Henry C	125
Weymouth, Herman C	117
Whipple, the late Col. Thomas J	187
Wiley, Dr. Rebecca W	179
Wiley, Rev. Frederick I	228
Wilson, Julius E	40
Wilson, Morgia Porter	90
Winnipesaukee Gas and Electric Co	94
Woodworth, Wellington L	91
Worrall, T. H	202
Wrisley, Dr. J. A	194
Young, Fred A	85
Y. M. C. A	227
Zebley, Summer Residence of Mrs. John F	238

www.ingramcontent.com/pod-product-compliance
Lightning Source LLC
Chambersburg PA
CBHW020804230426
43666CB00007B/849